A John Catt Publication

PREVENTING & COUNTERING EXTREMISM & TERRORIST RECRUITMENT

A BEST PRACTICE GUIDE

BY HANIF QADIR

First Published 2016

by John Catt Educational Ltd,
12 Deben Mill Business Centre, Old Maltings Approach,
Melton, Woodbridge IP12 1BL

Tel: +44 (0) 1394 389850 Fax: +44 (0) 1394 386893
Email: enquiries@johncatt.com
Website: www.johncatt.com

© 2016 Hanif Qadir

ISBN: 978 1 1909717688

Set and designed by John Catt Educational Limited

CONTENTS

PART A: THE CURRENT LANDSCAPE

PART B: TACKLING EXTREMISM

PART C: THE ISLAMIC STANDPOINT

I dedicate this book to my two best friends in the world, my dearly beloved brothers Imtiaz and Abid Qadir who were absolutely instrumental in helping me throughout my life and then to establish the Active Change Foundation. They bore the brunt when it came to difficult and dangerous moments and faced the challenges always with a smile, they gave me inspiration and hope. Sacrificing so much for the cause and then some.

Imtiaz was the one who kept on nagging at me to write this book so it can help others further away and those with less experience. Sadly they lost their own battle with illness and cancer in 2013 & 2014. They are greatly missed every single day. May Allah unite us in the hereafter in the gardens of paradise.

FOREWORD

Government and the media are awash with 'experts'. Experts on the economy, experts on politics, experts on everything under the sun. Nowhere is this more the case than in relation to violent domestic extremism, terrorism and the subject of radicalisation. Most such experts are self-appointed and operate from the basis of academic research. They seldom, if ever, interact with those at the cutting edge of the problem, individuals who have lived their lives trying to understand the complexities of what is undoubtedly the existential challenge of the twenty-first century. Real experts are thin on the ground, for whilst a few claim to have 'hands on' experience of radicalisation, there are fewer still who actually have real insight, born of seeing radicalisation and domestic violent extremism in all its forms whilst working to eradicate it.

Hanif Qadir is one such individual, he has that rare legitimate claim to be an expert by virtue of involvement and not just observation.

A 'religious' Muslim who is not deterred by the rantings of the right-wing press to demonstrate his adherence to Islam, Hanif has seen, close up, the way in which the cancerous perversion of his faith has blighted the lives of so many young British Muslims over the last two decades. He came to see, when first drawn into the net of radicalisation himself, that the recruiters who skulk in the shadows had little commitment to the religion that he, and millions of others across the globe, hold dear. He was sold a 'false prospectus' by calculating individuals whose motives had little to do with the enduring strengths of Islam or the pursuit of natural justice. So it was then in Afghanistan, and so it is now in Syria and Iraq. The shadowy figures behind the radicalisation of our young men (and women) want nothing more than to recruit foot soldiers for slaughter on dusty battlefields far from their homes in the United Kingdom.

Thus it is that the theme running through Hanif's important new book, like a golden thread, is that this waste of young lives and human potential must stop. It is the duty of all responsible citizens, teachers, youth workers, members of the medical profession, police officers, prison officers and indeed parents in the comfortable West, particularly Britain, to learn from this book and to challenge the perversity of radicalisation whenever and wherever it manifests itself. Unless we do, we risk losing an entire generation of young, intelligent and committed Britons to an obscure philosophy that seeks to turn the undoubted beauty of Islam into a nihilist death cult.

With compelling style, Hanif charts a path through the complexities of the challenge facing us, based upon two decades of working in the field. In this he is unique – there is no other practitioner in the UK with his breadth of experience. He offers, for the first time, a proper definition of radicalisation and how 'recruiters' work to draw the vulnerable into their web. He discusses de-radicalisation techniques and critiques the Government's 'Prevent' initiative. Lastly, he looks into a crystal ball and assesses what might be beyond ISIS and the current model of domestic violent extremism that we see today.

This long overdue book will be essential reading for all those involved in radicalisation and security issues in a broader sense, and I commend it to all such people and also to the general reader who seeks an understanding of what is undoubtedly the challenge of our age.

David Gilbertson QPM
Deputy Assistant Commissioner Met Police (retired)
New Scotland Yard

INTRODUCTION

There is a huge amount of research material by academics and think tanks focused on preventing extremism and terrorism, set out in very eloquent ways. Some of these papers are flawed or are only opinions, based on little experience or time working 'on the ground'; others are well-grounded and have real substance based on facts, evidence and case studies.

With this in mind, let me assure you that the contents within this book are backed up with facts, evidence from current real-life cases and personal experiences gained from working at the cutting-edge of counter-extremism and de-radicalisation. I have experienced huge challenges with some of the most difficult individuals in the UK and South Asia and I will set out how those challenges were overcome and how risks have been mitigated.

It is clearly evident that the problem of extremism and terrorism is increasing and new challenges are continuously arising. It is for this reason that I decided to add my experience of 15 years in the field, operating at a grassroots level and on the front line in the battle, to preventing extremism and terrorist recruitment. Hence, the primary focus of this book is to address extremism and terrorist recruitment within Muslim communities primarily, both here in the UK and abroad.

The purpose of this book is not to claim that I know everything. It is merely another source of education and information in my attempts to pass on to others the real and hard-won experience I have gained over the years. I believe it is essential we take examples from as many experienced sources as we can in our attempts to prevent extremism and terrorism. It is my intention that this work serves as a contribution to the experience and the learning that we all need, and it is my hope that it will assist in both changing lives and saving lives.

I am not an academic or a researcher. I am, however, someone on the ground dealing with the problem of terrorism and extremism every day and finding often very difficult solutions. I ask that the reader excuses my modest, plain English approach.

We all know of the conflicts around the world, in particular the Middle East and Africa, and how these conflicts have far-reaching consequences. With no sign of the solutions needed to establish peace in the near future, we see the impact of these conflicts on our streets and in our homes more than ever. Those regions have become prime training grounds for today's and, more worryingly, tomorrow's terrorists.

We now see that terrorist groups across the world, particularly in Syria and Iraq, **are** becoming extraordinarily skilful at recruitment, modifying religious and sectarian marketing campaigns to the digital age to suit their objectives within any given community. The usual prevention efforts are weakened by the lack of knowledge and (at times) the lack of willingness to understand the actual and real existing 'push and pull factors' or foreign fighter motivations. It is now evident that a re-energised, practical and more informed approach is crucial in order to more effectively equip frontline staff to play a critical role in addressing the problem. This book aims to serve that purpose by passing on knowledge and understanding of what has worked and how.

I will cover a journey where perceptions and views in general have changed the minds and attitudes of people from across the globe, primarily after the beginning of the War on Terror and subsequent terrorist attacks that have followed. The number of ideas and strategies that have been put in place to tackle terrorism has been overwhelming and challenging at every level. New laws have been applied and legislations have been written, and rewritten, time and again, and throughout this journey we have witnessed both good and bad practices that have changed the lives of many individuals, positively and negatively.

This book will cover my personal experience of being recruited into Al Qaeda as a foreign fighter and the rationale for joining them; my mindset, my attitude and behaviour, and why I eventually turned away. It will cover my efforts to dissuade many individuals from travelling the same path as my own, and the intense and sensitive work with some of the world's most difficult extremist and terrorist cases, and indeed the challenges and the benefits of working closely with partners and authorities.

The book's intention is to give the reader a greater understanding of the many misconceptions, attitudes, behavioural changes and internalisation of grievances, and identify critical intervention opportunities, but more importantly to draw many comparisons between my own experience and that of the different case studies included in this work. You will learn some of the many tactics applied by recruiters and the narratives they use, and hopefully I will provide you with a better understanding of how to prevent young men and women from falling prey to recruiters. It will examine why young men and women are more inclined to adopt a more extreme view. It will also generate an awareness and understanding of the risk of extremism within institutions, communities and even homes, where risks will vary greatly and change rapidly. That is why it is essential that every institution, individual and parent will need to give due regard to such risk.

I have to ask that you particularly think about the underlying factors and examine some of the 'push/pull' factors. These are crucial to any Prevent or counter-extremism initiative and if we do not consider them carefully, we are essentially missing opportunities and are ill-prepared to solve the actual problem. You cannot treat or cure anything without knowing the cause or the contributing factors at play. And I forewarn you that some of the factors I have included in this book can be a bit unsettling or may make you feel uncomfortable. They are not opinions or taken from second-hand sources; rather, they are fact-based arguments – arguments put to me directly by the cases I have worked with as well as the thousands of young men and women I have come into contact with across the world.

MY PERSONAL JOURNEY INTO (AND OUT OF) AL QAEDA

I will try to write the following in a way that will allow you to see what was going on in my mind: how I was processing the information, the language used by certain leaders and images of death and destruction and how I internalised these. It will demonstrate how, over a short period of time, my personality had completely changed.

I also feel the need to remind you that, aside from the facts surrounding the death toll of innocent men, women and children in Afghanistan, many of my opinions and views formed at that time (and subsequently revisited in this chapter) were misconceptions supported by 'structured' and targeted narratives, and that they were predominantly baseless. Any grievances you read here are based upon personal perceptions on the manner in which the War on Terror was executed. I am going to describe the extreme circumstances I encountered and how that exposure changed my personality. It will help to explain how far I travelled on a path towards self-destruction, and the reasons why I did so – simply because I failed to question what I was told without critically analysing anything.

In December 2002, after the US-led invasion of Afghanistan (the start of George Bush's so-called War on Terror), I travelled to the country from the UK, via Pakistan. My main intentions were to help alleviate the suffering of the many thousands of innocent civilians caught up in the bombing campaigns by the coalition forces and, more shockingly, being targeted by American soldiers on the ground. Although it is inevitable to a degree that innocent people will suffer as a consequence of war, I found it very hard to digest the stories that soldiers from the coalition forces were found to be indiscriminately (and often deliberately) killing civilians in order to shock and lower the morale within the ranks of the Taliban and Al Qaeda leadership. The images of dead children, parents and elderly people were brutal and very disturbing. It was very difficult for me to overlook this as simply 'collateral damage'. The general attitude of American leaders in support of their soldiers delivering 'revenge' for 9/11 shocked and saddened me.

The manner in which the War on Terror was unfolding and the number of civilian deaths I read about and saw on television news reports left me susceptible and receptive to extremist ideology, and so the process of my recruitment prior to travelling to Afghanistan was quick, easy and simple. I was approached by a local guy, a customer at the MOT testing station I ran, who knew that my brothers and I were always very helpful when it came to helping those in need and would do a lot for charity. He arrived one day with two other men, claiming to be raising funds for the innocent civilians caught up in the war and the children who had lost parents. They produced images and described what was happening in Afghanistan on a daily basis. I found it very easy to offer my support. My first thoughts were of my own kids and my elderly mother: 'What if it were them who were in such a position?' This really played on my mind for a few days afterwards, and it began to take hold, even more so once I began to watch the news more and more and search the internet.

Over the period of six to seven weeks I had met the same guys almost weekly for updates and to look at other ways of generating support for the victims. Our conversations were focused on how to stop this destruction from continuing and what action needed to be taken. After each meeting I became more upset with the language being used to describe Muslims and the Islamic faith by Western leaders and the media. I was hearing people expressing joy when bombs were killing civilians, describing them as 'ragheads', filthy vermin supporters of Bin Laden who deserved to be exterminated. I heard about many attacks locally on Muslim women and on shops. I began to feel my own customers, who were mostly white British people, looking at me strangely and acting more withdrawn. I mentioned these developments when I saw the two guys at the next meeting and they then began to explain how this was just the beginning of things to come. They kept on stressing that it wouldn't be long before Muslims were persecuted here in the UK because of the loss of life of British soldiers, and that the war would spread to other Muslim lands, targeting Islam and Muslims rather than 'terrorists'. I took this as the truth because of what I was experiencing personally, but also because of what I was hearing from other people.

11

Two days later I was called to another meeting, where I was introduced to an elderly man, who in fact looked a lot like Osama Bin Laden, but who was actually a Syrian who lived mainly in France. He carried himself very humbly and spoke with a soft voice in Arabic. One of the other guys translated for him, which I found very interesting as Arabic was a language I adored. The Syrian was incorporating certain verses of the *Quran*, which I related to, though I felt I had not previously understood. Not knowing whether he was manipulating the verses or not, I took it for granted that the Syrian was genuine and knew much more than I did because he was an Arab who spoke the language of the *Quran*. So, I naturally accepted what he was saying as the truth.

The Syrian was present and led every meeting thereafter and his presence made the meetings feel much more interesting and important, especially as they became more clandestine in nature. He reminded us of our duties as Muslims 'who have every luxury available at our feet and our homes', whilst our fellow Muslim brothers and sisters were being tortured and brutally killed by the 'crusaders'. He repeated that the War on Terror was in fact a religious crusade led by George Bush. I began to look deeper into historical events and underlying issues such as the ongoing events in Palestine. I read how Western governments remained silent whilst Palestinians were being slaughtered by an occupying force; and then about the First Gulf War, led by George Bush Snr, who attacked Iraq because it was trying to annex Kuwait, and how he was killing Iraqi Kurds. This I found most hypocritical, given that Israel was doing exactly the same thing with Palestine and the Arabs.

I was directed to look at certain websites, detailing how Muslims were being directly targeted for ethnic cleansing by Russians and the Chinese. I read reports about secret plans to divide Pakistan and I believed every single narrative that was put to me. I no longer felt I was British and I did not feel I could trust anyone outside of this new network I had been introduced to. I did not trust my own mother, my sister or my wife, as I felt they would not see eye-to-eye with me on what I now understood, and that they would never be able to see things as I did. I feared they would try to dissuade me from what I then believed to be the undeniable truth.

As far as I was concerned, my only allies were my two brothers and these three guys who I had met only a few months ago, and who I began to trust more than my family. At every meeting, we were instructed to take the battery out of our mobile phones and placed them under the mats in our cars, and we were searched by the three guys every time we entered the room. But I never once thought about whether I should search them, or asking whether or not they had left their own phones in their cars; it just never occurred to me to question why I was not trusted, despite me placing my own complete trust with them.

The meetings intensified, with conversations focused on how American soldiers were treating Muslims in Afghanistan and the rape of women and of young boys and girls. I was told about a special unit that was trained to rape young men and then let some of them loose so they can tell others of what happened. Many other stories were told about the brutality of the 'crusaders' and how they were stealing gold from villagers and how they were intoxicating themselves on cannabis before going out on killing sprees.

The way I was internalising these developments and how they were manifesting themselves in my brain was beyond my control and even though I was trying to look critically and with a rational mind, I found only one explanation: this War on Terror was more of a war on Islam and Muslims. George Bush calling the war a 'crusade'; an American general addressing his soldiers by saying, 'Jesus is with us in this war between good and evil'; Tony Blair describing 'an evil ideology'. The words were continuously going through my mind, day and night. My emotions were all over the place and my anger was rapidly building. The war was intensifying and spreading beyond the initial plan of finding and destroying Al Qaeda networks. It was generating deep divisions within the Afghan people, first and foremost, but also Muslims in general. I felt I had to do something more than just offer financial support for the victims and be more proactive in trying to prevent innocent Afghan children from being blown to pieces or orphaned. I felt I had to act to stop the death toll from increasing.

Then, as my emotions reached a peak, I stumbled across a website showing a photograph of American soldiers standing over a pile of dead bodies, mainly children. One particular soldier caught my eye; he was standing with his boot placed on top of the body of a young kid, whose eyes were still open. He was smiling for the camera, machine gun in hand, with a caption above him saying, 'We just kicked ass'. This sent me into a rage, to a point where I started to cry. I was unable to do anything from where I was. This sense of uselessness was driving me crazy, but it also made me believe more firmly that this was clearly a war on Muslims and an absolute revenge for 9/11: how could an armed soldier treat a young child like that, if he was not either intoxicated or on a revenge mission? It made me more determined to continue the course with the network I had joined.

I was angry at the Muslim leadership in the Middle East, especially the Saudis, who I felt should have responded to George Bush's 'crusade' statement, and other Gulf states who I began to despise due their lack of grit to stand up to 'the crusaders'. The Syrian man continued to tell me that the Arab leaders had failed the Muslim *Ummah* (community) and how they were only interested in personal wealth and saving their own positions as rulers. I was even shown a photo of the King of Saudi Arabia wearing a cross, depicting him as a Christian rather than a Muslim. I was shown the palaces of the rulers in Dubai and how much money they wasted on horses and women, whilst Muslims around the world were suffering immensely. I was shown images of almost all the rulers of Muslim countries laughing and joking whilst either sipping tea or alcohol with Americans or British leaders. Simultaneously, I was still being shown the images of dead, butchered children in Afghanistan, Iraq, Palestine and Chechnya, atrocities carried out by western regimes.

All this information and imagery completely threw me off balance. We discussed how all the leaders of Muslim countries, especially the Arab and Gulf states, were part of the problem and needed to be removed. After many meetings on this topic it became obvious to me that there were plans in place to do this first.

In my view at the time, it was crystal clear that the Muslim leaders were in fact selling out to the West. All these grievances were playing through my mind and pushing me further down into a deeper and darker hole.

I began to read literature I was given to look at in my search for the answers I wanted to hear, and examined many verses in the *Quran* which would justify the need to act. In fact, I flicked through most of the *Quran*, selecting certain verses that I related to and, without context, applied them to my own desires and beliefs at the time. I did not want to read verses of peace and the rules of warfare, and I certainly did not want to contextualise verses that would cause me to deviate from the path I was about to take. I was in an 'unconscious' state. In my mind and in my heart I was convinced that I needed to act and that if I joined these guys I would be doing the right thing.

During one of the last meetings I attended, the Syrian man took out a cloth resembling a handkerchief with Arabic writing on it. He told me that this was a message from the *Amir ul Mu'mineen* (commander of the faithful) and it had been endorsed with his seal of approval, reminding me that this was in fact exactly how our beloved Prophet (peace be upon him) relayed messages to his companions. He began to read it out in Arabic, which was translated by one of the others. He explained how the commander of the faithful was deeply thankful for my support and how it had helped change the lives of hundreds of orphans and widows, and he reminded me of the importance of continuing with this support. He further explained the urgent need for vehicles and manpower and how this was a fundamental duty for Muslims around the world.

After hearing my name mentioned in this message I felt deeply pleased with myself and became very emotional. I asked if I could have the cloth so I can take it back to show my brothers, and surprisingly I was allowed to do so, although I was reminded to destroy it afterwards. On the journey back to my workshop I kept the cloth in my hand, constantly looking at where my name was written. Each time I read my name I felt comfort. I was content that I was doing something right by my fellow Muslims and for myself too, for when I meet my maker. I took the cloth to a friend and had it translated in front of my brothers, just so they could feel a part of what I was experiencing and, in all honesty, to convince them that I was doing the right thing.

Looking back, this was clearly the defining moment for me. I knew it was time to take the next steps, so I booked my flight for the first week of December 2002. About ten days before I was due to travel, I went to meet the guys again, and found one of them absent. I was told he had had to travel urgently back to Afghanistan due to his younger brother being martyred in a battle. The Syrian relayed the whole story, explaining that some other *mujahideen* fighters had stumbled upon his body by following a sweet fragrance that lead them up a hill to a small group of mountain goats that were surrounding the body of 'the martyr'. I was told that the goats appeared to be guarding the body of this martyr and that the closer the group of fighters got to the body, the closer the goats drew towards the body, trying to protect it. Finally, the fighters managed to retrieve the body and bury it, as per Islamic ruling.

We sat for hours listening to similar stories, which had a powerful impact on me and others in the room. The Syrian man went on to talk about the Black Banners (flags) and how they will rise against the infidel and how the emergence of the '*Khorasan*' state was imminent. We were instructed to read up on these for ourselves from one of the books we were given, demonstrating the importance of participation in this *jihad*, no matter what.

In my mind and even though I did not need any further convincing, everything became crystal clear from that moment forward. All the conversations we had, the stories I had heard and the chapters I had been reading, were so overwhelming to me that I wrote up my will and handed it to my wife in case I didn't return. I explained that although I will be going to help the innocent victims, I may end up joining the *jihad* because of what I now understood. She tried to convince me to stay away from trouble and out of harm's way, and told me of how our children would suffer if anything was to happen to me. I argued that the kids in Afghanistan had parents too, but now they were orphans and alone with nothing and no one at all, and that the widows were suffering without their husbands. My wife is a very humble and caring woman who cannot bear to see others suffer, and these arguments helped me to convince her. Reluctantly she remained silent. But one thing she did say remained with me: that was to remember to conduct myself in the best possible manner and that every action I take must be strictly in accordance with the fundamentals of Islam.

I went to see my mother on the day I was to leave and told her I was going on a business trip. I asked her for forgiveness and to pray for me, she patted my back as she always did and reminded me, as she always does, to call her from the airport, call her when I arrive and to remember to call her every night. She then told me to return as agreed, to not extend my stay, which I told her was two weeks.

I travelled to Islamabad, where my brother-in-law received me at the airport before taking me straight to his home in the city. I rested the whole day and after waking up in the evening I asked to be taken out for a walk in Jinnah Park, from where I had been instructed to make a call back to London to ask for guidance on where to go and who to meet. After trying numerous times, I still could not establish contact with anyone. So I called my brothers to tell them I arrived safely and was waiting for instructions from the Syrian and the others. As I was walking back to where I was staying I noticed I had had a missed call, so I called back. It was one of the guys from the group, who told me to wait until Sunday afternoon and then call back for further instructions.

At this point I decided to go to the village in Azad Kashmir, where we had our own family home, with the intention of preparing it for the widows and orphans I intended to bring back from Afghanistan. I made arrangements for around 30 children and eight women to live in the ten bedrooms, which was quite comfortable considering the size of the rooms. I instructed one of my cousins to make sure the orphans were looked after properly in case I failed to return alongside them and left him with enough money to cater for six months, with instructions to contact my brothers when he needed more funds.

On Sunday morning, I returned to Islamabad and in the afternoon called my contact. I was given instructions to travel to Peshawar and in the early evening to travel to a mosque where I would be met by two people, who would somehow recognise me and take me on to Afghanistan through to Landi Kotl and onto Torkham. Following these instructions I set out on my next journey.

Looking back, this next phase of my journey was pivotal. Once I arrived in Afghanistan, almost immediately I began to witness some hard and brutal facts: the actual reality of what was going on. Here, I was set ablaze by the sheer lack of respect for human life by the very people I had travelled to support. There was no care for the innocent victims of the conflict. I saw how many of the

Taliban fighters had very little value for any human life, and witnessed the total hypocrisy of those who were claiming to represent fairness and justice, and indeed Islam.

I was appalled by the manner in which these people were dealing with the local Afghans and their attitude to those like me who travelled to offer our help. I saw kids being used as cannon fodder, old men treated like filth. Above all, I was furious with the arrogance of other foreign fighters from some of the Gulf states and Chechnya, who lorded a higher status over others. They treated the Pakistanis, Somalis and Bengalis like dirt. This, in my view, was totally against my faith and utterly inhumane.

To further their own agenda, and by using lies and deception and by capitalising on the suffering of others, the men I had been meeting with in the UK had given me a completely different picture to what was actually going on. This was far more criminal than anything I could imagine.

Of course, I had not expected the 'red carpet treatment' in Afghanistan. On the contrary, I knew I was going to a war zone and I expected shock and horror. But what I did not expect was that the very people who were flying the flag of Islam and claiming that the invaders were brutalising the locals were themselves guilty of doing exactly the same.

Kids were being groomed into becoming suicide bombers without even knowing what would happen to them, aside from being promised paradise for their parents and themselves. I watched them smiling after hearing stories of how they will be happy and will provide their parents and siblings with everything they could dream of in paradise. They were led to believe that all of their struggles and difficulties would vanish and their future would be in paradise with all of their loved ones and they would have anything they wished for. Hearing this was completely soul destroying. And especially so having heard the Taliban claim that this tactic was in response to American missiles and drones, and that they can use these kids as effectively as laser-guided bombs.

My head was throbbing with rage. An overwhelming desire to kill surged through me – yet it was a desire to kill those who I now saw with my own eyes to be the actual perpetrators. Contrary to all I had believed before, it was the foreign fighters, as well as some local Afghan Taliban, who I saw as arrogant and hypocritical. In my opinion, they were the people who had the complete disregard for human life – let alone any respect for Islam. Even though the Allied forces, led by the Americans, were the main cause of most of the death and the destruction, I could not accept people acting in the name of my faith, whilst contributing to the loss of innocent lives.

There was another very disturbing observation I made which I have thought about time and again ever since. The other fighters I met out there, even the ones being treated badly by members of Al Qaeda and the Taliban, were still hugely excited, energetic and committed to the cause. They did not see things as I did. Speaking to a few of them, they expressed their joy and happiness that they had an opportunity for *jihad* against the disbelievers, a chance which they would not have had if the Americans and their allies had not arrived in Afghanistan.

One particular statement I heard was: 'Allah has blessed us with this opportunity, because we do not have the means to travel to America or Europe, so Allah has sent them to us.' From what I could see, none of them seemed to be able to afford a decent pair of shoes, yet they all had their own weapons, some of which held together with rags and pieces of rope. Each of them equally prepared for death and speaking of this conflict as the birth of many more battles to rage. But I could not find a single voice speaking out against the hypocrisy rampant within their ranks, orchestrated by their leaders who were mainly foreign.

What I learned from the experience will remain with me for the rest of my life, and having been fortunate to walk away, without being harmed, I decided it was something I needed to address.

A very short period after I arrived in Afghanistan, I decided to return to Pakistan and I caught a flight back to the UK the following morning. Many readers will be asking how I got away and how I was allowed to leave. That is a different story and would require a lot more writing, but in short, it was challenging and hostile, and I consider myself very lucky to have left the country alive. I will leave it there.

After a few hours of being back home, I sat with my two brothers and explained in detail about absolutely everything I had experienced. Both were completely shocked and furious. We have always lived a life where if one of us was threatened we would come together and face the threat as one. If I was hurt then so too were my brothers, and it was our collective decision to seek out the Syrian and the other two guys – no matter what the consequences. We searched everywhere and even went back to the places we held meetings.

Looking back, I think it was a good thing we did not find any trace of these guys. It was like they had disappeared off the planet. Had we found them, I am certain we would have taken matters too far and perhaps ended up doing something very bad, even though they certainly deserved it.

My whole experience was an emotional rollercoaster; I was a willing participant, travelled the whole course and managed to survive its deadly and twisted curves.

My personality was ripped away and replaced with an unfamiliar one that was completely out of character. My loving relationships were almost severed and I had a complete lack of trust and respect for my mother, my sister and my own children. Had I been fully conscious, that would have been unthinkable for me to do. To think I would separate myself from my two beloved brothers was ordinarily impossible.

My emotions were abused and used against my better understanding to further someone else's agenda, instead of being used to sincerely help the innocent men, women and children I was sympathetic towards. My life was abused in a way where it was to be used as a sacrifice to support the objectives of men I knew nothing about. My faith was abused by ignorant and selfish individuals who did not respect the boundaries of Islam, a faith they claimed to represent, and one that I hold very dear to my heart.

The anger I had within me towards such people was so great and I cannot find the words to express it. But thankfully I believe that anger became the fuel that now drives my passion to prevent others from traversing the same path as mine. The continuing thought of my mother crying or my children struggling if I had lost my life has been nagging at me ever since and I believe it will continue for the rest of my life.

THE BIRTH OF THE ACTIVE CHANGE FOUNDATION

After trying to come to terms with my experience, I could not work anymore. I decided to sell the MOT testing station and urged my brothers to sell their tyre and exhaust workshop. The idea was to do something else, something more meaningful and focused on helping others. For three or four months after selling our businesses we just sat at home enjoying each other's company with our families.

One day we decided to find a place where we could do some community-based projects. We found an excellent venue right in the heart of the local community, which had previously been used as an unlicensed nightclub before being closed down by the police and local council due to gun crimes and drug abuse. We renovated the second floor and opened a health and fitness centre. The first floor was still used by another occupant as a Caribbean culture club, though this also ended up being closed down by the authorities for similar crimes. The landlord for the building had asked me to find some suitable tenants to occupy the first floor and gave me the keys to look after and show around potential tenants.

I was asked to investigate some young Asian boys who were terrorising a local estate, where elderly residents were facing the brunt of the boys' anti-social behaviour. I intervened and managed to convince the boys to refrain from hanging around the estate, though when one of the boys asked where they should go instead, I realised there was an underlying problem in the community, one which needed a long-term solution. I thought of an idea to get them interested in something they really needed, a place just to chill out and relax. So I asked them to come see me at our new building. The first floor had a pool table in one of the halls, although it was a bit broken. It was just the kind of hangout they needed. It was still in a bit of shambles as the previous occupier had ripped out all his fixtures and fittings and left the place in a bit of hurry. However, the pool table and some sofas were left behind and actually fitted the concept very well. The boys felt they had a place of their own where they could relax and where they were completely comfortable, without having people nagging them or the police chasing them. I asked them a few questions about who their parents were and if they knew me *etc*, which they answered without any problem.

Over the course of a week, as the little group began to get bigger and bigger, I had to think of other ways to keep them occupied and busy with positive things. I came up with table-top syndicate exercises and other such mental games which went down very well. Even though we had a broken pool table and a shabby set up, the boys just kept on coming in through the doors.

The project gave me complete engagement and real-time understanding of what problems affected the youth. It also provided me with an insight into how these young men were very vulnerable to recruiters of all kinds who could apply their narratives, just as had happened to me. The boys spoke quite frankly and openly about how they felt and what they thought about the War on Terror, feelings which I completely related to. A lot of anger was expressed and most felt they had to do something to prevent the death of innocent civilians. This was rapidly becoming familiar territory for me and I was increasingly becoming concerned about what would happen to these young men, and also about what they could potentially do to others.

I decided to speak to the local imam of the mosque right next door to our building, though as I did so he began staring into my eyes as if I was some drugged-up madman. I emphasized how severe this problem could become and how important it was that he addressed the parents of young people during his Friday sermons, as a protective measure to safeguard the youth. Sadly, the imam told me to stop worrying and to stop reading too many papers, because he thought the information I was trying to get over to him was actually something I had read or seen on TV. He clearly told me to be careful about reading into the plans of 'Westerners trying to make Muslims look bad'. He said that things were not as bad as certain people made them out to be. I argued that I was talking about real young men who I had spoken with, who were expressing some serious stuff, but the imam failed to appreciate my concerns. He passed it off as a conspiracy to undermine Muslims and Islam. Before I left his office, he insisted I kept quiet about such things and not to talk about them in front of non-Muslims as it would be seen as if I were doing the dirty washing of the Muslim community in front of them, and again tried to reassure me that the mosque was quite capable of dealing with such issues if they arose.

I could not resist myself; I went back inside and gave him some harsh truths about what was going on right outside of his office and in the very same street as the mosque. I told him that in fact he had a huge role to play in addressing the issues at hand and the emerging issues surrounding other young people expressing their anger about what was happening in Afghanistan. I was very firm with my points and gave him plenty of evidence, but it seemed to go into one ear and out of the other.

During the conversation, a few of the mosque committee members joined us in the room, and after listening to a few points they began to question what I was doing by allowing young people into my centre, which only promoted idleness and didn't teach them Islam. The argument rose to the point where they insisted that I should force those kids into the mosque or send them back outside, because I was spoiling them by giving them an alternative place to hang out instead of guiding them to the mosques. It was slowly becoming a shouting match where I didn't stand a chance of getting my point across. I asked whether I should instead allow them to continue in their anti-social behaviour and drug use, and was told by one of the members that it wasn't his or my concern, but rather that of their parents and the government or police. That was the general attitude amongst most of the elders. I had no option but to walk out in dismay.

Many days went by and discussions took place with other community elders and parents with the same attitude: ignorance and disregard. I began attending council meetings and lobbying my local councillor, Stella Creasy, with whom I began to get on quite well and who asked me to help move the young Asian males away from the local estate. She was one of two people at that time who took notice of what I was saying, the second person being Chief Inspector Ian Larnder (currently Superintendent). Both of these individuals were instrumental in helping me create more awareness of the problems facing young people and the wider community.

Stella Creasy then introduced me to another remarkable individual, who fully understood the dynamics of the street and the problems I was talking about. When we first met, Mike Jervis was the local council's 'gang's officer', and had seen some difficult situations dealing with gang issues. But noticing a firm correlation between gangs and extremism, and after a lot of emerging political issues, Mike left the council and joined the organisation I had set up (The Active Change Foundation). Many years later, he continues to work alongside me and the team at the ACF. Mike has helped me on many cases, and if it wasn't for his support it would have been extremely difficult to come as far as I have. Mike was, and still is, considered our 'brother from another mother' – a man equally as passionate about the work we do and the people it helps.

Even though we now had a few voices echoing the same issues, it took almost three years and the London bombings of July 7, 2005, for the local authority to actually realise there was a serious problem brewing and something needed to be done. By this time I had developed another very crucial and important relationship with the Met Police Muslim Contact Unit (MCU), within its Counter Terrorism Command. This unit was essentially a handful of very experienced and dedicated individuals who knew exactly what I was talking about and completely understood how to tackle the problem. Along with Simon Cornwall, another individual introduced to me later on by the MCU and who headed up the central extremism division within the National Offender Management Service (NOMS) and the Probation Service, these special people were instrumental in giving me the trust and the confidence to carry on with my initiatives to address the issues we faced. In fact they helped support me in reforming many individuals in the early days. These relationships also helped me forge through some great challenges and allowed me to get on with some very real prevention work, even though these were in the years before the formalisation of Prevent, the government's counter-extremism/terrorism strategy.

It would be safe to say that without the support of these incredible people, most of this book would not exist. Indeed many of the following case studies would not be studies on success, rather as statistics on terrorist acts by young men and women. So it would be entirely wrong for me not to acknowledge these individuals as the unsung heroes they actually are.

However, having already formalised the Active Change Foundation as a non-profit organisation, I continued to face some huge challenges from the very community I was trying to help. In fact I was hitting hurdle after hurdle and was blocked each time I approached the local authorities to deliver some real targeted projects – I was sent away without any help. I had no choice but to continue to pay for everything from my own pocket and it came to a point where I was rapidly running out of funds and could not see any hope of getting support from the authorities to continue. The rent was piling up and bills were coming through thick and fast, even though my two brothers helped as much as possible and gave me the financial backing when I had exhausted everything I had of personal wealth.

I found out later that my older brother had sold his house to keep my work going and to allow me more time to face off the opposition that had mobilised against me, in their efforts to silence me. As I mentioned before, my brothers and I were very close and if one was threatened we took it as if all three were. Though the local opposition continued, both of my brothers became much more actively and openly involved in my work. This caused further waves within the community, but it helped me to carry on with the real preventative work and to help many young people – again, this was all done before the official Prevent agenda was formalised in late 2006 and early 2007, when the Home Office created the Office of Security and Counter Terrorism (OSCT).

On August 10 2006, something happened that changed everything. 13 young men and one young woman were arrested for planning the biggest terrorist plot since 9/11; now commonly known as the Airline/Liquid Bombers, or the Overt Plot, where a number of trans-Atlantic airliners were to be hijacked and exploded before landing in the USA. All of those arrested were from my local area, aside from one, who was from the Thames Valley region.

When the story broke, the world's media descended upon Waltham Forest, and everyone in a position of authority, including local imams, were faced with a media onslaught. At one point, there were 75 journalists and their crews waiting outside the centre to interview me about the plot and the young men involved. A number of journalists went as far as looking into some of my previous interviews going back as far as 2004 and 2005, prior to the London bombings, where I warned the authorities of a problem like this coming our way. Almost every single media outlet quoted me saying exactly that, which clearly did not go down too well with certain people in the local community, especially those in the local council. In fact one press media network decided to carry out an investigation into everything I spoke about and what was going on within certain departments and institutions.

In hindsight, though I was not playing the political game very well and only said things as they were, being totally honest about what was going on, I was blatant and loud and I was drawing too much negative attention to the local borough and that was not at all beneficial for me or my work going forward.

It was an experience from which I learned a great deal and I reasoned that I needed to be more careful and sensitive when talking about my passion for protecting people in my community. I learned that tackling deep-rooted community problems can only be done at a 'political' pace, and with the support of certain influential individuals. What I was struggling with was the fact that, at times, I needed to get things done at a much faster pace in order to establish an effective support network for some of the young people I was trying to help.

Towards the end of 2006, my brothers and I had completely run out of funds and options. The rent for the centre was in arrears and the bills were way overdue. It looked like the end of the organisation and the end of my interventions. Judging by the intent and mood of some people in certain institutions, it seemed we were doomed to fail. We had reached our lowest point.

However, just at a time when I had lost all hope, after a CNN interview between myself and Christiane Amanpour called 'The War Within', we were approached by an organisation known as Forward Thinking. They sent out a remarkable gentleman looking for us, Mr Yusuf Desai. This man walked all around Waltham Forest and went into every local institution and mosque searching for me or my brothers. Finally, in the evening, he bumped into my older brother who brought him into the ACF centre. This is where things began to change for the better. After a few days, via Yusuf we were introduced to Chris Donnelly, a very polite and generally quiet gentleman, but someone who made a very loud bang when it came to garnering support around us. Chris has been a special advisor to four consecutive NATO generals and was a very well-known strategic thinker who has advised many senior ministers within the UK establishment and around the world. Chris found our work interesting and of the utmost importance and began to mobilise his own support network to aid the delivery of our aims and objectives.

We managed to convince the landlord to hold off until we found funds to pay him, which also allowed us to deliver some great projects, and, whilst doing so, Chris managed to introduce more people to our work. We were forming a highly credible network of remarkable individuals who continue voluntarily to support our high-risk but very important work to this day. Later, Chris and Forward Thinking introduced another very special gentleman with an absolutely huge level of integrity. David Gilbertson, who was then Deputy Assistant Commissioner for the Metropolitan Police and who served in the police force for decades before retiring, came along voluntarily and began applying his skills and guidance, helping shape the Active Change Foundation into a professional, well-oiled and well-structured charity, ready and able to meet the challenges ahead.

From this point forward and with a renewed level of confidence, I was called to deliver talks and presentations and share my experiences with some very high-profile institutions and individuals. To mention a few: Governor Sununu, Chief of Staff in the White House; Farah Pandith, head of European and Eurasian Affairs in the US State Department; UK Chief of Army Staff, General Nick Parker; UK Home Secretary Jacqui Smith; Hazel Blears, UK Secretary of State for Communities and Local Government; and others. Additionally, I regularly delivered monthly training to new and existing OSCT Home Office staff and quite often helped educate the Met Police on issues within mainly Muslim communities.

In early 2007, we were approached by the Home Office, who asked me to put together a proposal and outline a plan of action to prevent the growth of violent extremism and terrorist recruitment. We quickly put a document together and, to our great surprise, it was accepted and funding was granted. By working tirelessly and endlessly, we were beginning to demonstrate far and wide how effective our work could be in protecting young people from terrorist recruitment. We used our newly awarded funds very wisely and doubled our efforts to prove how far small ideas can go when they are backed with resources. In the years since, we have continued with our efforts and to this day we are considered as perhaps the best organisation in the world at addressing the problem of extremism.

My personal journey into Al Qaeda networks has allowed me to fully understand their *modus operandi*, how they think, how they communicate, the narratives they use and how they adapt to the times, their objectives, their knowledge and indeed their values and beliefs. It is with this understanding that we have managed to prove successful over the years with work and cases which have added on to this experience, and we continue to learn a great deal more. Working with many different partners and institutions has also provided us with greater insight, allowing us to develop our models over time, and as we experience greater challenges with high-risk cases we have to adapt our strategies to meet the demands. We have positively shaped and changed the lives of many vulnerable young men and women and this has also afforded us a huge amount of experience in shaping our models to meet the challenges ahead.

WHAT IS RADICALISM?

The major issue in question is the phenomenon most commonly understood as Islamic-based radicalisation and violent extremism, and it is that issue that I will focus on in this chapter.

Firstly, however obvious a fact it may be, it is necessary to remind ourselves that not all violent extremists are motivated through Islam, nor indeed inspired or reinforced by religious enthusiasm of other faiths. Nationalism, emotional responses to conflict or social, economic or political reasons may be the cause. Religion may be irrelevant, or it may come to be an issue as the contention develops, thereby obscuring the fundamental cause and becoming a distraction and a complicating factor in evaluating and indeed addressing the problem.

Secondly, the universal use of the word 'radical' in this context is unfortunate. Radicalism has a proud history in many political cultures, those of the UK and US included, where radicals pursued causes such as electoral reform and the abolition of slavery. When Christianity went through its painful reformation, it was driven by radicals, not moderates. Now at least, we can cope with the contradiction of the fact that being 'radical' can be either good or bad, depending on the circumstances and on the viewpoint of the user. But commonly giving radicalisation a negative connotation in terms of religious fervour can easily lead to the assumption that it always leads to violent extremism.

Not only is this not true, but the risk is that we become blind to those religious radicals – secular, observant and politically motivated – who share liberal principles, support representative government, popular participation in politics, transparency, good governance and economic development with the cooperation and partnership of the international community. These 'radicals' are essentially reformists who are, in fact, in conflict with the fanatics who advocate violence to achieve their aims. Such radical reformists include secular

Muslims, observant and conservative Muslims, Christians, Jews and members of other religious faiths, as well as many in Islam who follow the actual Salafi methodology but who genuinely advocate participation in the social and political life of the country in which they live and are in fact part of the solution instead of being seen as part of the problem like many would like us all to believe.

Failure to understand this dichotomy in the nature of radicalism can blind people to potential solutions, where those most at risk can be diverted from resorting to violence by helping them to espouse radicalism in a different way, or by engaging them in traditionally conservative religious practice as a bulwark against any tendency to violence. Unfortunately, we are stuck for now with the term 'radicalisation', widely understood in a purely negative way. We will use the term in this book as such because of current convention. But we should be particularly aware in planning that fanatics and extremists need to be studied and understood as being distinct from radicals. Under this definition, Al Qaeda, ISIS and others alike are violent fanatics and extremists, not radicals.

Thirdly, when trying to address the issue of the Islamic-based radicalisation that leads to violent extremism, a better insight will be gained if, rather than considering this as 'Islamisation' as many will argue or as it is now more commonly known, we take our starting point as this phenomenon simply being 'extremism'. That is to say, the most significant and weighty factors which in today's world initiate and stimulate the radicalisation process, especially in young people, are not initially or essentially religious, but are usually based in perceived injustice, empathy, grievance and in some cases deprivation. The use of religion (or rather the interpretation and practice of the faith by the individual), the organisation, and the recruiters (or the self-recruitment process) will then often provide the psychological framework to explain the causes of the motivating injustice, to justify the resort to violence, and to sustain the fervour to implement it.

This last point is crucial when taking into consideration the dynamics of the phenomenon of violent extremism, and it underlines the importance of the timeliness and currency of the evidence one takes into consideration when making the all-important first assessment.

The evidence from my experience is that in the past couple of years a lot has changed in the process through which individuals advocate violence using faith as a prism. It used to take quite a long time for an individual to immerse themselves in religious interpretations to the point where they advocated or carried out violence in the name of their faith. Now, it seems, this process is taking only a matter of weeks. More recently this acceleration in many cases appears to depend on the state of affairs across the Middle East and in mainly Muslim countries coupled with a religious 'radicalising' to a point where the individual takes on the mantle of faith to take the first steps to advocate or legitimise participation.

This is perhaps the most significant development that we need to understand better, especially due to the referencing within religious texts of those areas where conflict is increasing. For example, Syria and Iraq, more generally known as Sham and referred to as 'the place where the major battles and indeed the final battles against the enemies of Islam will be fought'. More individuals are looking at this as a religious obligation, that participation is a must. The individual's belief, or the interpretation of that belief, is that the faith compels them to act. Of course, this is not the case, but it is what many young people are led to believe; it is the argument made and professed by extremist groups and hate preachers. Without clear explanations and guidance of their faith, I'm afraid this will become more prevalent within young people and indeed their communities.

These distinctions are not splitting hairs. They are fundamental not only to gaining an understanding as to the processes at work within an individual, an organisation or a community, but also to approaching the planning of an intervention which can help to solve the problem.

The radicalisation process and the rationale behind it

The process of radicalisation takes shape through a number of different mediums, but more often it is a targeted strategy implemented by an individual or a group via direct as well as indirect contact (physical or via social media). This strategy requires interaction or engagement which is then built upon through conversations. These conversations are followed up with some 'facts', often distorted and manipulated to suit both the circumstances and the individual on the receiving end.

An example: *"In Afghanistan the Americans are responsible for killing thousands of Muslims, women, kids and the elderly."* This is a fact, but there is more to it than this one-line sentence. There are other tempting lines that I have heard are used and exploited by the recruiters. *"Donald Trump wants to ban Muslims from the USA. It is a crazy, radical statement, but then look, millions of Americans support him."*

"The whole world is turning against Muslims, they fear Islam, that's why they are finding new ways to attack us."

"Can't you see what's happening? In Syria, Bashar Al Assad is butchering thousands of Muslims, yet no American or British intervention comes to stop this, like they did in Iraq with Saddam."

"Muslim lives don't matter – look at how non-Muslims come together in solidarity when non-Muslims are killed, yet they ignore the deaths of thousands of Muslims on a daily basis in Iraq, Syria, Palestine, Pakistan and Kashmir."

These are just simple narratives, but lead on to fuller conversations which will change track at times when needed. The key objective for the extremist groups and the recruiters is to raise curiosity and thought.

We know historically that revolutions have been created through simple conversations. It is exactly the same strategy that is applied now and certainly will be in the future. However, the current establishment policy to address this issue is to try to shut down conversations. This is a bad strategy, one which creates further problems as those conversations go underground, develop into whispers and subsequently the formation of ideas. Through this process, ideologies are born and a journey is mapped out. It is the same process which has happened countless times throughout history.

We need to appreciate that the process of radicalisation is shaped through engagement and relationship-building, firstly by engaging and then finding common ground with the subject. From this point forward the conversations are instrumental in creating an appetite, which then generates the ideas and then the mindset can be established. In fact, it is the exact same process that I have applied successfully on numerous occasions to de-radicalise an individual.

What we need to understand quite clearly is that engagement is the primary key, this is what starts the process. Only after engagement can a relationship be built between the recruiter and the vulnerable, creating the platform for conversations. It is then the skill of the recruiter (or intervention provider or the mentor, in the de-radicalisation process) to shape those conversations accordingly. This is how extremists operate and establish their roots within communities and institutions.

With regards to Islamic-based extremism, the foundations have already been firmly set for extremist recruiters to exploit and build upon. These foundations are by way of past and current conflicts overseas and our roles or lack thereof within them. The critical mistakes being made by Western powers (like the invasion of Iraq, and the non-existence of WMDs, the unresolved Palestinian-Israeli conflict and many others of this nature) have created the fertile ground. And on top of these issues, there is a clear and precise strategy laid out by groups like Al Qaeda, ISIS and others to drop information and use the death and destruction of innocent lives to further their own sinister ambitions. The radicalisation process becomes easy, quick and effective, in the main due to our own mistakes and lack of understanding of the constructs and sentiments of our communities.

I know many will disagree with me on this, but quite frankly it is at our own peril: failing to accept these facts is failing to address the growing problem of violent extremism. Foreign policy has been and will continue to be one of the major springboards from which violent extremism is launched and will be legitimised through whatever means, especially using a faith prism.

We can continue chasing our phantoms by blaming the growth of extremism exclusively on 'identity crisis, alienation, depravation or ignorance', but in reality it has been Western foreign policy that sits right at the top. And whilst I accept that the other vulnerabilities need to be seriously considered and addressed individually, in regards to violent extremism they are merely contributing factors. If we go back pre-9/11 or even further back, we have had black and ethnic minority people living in some of the most deprived areas within Europe, the UK and other parts of the Western world, who have been alienated, underachieving in school and in life in general whilst also having experienced the worst kind of racism. Yet we never experienced the growth of extremism or terrorist acts like we are experiencing currently.

Over the many years working on this issue, the majority of cases I have worked with have taken the first steps towards violent extremism because of Western foreign policy and the narratives used by recruiters, especially since the 'War on Terror' began. I can very easily follow hundreds of unqualified theories and tell you that the process of radicalisation is X Y & Z, whilst in fact it is not. And whilst I also accept the fact that each individual case is different, I cannot ignore the fact that 99% of the cases have one argument in common and that is that the radicalised individual believes that *"the war on terror is actually a war on Muslims and Islam"*. This then makes the process of radicalisation within Muslim communities pretty easy and uncomplicated.

PART A
THE CURRENT LANDSCAPE

WHAT THE UK GOVERNMENT IS DOING

WHAT IS PREVENT?

The general consensus is that everyone considers an act of terrorism to be a physical act of violence that causes death or severe injury. In reality the UK faces a number of terror threats that seek to attack the infrastructure of the country, our corporations, our energy plants and indeed to disrupt cohesion amongst communities. The government response must therefore take into consideration a multitude of potential threats and develop a response. However, whilst intelligence can mitigate risk and in many cases foil attacks it is important to understand that intelligence alone cannot stop all attacks.

It is the responsibility of the Home Secretary, in conjunction with the intelligence services, to set the level of threat and communicate it to the public. The range of threat level is set out below:

- Low, meaning an attack is unlikely
- Moderate, meaning an attack is possible, but not likely
- Substantial, meaning an attack is a strong possibility
- Severe, meaning an attack is highly likely
- Critical, meaning an attack is expected imminently

Between 2007 and the present day the threat level has fluctuated between 'substantial' and 'severe'. With this likelihood it is important that the government have a range of options. In this sense the Counter Terrorism Strategy (Contest), which was first published in 2006, set out a number of strategic objectives known as the Four Ps:

- Pursue: To stop terrorist attacks
- Prevent: To stop people becoming terrorists or supporting terrorism
- Protect: To strengthen our protection against a terror attack
- Prepare: To mitigate the impact of a terrorist attack

To achieve strategic clarity, the government's tactical approach was to utilise policy and legislation to empower the statutory sector, civil society and faith institutions to address terrorism. A range of counter-terrorism and security acts came in to force which looks at all aspects of the Four Ps. The most controversial component of the Counter Terrorism strategy is the Prevent strand, controversial due to the subjective nature and assessment tools required to prevent someone from becoming a terrorist or supporting terrorism.

Preventing someone from becoming a terrorist or supporting terrorism works within a space where no crime has yet been committed. This is known as the 'pre-crime space'. In this space the obvious question by campaigners against Prevent is 'How do you know that a person is likely to become a terrorist or support terrorism?' This is a legitimate community concern. In response to these concerns we must acknowledge the fact that there are people from within those very communities in the same space who have been and are continually plotting and planning acts of terror, recruiting our young people and also deciding to travel to fight or support the terrorist ideals. And we also know that, given the space, extremist recruiters will exploit the hearts and minds of our young people. The Prevent strategy is therefore in place to protect individuals from such exploitation by providing mentoring and support networks in order to safeguard young people.

The government's operational Prevent strategy response (2011) set out three objectives known as the Three Is. All organisations working within the pre-crime space should address one or more of the following:

- Respond to the **Ideological** challenge to terrorism and the threat posed by people who promote it;
- Prevent **Individuals** from being drawn into terrorism and ensure that they are given appropriate advice and support; and
- Work with sectors and **Institutions** where there are risks of radicalisation that need addressing.

However, having an operational response without operational scrutiny is simply bad strategy. Someone at the lowest operational level has to hold responsibility for the implementation of the Three Is. This falls to be the responsibility of the local authority and the police. The Crime and Disorder Act 1998 put a responsibility on all local authorities to work within a multi-agency framework to address risk and provide 'transition platforms' to create opportunities for change. In its most positive sense the theory is that a person with a chaotic lifestyle faces many challenges, and only with the main support of the statutory sector providing a holistic approach can we address all the needs of the individual or family. No single agency can create the change.

In the current climate of Islamic extremism, the actual problems for the statutory sector are, firstly, that they do not really have the reach to the local community; and secondly, that there is a capability challenge of how to deal with an ideological issue, because civil society and faith institutions do not form part of the permanent membership of the multi-agency framework. Without people to assist the Prevent implementation strategy, it will fail as a subject of fatigue, due to lack of human resource, expertise and community impact.

There was a further issue, which was that no one actually knew within the framework what the act of preventing people from becoming terrorists or supporting terrorism actually meant to them in their working life. The government decided to implement training to 'Raise Awareness about Prevent' (RAP) in the statutory sector. All practitioners were required to attend such courses. However that training in itself created a few problems when a flood of referrals, mostly inappropriate, quickly followed.

It illustrated a number of flaws. Firstly, the RAP training should have been followed up with further enhanced training, on aspects such as effectively identifying clear indicators, managing individual cases, signposting, and ensuring that cases were referred appropriately. Secondly, not many practitioners or frontline staff fully understood the underlying problems in individual cases, and indeed they never really had a grasp of the community dynamics underlying them. Finally, the issue we are being tasked to address is an evolving one, which requires continual study, expertise and research and subsequent adaptations to the approach; there is no one-size-fits-all solution and there never will be one.

Thankfully, the situation has since changed remarkably and there is now a lot more emphasis on generating further awareness and support. Understandably, this is a subject that has thrust many of us into very unfamiliar territory and has required us to rapidly adapt our methods, which in all fairness the government has also been doing over time, although at times ill-advised methods have been applied, causing significant damage to its brand. Our obvious and natural default position has been one where everyone questions the establishment and wants to know why such threats are still being faced. What is being done? How are we supposed to tackle the problem without any real expertise? There are many more similar questions that are still being raised, and yet we fail to appreciate that this is a sensitive area and it is a learning process for everyone, including the senior civil servants and indeed the government. Saying this, I do advise the government to understand and appreciate the risks attached to Prevent or counter-extremism work and adapt themselves to both face and support those who are dealing with the risks that are and will inevitably come about.

It is a challenging process and I believe we also need to be prepared to 'learn on the job' and as we go. This road will continue to be traversed for a long time to come, but this is something we all have a duty to do, in order to safeguard our communities, our national and international interests and the lives of our young people.

CHANNEL

In 2007 it became clear to the police and the government that there were a number of people that were clearly at risk of radicalisation, but did not pose a direct threat to security and did not warrant criminal proceedings. It was decided then that a process must be adopted to disrupt the recruitment of these young people and address their vulnerabilities or grievances. As no crimes were yet committed this fell within the operational strand of Prevent. The early intervention programme, Channel, was piloted in 2007 and was rolled out nationally in 2012.

Channel is a key element of the Prevent strategy; it is a multi-agency approach to safeguarding children and adults from being drawn into extremism or committing terrorist-related activity. It is based on early intervention to protect and divert people away from the risk they face before criminal activity occurs. The programme uses existing collaboration between local authorities, statutory partners (such as the education and health sectors, social services, children's and youth services and offender management services), the police and the local community to:

- Identify individuals at risk of being drawn into terrorism;
- Assess the nature and extent of that risk; and
- Develop the most appropriate support plan for the individuals concerned.

Using an assessment framework that determines both the level of risk posed by the individual and the subsequent support required, the Channel process evaluates the scale of vulnerability and also the individual's potential for violence. It allows the assessment panel to learn more about the unique factors in each case and to best evaluate the whole process. In all cases referred, the nominated 'intervention provider' will be tasked to provide targeted mentoring based upon his or her experience and suitability.

The programme has faced and still faces a number of challenges. After a number of high-profile plots by terrorists, Islamic extremism took precedence over all other threats posed to communities. And because of this, it was natural that Muslim communities developed hostility to a system that effectively pointed the finger of blame at them. The anti-Prevent lobbies developed and began instigating fear and mistrust amongst communities, predominantly Muslims.

Rallies and community meetings were organised and the scaremongering began. In the intervening years, this dissention has increased. And the extremist recruiters have taken advantage, by targeting the people who openly attended these anti-Prevent rallies simply because they had made a visual declaration that they were in some way disaffected by government policy, which they felt was deliberately targeting them due to their faith.

A few years back, it was the police and local authorities that made most of the referrals to the multi-agency boards. The initial premise of that referral was that the police had met or had knowledge of the individual and had deemed them a risk. This gave rise to the concept that the police were effectively spying on the Muslim communities and taking matters further, with an ulterior objective and where no evidence of a crime yet existed. To the critics, any other organisation – such as NGOs, civil society and even faith institutions – also involved in Prevent and Channel programmes were similarly a part of this 'spying' regime.

In 2011, the Prevent strategy first took into consideration referrals from other agencies and families. This raised another issue: that local organisations did not have the vision to see the wider picture. It meant that a vulnerable person could be actively recruited into a terror cell, and no local agency would assess matters arising from activity outside of their remit and boundaries. It was therefore necessary, in order to provide advice and support for the multi-agency partnership, for organisations to determine whether there were factors outside of their reach that needed to be considered. To achieve this they would have to share the referral with the police, who could then look further into the matter and seek out any intelligence that could assist with determining certain facts surrounding the referral.

Legislation was also introduced that meant it was the police who decided whether or not the referral went to a multi-agency Channel board meeting – where the Channel board either accepts or rejects a referral. If the referral is accepted, in some cases, depending on the level of risk, a decision is made to safeguard the person through a designated mentor known as the intervention provider. If the risk is considered to be low, the use of some other mechanism available to the multi-agency panel will be sought.

It must be remembered that any remedy, whether through the Channel process or the safeguarding process, requires voluntary participation. An intervention could not happen without the person's consent. In the case of a very young person, that consent must come from their parents. However, I believe this is now changing and that every referral to Channel would mean compulsory participation, which, I believe, is a bad idea and will certainly prove quite difficult in practice.

Every individual case is based on three different factors, which can be found in the statutory guidance notes set out by the Home Office. These factors are categorised as:

- **Engagement** with a group, cause or ideology
- **Intent** to cause harm
- **Capacity** to cause harm

Although these seem pretty limited, they expand into separate dynamics, which include the 22-point vulnerability assessments as set out below:

Engagement with a group, cause or ideology

Engagement factors are sometimes referred to as 'psychological hooks'. They include needs, susceptibilities, motivations and contextual influences and together can map the individual pathway into terrorism. They can include:

1.   Feelings of grievance and injustice

2.   Feeling under threat

3.   A need for identity, meaning and belonging

4.   A desire for status

5.   A desire for excitement and adventure

6.   A need to dominate and control others

7.   Susceptibility to indoctrination

8.   A desire for political or moral change

9.   Opportunistic involvement

10. Family or friends involvement in extremism

11. Being at a transitional time of life

12. Being influenced or controlled by a group

13. Relevant mental health issues

Intent to cause harm

Not all those who become engaged by a group, cause or ideology go on to develop an intention to cause harm, so this dimension is considered separately. Intent factors describe the mindset that is associated with a readiness to use violence and address what the individual would do and to what end.

They can include:

14. Over-identification with a group or ideology

15. 'Them and us' thinking

16. Dehumanisation of the enemy

17. Attitudes that justify offending

18. Harmful means to an end

19. Harmful objectives

Capability to cause harm

Not all those who have a wish to cause harm on behalf of a group, cause or ideology are capable of doing so, and plots to cause widespread damage take a high level of personal capability, resources and networking to be successful. What the individual is capable of is therefore a key consideration when assessing risk of harm to the public. Factors can include:

20. Individual knowledge, skills and competencies

21. Access to networks, funding or equipment

22. Criminal capability

Some further explanation of the three categories

An individual may be of a genuinely decent nature, but due to his or her affiliation with a group, who may have a certain cause and ideology, there are concerns. These might include emotional hooks; identity; belonging; protection; a desire for adventure, status and control; family member or peer involvement; or, most importantly, the susceptibility to indoctrination.

This is the 'engagement factor'. As the phrase goes, 'You are judged by the company you keep', and it rings very true in this sense. Even though an individual may not share the views, sentiments or grievances of his/her peers, the engagement with that group raises considerable concern, and would definitely need exploring further. Let's take the three girls from East London who sought to join ISIS in 2015 as an example of this, where engagement created an appetite and the space for indoctrination.

The same can easily be said with regards to 'intent' and 'capacity' to cause harm, especially when considered in light of some worrying engagement factors. If an individual, or their social group, harbours any kind of grievance, has any criminal history or has adopted a particular ideology similar to that of ISIS, Al Qaeda or any far-right ideology not conducive to mainstream thinking, then the intent and the capacity to cause harm will be determined by consideration of a number of additional factors. This includes a sense of injustice or victimisation, 'them and us' thinking, attitudes that justify violence, *etc.*

In this aspect, consideration needs to be given to the underlying factors with regards to conflict, immigration, the War on Terror, the Syria/Iraq situation and the Palestinian-Israeli conflict. These current and emerging conflicts are aggravating the situation, prompting a sense of victimisation and consequential radicalisation of Muslims and non-Muslims alike.

This is now adding to the grievances of many, and in turn will cause ordinary individuals to either mobilise into groups or act alone. The intent and capacity to cause harm will follow as a natural progressive factor. Let me be very clear on this aspect, because we cannot be blindsided by the outdated rationale or notion that 'not all those who wish to cause harm on behalf of a group, cause, or ideology are capable of doing so, as plots to cause damage take a high level of personal capability'.

I need to emphasise that, given the current climate, this line needs to be re-evaluated and restructured. Access to funding and equipment, having the skills, criminal capability or being competent are indeed serious considerations that need to be made, but they will not always be the defining factors. Taking each other factor on its own allows us to appreciate them in their own capacity.

Having an 'intent' to cause harm is something we must take seriously, along with having the 'capacity' to cause harm. But we cannot ignore 'engagement', or classify it only as low risk. It is crucial that we look at the engagement factor as a significant concern in our attempts to identify early indicators to prevent extremism. If the 'engagement' is not addressed, the individual will naturally develop an appetite for intent as it progresses through the engagement – 'Where there's a will, there's a way'. Capacity to cause harm will be an inevitable outcome. Where you find all three factors associated to the individual, then it would be obvious that you raise a number of clear red flags and get the right people on board as a matter of urgency.

Many people may raise concerns as to why it was the police who took the lead on Channel referrals, and to an extent I can understand the concerns here. However, I have hard-won experience in this regard. Early on in the development phase of Prevent, I was in the process of trying to move an individual away from a certain network, which was actually involved in plotting an attack. We put all the mentoring to work and managed to garner some support from external service providers, but the local authority at that time could not see or indeed understand the high level of threat that was posed both to and by the young man. As a matter of urgency, we needed additional support for the individual but it was not forthcoming, and I had no choice but to get the police on board. They understood the risks and because of their involvement, people in the local authority subsequently began to take the case more seriously, which then helped us to get all the support we needed. This was at a time when Channel was being more softly implemented at a community level and was still in its embryonic phase.

On the whole, the situation has changed dramatically and indeed for the good, where local authorities are taking the lead on all Channel cases and are well-informed of its processes and its needs. In fact it is safe to say that Channel in its current phase, although it is not perfect, is by far the best initiative we have to help individuals to move away from the criminal space and from being recruited into terrorism. There are, however, some improvements that need to be made, particularly by the police in certain areas, and especially when trying to engage with a potential vulnerable young person.

An example: a young person has been referred by a relative due to conversion to Islam and becoming less engaged with family. Concerns are raised when the young person decides to travel at short notice to the Middle East. The relative is worried and so calls for guidance and support. I raised the call to Channel officers who then decide to pay the young person a visit in the evening and pose questions, such as: Are you involved in an extremist network? Do you support ISIS? Are you planning anything dangerous? The young person automatically assumes the relative has some involvement in this and breaks off communication. And the result is that the young person becomes disengaged with no further support or access to information via relative.

This is an actual real live case example and has resulted in complete mistrust towards the relative who was simply looking out for the young person's best interest. It has also caused a rift between the family and the police, who engaged with the young person without first considering their abrupt approach.

I also believe we are now in a better position to identify those who have no real need for Channel support, but who have tried to exploit its multi-agency support network by acting out as if they were adopting extreme views and were thinking of joining a terrorist group. We have experienced individuals who have tried to play the system by using the Prevent agenda in order to receive support or find work. So there is overwhelming evidence available to support Channel as a successful concept for positive progression. With any kind of government initiative, especially of this nature, there are and will be mistakes made. But on the whole and in some areas, Channel has been quite effective and successful.

Many critics will disagree with my view, and of course that is their right. But I think it would help persuade many people of the merits of Prevent and Channel if we could highlight the hundreds of success stories where young men and women are now much more focused on their education, careers and personal wellbeing. Not to mention the many who have become positive role models and activists within their respective communities or indeed those who have taken up preventing others from becoming terrorists. There are a huge number of cases that I can personally reference, and it gives me great pleasure in doing so. I'm very hopeful that in the near future we will be in a much better position to showcase all of the successes around this agenda which will certainly assist in getting real and effective community 'buy in'.

A message to the 'Prevent critics': when I first approached community elders and leaders in the early days going back to 2003, I was reminded that they do not have the responsibility to deal with such issues. Instead they insisted that it was the police and government's responsibility to deal with these problems. I beg to differ slightly: I feel communities must lead on tackling this problem with the backing by government and law enforcement agencies.

My point being that the increasing anti-Prevent lobbies do not have a leg to stand on in most cases, especially since most of them had removed themselves from being a part of the solution when the problem was still embryonic. I am witness to this as perhaps being one of the first ever to raise the concerns around 'extremist recruitment' within our communities way back in 2003.

THE 'DUTY OF DUE REGARD'

In July 2015 the Counter Terrorism and Security Act 2015 came into force. This is the Act that was dubbed the 'Snooper's Charter', in reference to the government's proposal to have access to social media platforms such as Facebook and Twitter of individuals of concern.

In addition, the government placed responsibility on the statutory sector to identify people who could be drawn into extremism. This means that any specified agency within the statutory sector including health, housing, education, and police must now have regard for people falling into extremism or on a path to radicalisation.

But what does that mean? Many questions have been raised. If a teacher sees a young Muslim growing a beard and studying his religion more intensely than in the past, do they refer him as a potential threat? Or what about a health professional whose client is looking at 9/11 videos as he believes there is a global conspiracy for a new world order: might he be a 'lone wolf'? What about data protection: what information is appropriate to share and what is not?

The 'duty of due regard' – also known as 'the Prevent duty' – is an equality duty that has legal case law attached to it. It outlines the duty of specified authorities to 'have due regard to the need to prevent people from being drawn into terrorism'. The perception is that the government seeks that all agencies make it a priority to remove discrimination and injustices from their practices, as a means of reducing the possibility of a grievance that can then be exploited.

However, if the teacher, doctor, or the fire-fighter has no knowledge of the facts surrounding government foreign policy, or does not have any kind of understanding as to any underlying factors in individual lives, then many of the most concerning cases will be missed.

Michael Adebowale and Michael Adebolajo, the men who murdered solider Lee Rigby in Woolwich in 2013, stated their grievances that the UK were participating in acts to kill innocent Muslims abroad. Any local duty at that time may not have been able to deal with this narrative. However the duty to assess vulnerable individuals through a number of prisms might have identified the trajectory of the men. In this way it would have been possible to intervene at an earlier point had such a duty been in place.

There are many practitioners of all disciplines who are confused and are unclear, irrespective of guidance of what they are supposed to do. A simple explanation is that the duty applies the responsibility on a specified authority to develop the capacity to reasonably foresee a person potentially falling into extremism or terrorism, and then to apply measures which are reasonably practical, such as an internal or external intervention if deemed necessary.

The terms 'reasonable' and 'foreseeable' may at some point be tested in law, in regard to the level of knowledge the organisation sought in order to recognise the problem. Currently the most robust approach is that all institutions must attain **common knowledge** (what is generally known about people falling into extremism or terrorism), **industry knowledge** (what the central departments issue as guidelines about people falling into extremism or terrorism), and

expert knowledge (what specialists and experts say about the changing trends in regards to people falling into extremism or terrorism).

Naturally, no specified authority wants to be responsible for being the body that did not prevent someone from falling into extremism or terrorism, because the reputational risk is too high. But acquiring the knowledge is only half of the responsibility. The greater responsibility is what to do with it: what measures are reasonably practical?

'Reasonably practical' concerns the application of resources; it is about the steps that an authority takes to mitigate the risks that have risen from the knowledge they have acquired. An assessment of that level of risk must be made, to allow the authority to make a decision on whether to refer the case, and subsequently to share information about it. Often, practitioners do not refer a case as they feel that they may initiate a process that could lead to the criminalisation of an individual, but it is worth noting that this is a misconception when dealing in a pre-crime space.

To overcome practitioners' fears, the government has a secondary door for referrals through a Multi-Agency Support Hub (MASH). The MASH can present an individual to the Prevent case management practitioners, who can then decide whether there is a need for a referral to the Channel process. The question then arises, what do you do if the individual does not meet the Channel threshold and the risks identified are not mitigated?

The duty that 'reasonably practical' action is taken once a risk is identified sometimes means that the institution has to perform an intervention, either itself or by bringing in a third party. This decision is made after the specified authority considers the benefits over the costs:

a.   Tasks required in order to mitigate the risk

b.   Inconvenience to the specified authority

c.   Money and other resources required to address the issue

d.   Efforts required by internal pastoral care staff to achieve the objectives

UNDERSTANDING THE UNDERLYING ISSUES

In order to fully appreciate the length and breadth of the problem we are facing, including the many challenges ahead, we need only look at some of the factors and major trigger points that resonate amongst young people in our communities. We need to look at this as an illness of some kind and treat the problem likewise. Without going over the cause or contributors to the cause of the illness, we will struggle and second-guess the actual cure. In order to do this, we need to accept some hard facts, which I know will disturb many people and might even push a few into a mode of denial. I say this because I had a gentleman who was taking part in some training walk out in the middle of the session because he could not bear to listen to some of the narratives used by young Muslims. (A few of which are listed below.)

However, if we are truly intending to address the huge challenges ahead then I'm afraid we have to swallow a few bitter pills. And I say this with sincerity, through hard-won experience and based upon real facts, having engaged with thousands of young people, and worked on hundreds of cases that share common threads.

For any Prevent initiative to work successfully, it is critical to fully understand all the underlying issues relevant to the subject, as well as those in the hearts and minds of our communities. Without a doubt, young people are the prime target and the most vulnerable and so we must first and foremost appreciate the fact that they will be wary and sceptical of any initiative that is being put their way, especially by those who cannot relate to them or that they cannot relate to.

Let us look at some of the key underlying historical issues that need to be understood. Although many individuals in government and many research academics will argue otherwise, the actual fact is that objections to foreign policy are at the forefront when it comes to young people and their grievances. Almost every single case I have come across has one common argument, starting from the Palestine-Israel conflict, to the First Gulf War, the War on Terror and then so on and so forth, with Syria and Iraq being the new common thread. Attitudes adopted by all the cases correlate with how I felt when I was recruited; the language used by George Bush and Tony Blair prior to the War on Terror and the Second Gulf War resonates deep into the hearts and minds of every case I have heard of and amongst the young people I have met and engaged with. We must not lose sight of the historical conflicts where Western nations have played a major role, as well as the more recent ones such as the Second Gulf War, where thousands of innocent people were killed or displaced in a campaign that was significantly based on false information about weapons of mass destruction. For many young people, this is still an ongoing issue.

Young people often see things very differently to other sections of the community and now that they are much more engaged with each other thanks to communication technology, they are able to look at multiple sources of information available 24/7, and they do not trust mainstream media networks such as the BBC, Sky, CNN or FOX, who they feel are part of the problem in creating an anti-Muslim environment. Social media platforms allow for information to be shared instantaneously and in a very raw state, whilst also allowing fanatics to spew their ideas and narratives across the globe without any difficulty. Accessibility to these social media platforms has become very easy due to technological advancement of smartphones, and this in itself poses huge challenges for anyone, especially parents, who find it difficult to monitor their child's online activities for fear of breakdown of relationships due to a perception of mistrust. Similarly, frontline staff in educational institutes or elsewhere cannot invade the student's privacies, and in fact are very limited to what they can do in this circumstance, which is entirely understandable.

Therefore the social media space becomes, to a certain extent, ungoverned and ultimately allows unscrupulous individuals to operate freely. The information dumping strategy applied by extremist groups, where they become very active in dropping or reminding people of what is actually going on and where, mostly provides misinformation, but backed up with a few facts. This works either way, and often generates an element of curiosity, which in turn can change the attitudes of young people in a number of different directions. I will explain in more detail about the information dumping strategies in another chapter.

Information is spread more rapidly than ever before and we now live in times where accessing information about conflicts around the world is quick and easy. Young people see these conflicts on their phones, TVs and other media devices on a daily basis and are exposed to the gruesome reality of death and destruction in many parts of the world, often in places where many of their families have originated from.

Here are some examples given in some of the cases I have worked on, where a vulnerable young person has cited foreign policy as one of the motivating factors in their heightened grievance:

- The US, Britain and other Western countries are not protecting Syrian Muslims being killed by Assad; instead they are killing the ones who are trying to establish Sharia.

- The sexual abuse of boys by Afghan allies and the reports that US soldiers were told to turn a blind eye and instructed not to intervene even when their Afghan allies have sexually abused boys on their military bases.

- George Bush Jnr's continued use of biblical connotations. Following the 'crusade' statement, he went on to say: 'Either you are with us, or you are with the terrorists.' The Synoptic Gospels attribute the following quote to Jesus of Nazareth: 'Whoever is not with me is against me, and whoever does not gather with me scatters.' (Matthew 12:30).

- The Afghanistan container massacre, otherwise known as the Dasht-i-Leili massacre, of 2001, which saw the killing of hundreds of prisoners who were shot or suffocated to death in metal shipping containers while being transferred to a prison by forces loyal to Afghan warlord General Rashid Dostum. And indeed the subsequent cover-up by members of Congress, the White House and the US military.

- The killing of 16 Afghan villagers in Kandahar in 2012 after US soldier Robert Bales goes AWOL.

- Abu Ghraib prison and the physical and sexual abuse of detainees there by US soldiers and the CIA.

- The Israeli use of heavy weaponry and illegal cluster bombs on Palestinians and the number of young children being slaughtered by the Israelis, without any significant response from the Western leadership. I have heard young men and women tell me that they now feel that Muslims are considered less human than others; when a Muslim is killed, they feel little consideration is given, whilst the killing of non-Muslims is considered as an act against humanity and gets more air time in the media.

- More recently in November 2015, the press reports that 'U.S. drone operators are inflicting heavy civilian casualties and have developed an institutional culture callous to the death of children and other innocents', according to four former operators. It was claimed that drone operators refer to children as 'fun-size terrorists' and liken killing them to 'cutting the grass before it grows too long', while also describing widespread drug and alcohol abuse. (Murtaza Hussain, The Intercept)

The list goes on and these are just a few of the thousands of narratives that are being interpreted as a full-on crusade against Muslims.

By choosing, or let's use another word, by *failing* to accept that foreign policy or the grievances identified previously have nothing to do with aggravating an emotional or sympathetic mind that tends to lean towards a sense of injustice, we are completely misguided to say the least. I must emphasize this fact that, by ignoring this, we are by default significantly contributing to the problem.

More recent events have added a greater sense of victimisation and a perception that Islam is under attack, such as the new laws prohibiting the veil or headscarf being worn in public in the UK's close neighbour France. The French government's approach has unsettled thousands of people across Europe, with the fear that it will soon be applied by other European governments.

This attitude towards Muslims, who have witnessed other attacks upon their faith and their beloved Prophet by cartoonists and filmmakers, has been taken by some youngsters as a provocative act designed to push young men and women over the edge. They feel that they cannot remain silent in the face of this aggravation and that they are being forced to react in ways which can then only be categorized as 'extreme behaviour' – with the effect of ultimately proving that Muslims are potential terrorists. So the general feeling is that of complete mistrust in government and one of being targeted deliberately.

There are thousands of grievances and arguments put forward by young people. Many are crazy and simply vulnerable and paranoid minds at play. However, there are some real and legitimate arguments that need to be appreciated and discussed. Counter-arguments do not often work if we ourselves fail to accept the underlying issues as contributing factors, and try to at least build a relationship with the individual. It is essential to adopt this approach in order to examine ways of managing grievances and identify ways for young people to air their concerns in a positive manner and create diversionary opportunities.

Another significant problem, which we all need to take into sincere consideration, is the fact that we have not invested enough in educating our young people on critical thinking skills. Their lack of being able or willing to critically analyse information is indeed a problem that is putting them at continuous risk of being manipulated and abused by recruiters.

I cannot emphasize enough in this regard, so I leave you with these few words in this chapter. **Know your subject.** Ensure that you have an in-depth, up-to-date understanding of the progression to violent extremism as a phenomenon, including that of the religious dimension in all its rapidly evolving complexity. This includes: why people become extreme; how people are driven to become extreme, *ie* what stimulates the process and how this process escalates; who are the most vulnerable and at risk; and why.

Our direction must change and our attitudes towards these key grievances need to be more considerate. Sometimes just having the difficult debates around such issues, if you are prepared to listen, can in many cases alter the trajectory of a young mind.

CURRENT AND FUTURE CHALLENGES

Every terrorist group dwells in its own moral universe, adopting a value system and worldview that compels it to exterminate anyone or any idea that opposes it.

The current challenges are huge and are in part due to the current changing nature and emerging conflicts around the Muslim world, and the general negative perceptions of young people surrounding these conflicts. Young people want to know more about what is going on and what they can do to help prevent the loss of innocent life. This puts them in a space where their inquisitive and curious nature leaves them at risk. As mentioned previously, another major contributor to the problem is technology, which has rapidly changed the way we communicate and engage. Trust in authority and leadership is declining at an unprecedented rate and the established media networks are seen as, at best, selective, biased, and untrustworthy. This has created a shift towards alternative media sources where information is much more accepted as factual and reliable. This is exploited by many extremist and terrorist networks that fully appreciate this trend, and find ways of dumping multiple strands of information in a manner that becomes more credible and acceptable by their intended audience. Of course, most of this 'information' is incorrect and is deliberately designed to grab at the emotions of the young impressionable mind.

Ever since the Syrian conflict attracted mainstream headlines and the brutal Assad regime prompted an exodus of innocent women and children fleeing their homeland, followed by the subsequent birth of ISIS, we have witnessed a lot more young people gravitating towards what we feel is an extremist ideology. Yet in their view it is simply being sympathetic as well as having a sense of religious obligation to help and prevent such atrocities from happening, even by way of force which will mean killing the perceived enemy and indeed sacrificing themselves if need be.

Although this has posed huge challenges, we have still managed to dissuade and prevent hundreds of individuals from actually being recruited into extremist networks. However, since the emergence of ISIS and the re-branding of Al Qaeda, we are now facing a much more potent and challenging threat, one which has become expediently virtual, fluid and unpredictable. This threat is posed by a committed network of individuals who are well-versed in modern communication strategies and are establishing new methods on a daily basis. They operate in the space where most young people are present, be it physical or virtual. They also fully understand how to relate to young men and women from very diverse backgrounds and from different religious belief systems.

ISIS, Boko Haram, Al Nusrah, and all the other terrorist groups who fly the Black Banners, are applying a narrative that is posing a huge challenge and what supports their narrative is the lack of genuine consideration by European establishments for the growing trend of anti-Muslim hatred. By default, this then supports the ideologies spewed out by every extremist group or individual and in turn generates mass gravitation of young people towards a *jihad*ist mentality. It is immediately difficult to reason with vulnerable individuals when they are told 'Don't trust the *kuffar* or those who align themselves with them. Non-believers are your enemies and not your friends.'

Foretold prophecies are, in many ways, being realised because of the many conflicts and general attitudes towards Muslims. ISIS is constantly reminding Muslims of the 'end of days' prophecy, which pinpoints an area in Syria known as Dabiq. The '*Mahlamaah Al Kubra*' (the Greatest War) will be fought at Dabiq and every Muslim is commanded to travel there, even if it means they crawl on all fours over a sea of ice, and join those who raise the Black Banners. ISIS constantly send out reminders that "you will never be accepted amongst the non-Muslims" until you leave your faith, and even then your colour will be different and you will never be at peace.

In Europe and elsewhere in the western world, extremist recruiters are pushing out a narrative that is actually being confirmed by many European governments and the institutions within, by encouraging or in some cases 'suggesting' that Muslims adopt a more western or 'British' Islam which in itself poses a number of questions and indeed varying challenges, simply because there is no such concept of a 'British' Islam and it would be completely futile for us to even endorse or suggest such a concept. This will continue to push the very communities that we need to work with further away, in fact it is safe to say that doing so or even being seen to be supportive of such an idea will increase the numbers of young men and women disengaging and/or leaning towards a more extreme interpretation of Islam. Disengaged communities and young people and the acceptance that the narratives espoused by extremist groups are in some way being realised will become more prevalent.

The environment that this would create for the terrorist and extremist recruiters would make it impossible for any Prevent initiative to succeed. Such an environment would also feed the far-right groups and evangelical groups from across America and Europe, who equally promote this as a religious war against Islam. There are thousands of arguments and narratives that have shaped the attitudes of millions of individuals from across the world, both young and old, towards intolerance and violence by using faith as a vehicle to set divisions.

Coming back to my main point on the foretold prophecy, this in itself poses questions around the identities of the foretold (prophesised) ones raising the Black Banners. Is it ISIS, Boko Haram or Al Nusrah? Or should we expect another group to become prominent? Indeed, is this prophecy actually authentic? Whatever the answers may be, it does not change the fact that a lot of people firmly believe in them and openly support them or are either secretly sympathetic towards those who claim to be the defenders of the faith by raising the Black Banners. Again, these narratives then give wind to the sails of far-right extremists who use them to whip up further hatred, which can manifest itself as attacks on innocent law-abiding Muslims. You can then imagine how things can escalate when these events become more frequent and more hostile.

So if you can take on board the significance of the extremist narratives and then the growing anti-Muslim hatred, be it perceived or fact-based, then you must understand the fact that interventions are critically important. Teachers and other frontline staff must appreciate the many different issues affecting our young people in multiple ways, and it is essential that we consider these facts whilst we engage and communicate with them.

As we witnessed the 'premature' eradication of almost all of Al Qaeda in Afghanistan, we find them re-emerging with vigour and much more potency. With this in mind, we must seriously consider what will come after we have 'eradicated' ISIS? What shape, form and narratives will emerge after ISIS is defeated on the battlefield? In fact are we actually fighting on the right battlefield? Can we seriously beat terrorism by killing all the terrorists?

The most significant challenge will be to withstand and prepare for what comes next, which means what we do now and how we do it will determine our success or failure in the months and years ahead. Every single terrorist group, be it big or small, requires human resources who are recruited from within communities. It is therefore crucially important that we deny them the space or the opportunity to operate within our communities or within the hearts and minds of our young people. Let's beat them to it and starve them of the human resource they need to continue and indeed grow. This is in my opinion the only way to truly defeat the terrorists who completely rely upon their recruitment of people.

IMPLEMENTING PREVENT AT A LOCAL LEVEL

The government's response, and the many initiatives designed to address this growing issue, have not always been well received by communities in general. In fact, we have experienced a growing disconnect between these communities and local government, and increasingly the younger generation is feeling a sense of victimisation, due to both the manner in which Prevent initiatives have been delivered and the perception of Prevent. In some areas and under certain circumstances, these initiatives have been poorly delivered as well as poorly sold. Inevitably and with any such kind of program, it is expected that mistakes will be made, and critics and, in some cases, extremists masquerading as community 'do-gooders', will snatch at any chance to undermine Prevent.

It goes without saying that the statutory 'duty of due regard' will certainly increase this sense of victimisation and, in turn, will potentially generate a 'shut down' mentality. This has been noted after holding many workshops with young people of all ages: that they fear they cannot discuss matters relating to extremism or Syria, they feel they cannot even show any kind of empathy towards the victims of conflicts in Muslim countries, because they could be potentially labelled an extremist. There is a good chance that this will force the perceptions and sentiments of young people to become further internalised and allowed to manifest in an uncontrolled manner, only to resurface and be expressed in a potentially harmful way. In effect it could even prevent you from actually delivering Prevent strategies simply because there is a fear even to discuss matters relating to terrorism or Syria for instance. If people cannot discuss matters that affect them in an open environment or even in a classroom then this leaves the matter to be internalised or to be discussed elsewhere without controls in place.

During my work with young people, especially on Prevent/CVE, I had the chance to interview some young people willing to share independently how they felt about Prevent and how the strategy affected them. In one of those interviews, one young Muslim female opened up and explained what effect the Prevent Strategy is having, not only in her life as a pupil, but in her attempts to seek more knowledge of extremism and terrorist recruitment.

During our interview, the young girl complained about the lack of spaces in which she was able to address her appetite or desire to know more about radicalisation and what effects this has on the life of those who have been radicalised. Most importantly, the girl felt that she could not openly address this desire as, being Muslim, she feared that the school could possibly misinterpret her point and report her to the authorities. She pointed out that she has already been treated as suspicious because of her engagement with the Islamic Society of her school and that her emails have been monitored. (This could be fact or it could be a perception, but either way it is her belief.)

However, we could not redirect her desire to seek more knowledge on the topic, rather we decided to look at ways in which she could achieve her goals and support our objectives at the same time. Essentially we helped develop her capacity to manage the knowledge and information she would be exposed to and build her resilience to digest it. She ended up participating on one of our young leaders' programmes and is to this day involved in helping us prevent other young people from being radicalised.

Another example case arose in July 2016, where a young 17-year-old female had issues around doing some work on a contentious subject. She sent us an email, part of which I have added here for your understanding and in the hope that such matters can be avoided or managed better in the future:

'I feel ACF provided me and others a safe space to talk about subjects we cannot discuss or even include in our work at college. Like, I remember in college I was doing an extended project qualification and I decided to write an essay on the Middle East, in particular the issue between Palestine and Israel. The Head of the EPQ called out and said, basically I can't discuss this topic because I'm gonna be biased because I am a Muslim so 'supposedly' I'm gonna take the Palestinian side when writing the essay. So I asked him – what am I supposed to do now? He responded by saying; 'Maybe change your essay about something else, You can talk about the Middle East but not as specific as Palestine and Israel. You can discuss what's going on in the Middle East in general terms.' It was very shocking for me to hear this, so I had to change my essay instead of around talking about the outcomes of the 6-Day War. I had to change it into a historical debate. And when I came to ACF I was introduced to Mike (Jervis), where I was able to discuss this issue openly, so I told him about my essay and what happened which he found equally shocking, but he allowed me to discuss and have a debate about the issue of Israel and Palestine which helped me understand things a lot better than I previously thought, so I feel like ACF is a much safer space to talk about these things while in college I am restricted completely.'

The fact that the school's implementation of the Prevent strategy has concurred with the diffusion of fear among the pupils in their desire to know more about radicalisation or discuss certain, often contentious topics within a protected context (the school's premises) makes me wonder to what extent the Prevent strategy is actually redirecting these desires towards territories that cannot be safeguarded, such as social media platforms or other environments.

The question really is, is the Prevent Strategy affecting young people to the point that they feel the need to further understand what it is that the strategy is actually attempting to protect them from? And if this is the case, what have we in place to address this concern?

I know from experience that allowing for debate and conversations to continue, in safe spaces of course, is actually very helpful and it does afford you a lot more of an understanding on what is going on within the hearts and minds of our young people. This then enables you to shape effective and proactive programmes with the young people on board as part of the solution (instead of being a part of the problem) to prevent extremism in all its forms.

Every institution that employs a Prevent officer, especially our Local Authority Prevent leads, needs to be well-educated on local sensitivities and has to sincerely consider these sensitivities as an important aspect, especially when certain initiatives are to be delivered. I have found a number of officers completely disconnected from their local communities and in some cases quite ignorant of their cultural or religious needs. It is a fundamental flaw if the Prevent lead or the person tasked with a Prevent responsibility does not connect or communicate with their local people.

It is imperative that all front line sectors, including NGOs, have a basic understanding of the local community dynamics and, if possible, a degree of knowledge of the many cultural and religious complexities. However, whilst there is a clear strategy implemented by central government, there seems to be a disparity at tactical and operational levels. The tactical problem is that many local Prevent leads do not often have the capacity or the reach to engage at a local level with local groups and institutions. Operationally, those who have the reach do not have the tactical back-up, which means their local institutions will not be enabled to support or even deliver upon the Prevent objectives.

A clear example would be where a local mosque understands theology and the practices within their respective faiths very well, but lacks the competency and the knowledge of safeguarding or preventing an individual from extremism or terrorism, or from being recruited. This is where the Local Authority will fail in effective delivery of the Prevent strategy and it will further exacerbate the growing negative perceptions of the Prevent agenda.

Before 2011, local Prevent leads, both from the councils and the police, were well engaged in their communities and with most NGOs and faith houses working at grass roots. There was a lot of engagement and partnership work going on which actually created an effective community 'buy in' to some extent. This allowed for ease in establishing information-sharing protocols and it actually generated a degree of trust between communities and the establishments. It helped build mutual understanding, which enabled Prevent to be delivered effectively and without much hindrance.

Over the years this has changed and trust between groups and authorities has eroded; not many NGOs have knowledge of who the actual Prevent leads are, let alone what is going on.

Whilst I know of some remarkable individuals who have been very successful Prevent leads over the years in a few areas across the UK, sadly I have found many who really need to either significantly improve their game or give way to more experienced people. Not that they are not well intentioned. On the contrary, their intentions maybe genuinely good. But unfortunately they do not possess the right kind of experience and determination in delivering Prevent locally. At times, they can actually be a hindrance to the process, which could potentially prove damaging if not entirely dangerous. And this is where the whole agenda finds itself being heavily scrutinised by those who oppose it, and in particular those who seek to undermine it. Here are some key considerations for Prevent/Community leads:

- Know your audience and local circumstances. Make sure you understand the idiosyncrasies of the local situation through and through, including the situation and attitudes of the relevant communities and their constituent groups.

- Know what other initiatives are going on locally. Assess all other direct or indirect Prevent interventions that have been or are being done: what has been their impact? Do not be beguiled by overly simple metrics of 'output and assumed impact' provided by those who might have a vested interest in demonstrating a success, no matter what the real outcome. Remember Lenin's dictum: 'Trust is good, but checking up is better'.

- Stand back and see the bigger picture. Understand the external influences on the situation which cannot be controlled, and how these will affect the plan. It is all too easy when faced with a difficult situation to lower your horizons and get sucked into looking only inwards.

- Work closely with every single religious/cultural institution and exhaust all efforts to maintain healthy, working relations with them.
- Where possible, engage with young people (not selected audiences) and establish facts and current narratives for yourself.
- Do not rely on second hand information or 'community gatekeepers'.
- Do not try or be seen to shape or introduce a 'western or a moderate Islam' when dealing with communities. (This will inevitably support and endorse all the extremists narratives and push your communities away)

CRITICS AND ANTI-PREVENT LOBBIES

It is quite common knowledge that Prevent is being seen as specifically targeting Muslim communities and has generated quite a few anti-Prevent groups as well as some outspoken critics. I would like to point out a few hard facts that may not sit very well with a lot of people. However, it is important to accept the fact that Prevent, while not exclusively so, *is* predominantly focused on Muslim communities, though it must be noted that there is also a clear focus on far-right extremism as well. We must acknowledge why it is targeting Muslim communities more so than others. The fact is that most (if not all) of the current threats emanate from within Muslim communities and the majority of plots that have been carried out or foiled involved young Muslims.

There is significant evidence (also corroborated by my own personal experience) that most extremist and terrorist network recruiters are directing their attentions on young, impressionable Muslims, and the focus of the terrorist groups, their supporters and their marketing campaigns are equally and specifically targeting Muslim communities with their recruitment. It is therefore common sense that Prevent work needs to be largely focused on Muslim communities, in order to safeguard them from being abused and manipulated.

The prevailing attitude of people both within the Muslim communities and outside is that Prevent is becoming a Muslim witch-hunt. Critics of the Prevent agenda are increasingly promoting their own opinions. In doing so they are agitating an already volatile community who believe this new statutory duty is designed to control Muslim expression and that it is part of a government strategy to implement a more 'British' Islam.

Two points come to mind here, and both have their own challenges. The first is to counter both the disruptive and the destructive narratives of the extremists, whilst the other is to argue with the emerging hostility of the critics, who are essentially posing equal threats both to our young people as well as to the wider communities.

Whichever narrative we look at in these two circumstances, effectively they are both radicalising our communities. In fact it can be said that the critics are causing equal damage by undermining most of the excellent work being undertaken by groups and individuals delivering Prevent work, as well as the statutory duty, in turn creating a 'hesitation' mentality, which will ultimately hamper our institutions' and communities' abilities to deal with the problem. This disruption allows the extremists a wide berth, as it allows them additional opportunities to target our young people, also enabling them to do so with ease.

If we make a mistake by wrongfully identifying an individual deemed to be on a path to extremism (which is inevitable given the number of cases we work with), we often face a situation where the individual may be subsequently supported by the anti-Prevent lobbies, and consequently become more inclined to feel a sense of victimisation and then gravitate towards the extremist narrative.

Experience tells us that extremist sympathisers and critics of Prevent have somehow found a way to engage with such individuals, reinforcing their own narratives, pulling the person further away from the natural protective factors that were ordinarily in place. This then creates an environment where the individual has no control whatsoever over the circumstances he or she is now faced with. That is when the rollercoaster ride begins. It is important to realise that when we expose young people to ungoverned environments beyond our, or indeed their own, control, we are adding to their already existing vulnerabilities.

We must also consider another very significant contributing factor. Whilst it is understood that groups like the English Defence League, Britain First or Patriotic Europeans Against the Islamisation of the West (German: Patriotische Europäer gegen die Islamisierung des Abendlandes, abbreviated to PEGIDA) have not caused any major terrorist destruction on the scale of Al Qaeda, ISIS, Boko Haram and others, there is a clear and present danger emanating from within these networks in that they are causing a real sense of fear for peaceful, law-abiding citizens. On one hand we find ISIS/Al Qaeda trying to pull individuals towards their ideology (a rock) and on the other we find the far-right groups pushing decent law-abiding citizens against the wall (a hard place). The more vulnerable citizens then begin to rethink their options. The language being used by the far-right groups, sometimes echoing the famous Enoch Powell 'Rivers of Blood' speech, is powerful and emotional and is designed to speak to the hearts of those uncertain about where they fit in to British multicultural society. These are very real concerns.

In my experience, the extremist narrative and the critics of the Prevent initiative pose an equal obstacle to effective tackling of extremism in our communities.

Whilst governments understand this issue, in the past there has not been an appetite to showcase the effectiveness of Prevent across communities, which would demonstrate its success and thus reduce the criticism and create the space where practitioners can continue their work on a level playing field.

The more significant threat that the 'anti-Prevent' lobbies pose is the fact that they may even unite and 'take the hill', so to speak. This will cause a challenging reality, where communities will gravitate towards their calling and their agenda, which will result in little engagement between Muslim communities and the establishment. In short, it will be a matter of time before certain groups will create their version of Prevent; indeed, this has already been 'whispered' about within certain communities. This has far reaching consequences, especially if these groups have access to communities through the faith institutions and community 'gate keepers'. So the actual official Prevent program loses ground rapidly and causes disengagement, which then poses different challenges to everyone who has a stake, be it Police, security services, experienced interventionists, school teachers and indeed the government. Any Prevent-related ambition will prove absolutely futile if and when this happens.

This is why a radical shift in our approach is needed, and it must consider the emerging challenges from equal sides. Whether ISIS/AQ designs change and become more fluid than ever, or whether community or faith groups try to develop their own models of Prevent. Governments and other actors on the ground like myself need to appreciate and recognise how to adapt to meet the tide at the shore. We essentially need to change the growing perception that governments are hostile towards potentially 'volatile' Muslim communities, because this is where extremists and indeed anti-Prevent critics will always thrive.

ADDRESSING THE ISSUE ON AN INTERNATIONAL LEVEL

An additional challenge we need to address is the lack of attention given to the African and Afro-Caribbean communities, both in their own countries and across the world. We can see by glancing at terrorist groups like Boko Haram or Al Shabab that there is a huge drive at recruiting individuals from this demographic, who find it very easy to relate to their problems, of which there are many. Boko Haram leader Abu Bakr Shekau mentioned in a speech that 'The Nigerian government is attacking us because we are Muslim and nothing else, because we will continue to believe in Allah and stand by what God has said'. He continues to maintain that 'they must continue to fight for the survival of Islam'.

These are very powerful statements especially when half the country is Muslim and is experiencing difficulties, be it employment, health care or other opportunities that they are being denied. It is fact that there is very little real energised focus on providing support or interventions for this demographic, even from their respective governments, and subsequently we are witnessing huge numbers of new recruits joining these networks in places like Somalia, Nigeria and Cameroon, simply because their governments are lacking in resources, experience or even the political will to challenge this growing phenomenon.

Equally, whilst we can argue that there is a lot of knowledge and experience around this issue on an international level, there seems to be a disconnect between governments and non-governmental organisations. This gap in the sharing of knowledge or providing practical solutions is essentially preventing the formation of an effective network of experienced individuals to tackle this particular threat in many Third World countries.

Given the current situation in the Middle East, including the ongoing killings in Palestine and Israel, and the events across Europe, especially in Paris, it seems the threat is becoming much more serious. It is knocking on our doors ever more so than before, and it does not discriminate between faiths or colours. It is more fluid than ever and it is breaching all the existing norms. ISIS has its own 'red button' with activists living and operational in almost every country, especially within Europe and North Africa, and whilst we look into the usual quarters or try to examine where or from which demographic the threat is more likely to emerge, the ISIS/Al Qaeda leadership have their fingers on that button. The attacks in Paris in 2016 were a clear reminder of this and one which highlights the critical importance of effective work with vulnerable youngsters.

Terrorists of all kinds, especially the likes of ISIS, will continue to radicalise our young people and threaten our way of life in their attempts to try and disrupt communities across the globe. The attacks in Paris and the attitudinal shift by the French establishment are testament to the fact that ISIS have in fact radicalised the whole French nation, in one sense or another. The French government has not been immune. Consider statements such as 'We will be pitiless and merciless in our strikes against ISIS', and the authorisation of multiple air strikes on Raqqa, even though it was inevitable that innocent civilians will be killed. The lack of regard for the potential deaths of innocent people not only serves to further radicalise or legitimise the extremist narrative, but will undoubtedly create a new wave of terrorists who will ultimately seek revenge.

In essence, people are being radicalised as a consequence of the terrorist attacks. Losing our rationale and our sense of better judgement is only going to play to the strengths of the extremists, who have given thought to their every attack. I am in no way alluding to not taking action, but rather suggesting we need to be measured and our actions need to be proportionate.

The Middle East is rapidly becoming ever more volatile and recruitment is taking place at every level, including within institutions ordinarily opposed to such extremist ideas. Governments are beginning to realise that doing nothing is no longer an option and that a real and serious focus must be applied at every level. The Saudi regime in particular has a huge challenge on their hands in this regard, with a significant presence of extremist individuals and networks operating both within the Kingdom as well as in neighbouring countries.

This said, the Saudis do have a large number of highly notable scholars who have become quite vocal in opposing extremists and their sympathisers, and the leadership has been giving serious attention to this huge threat for quite some time but a lot more must be done. Elsewhere in the region there is a lot of emphasis on fighting terrorism and extremism abroad, but little focus on addressing the growth, networking and recruitment of extremism within certain countries. Every Arab nation needs to implement some real and genuine efforts to engage and shape their youth and wider communities, before they are revolutionised by others who do not share their nation's ideals or visions.

We can see a lot of resources being applied to research and think tanks but very little – in fact, almost nothing – is being done at a grass roots level to actually counter violent extremism. The fact is that the Middle East and Gulf regions are primary targets of terrorist groups who have always held it as their main ambition to overthrow the rulers and seize control. Whilst I accept there are many security measures in place to deter them, I find it worrying that nothing of real substance is being done to actually prevent the tide from coming in the first place.

My engagement with many leaders across the world has helped me understand matters much more; in fact, I found that in some countries, including within Europe, many individuals in authority, even at ministerial level, harbour grievances around western foreign policy. This is something that has and will create the 'domino' effect in particular when such countries are becoming ideal breeding grounds for extremism. If the state of someone in authority is of an extreme mindset, then one can only imagine what the attitude of the general population is. Yet it is often an unconscious statement or view which can be taken as legitimate by the average mind.

One of the more worrying emerging issues brewing at a rapid pace is the sectarian conflict between Shia and Sunni Muslims which, although has been a historical problem, has now become much more hostile and intense. In Pakistan, for example, there have been reports of mass murder of Shia Muslims across the country and, in some cases, with the apparent blessings of some elements within the nation's security forces. Iran and Saudi Arabia are on a war footing, which is a feeling that is spreading ferociously across the region. Iranian-backed Houthi rebels are launching hostile attacks in the Saudi Kingdom, with further potential attacks being launched in the Holy cities within the Saudi Kingdom. We also know of the existing sectarian conflicts growing ever more vigorously within Iraq, Yemen and Syria.

In almost every single Western country there are large groups of Shia and Sunni Muslims, and each side are watching the developments unfold. And I believe that each group are waiting for 'the call to action' from their scholars, or from those whom they see as their leaders. For the Shia, this is the Iranian clerics who have already called for Jihad against Sunni Muslims in the conflicts of Yemen, Iraq and Syria. I think it is merely a matter of time before their call expands to action beyond these areas.

And should there be a clear violation of the Holy sites in Saudi by any Shia or Iranian-backed group, the war will certainly spill over to other areas. Europe, America and the UK could very easily become the battlegrounds where this sectarian conflict could expand. It goes without saying that this is where the whole clash could turn into a global nightmare, with the battlegrounds becoming broader and undefined.

It is therefore important that we take notice of these developments and initiate our collective responses in a timely fashion. Our proactive approach can limit, if not eliminate, the possible threat that such developments can pose. Recognising any change in behavior, any attitudinal shift, or listening to emerging narratives can give us vital clues to help us stop matters from escalating. Otherwise, and without wanting to indulge in scare mongering, I believe a further spark could ignite a potential global sectarian inferno that will have no boundaries.

Ordinarily stable countries could easily become volatile and instable in a matter of days, should there be a rapid expansion of terrorism and its networks. We know from recent experience that the instability caused by terrorism has been disastrous and it can undo other potentially positive developments internationally. The Pakistan-China Gwader Port project is an example: it has the potential to bring about enormous positive for both China and Pakistan. The vast amount of resources put into this project by China has been one of the largest investments China has ever made. But even a project of this size and scope could prove vulnerable if terrorism destabilises the region. It is a matter for the Chinese and Pakistani governments to look at these issues with vigor and determination to address the issues now – and not only through armed forces, but also through conversations and participation of both state and non-state actors.

IN CONCLUSION

There is a need to create a genuine network of well-grounded and established practitioners, and indeed academics, to help develop institutional learning and to build up an accessible 'critical mass' of experts who can concentrate their time and energy on increasing their expertise and disseminating their wisdom and experience. Even when agencies attempt honestly to conduct post-operational evaluations, these tend to end up as 'lessons recorded' rather than 'lessons learned'. I accept that we have the Radicalisation Awareness Network (RAN) in Europe, but in all honesty and after attending a few of their gatherings and speaking to many of the participants who have their own reservations about RAN, it seems to have developed into more of a 'talking shop' than anything else. This is not to say the idea behind the RAN was not a well-thought-of concept, indeed it is a brilliant idea, but it lacks serious practical learning and it has not produced much in the way of real impact. The RAN can prove highly useful and successful if its direction changes slightly and the learning that can come out of it is used effectively and practically at grass roots level.

As mentioned previously, the causes, circumstances and mechanisms of violent extremism and terrorism are themselves constantly and rapidly evolving and it is futile, indeed misleading, to base one's understanding of these factors on a snapshot of any particular moment.

Furthermore, this ongoing evolution often renders some experience quickly obsolete. Consequently, experience and evidence need to be constantly revalidated before they can be relied on. Some factors persist, others change rapidly or at a rate varied by location or circumstance. The problem is to distinguish between the two.

In such a rapidly changing environment, no planned Prevent programme can be based completely and solely on past experience; it needs to be ready to innovate and experiment, to be adaptable, and to be ready to 'learn on the job'. This does not normally fit in with institutional or government requirements, but it is certainly an important fact we must acknowledge.

For example, before ISIS emerged, whilst we were dealing with Al Qaeda-inspired extremism and terrorism, which in itself posed many challenges, we found a rapid shift in attitudes, narratives and behaviours which we needed to quickly understand and put measures in place to address. Jihadi John and ISIS took many people completely by surprise; where ordinarily we could use the brutal and barbaric murders as preventative measures by referencing religious texts or pulling on human emotional chords, our attempts initially proved futile. We found his barbaric behaviour became a flavour many young people enjoyed. We also found young people promoting the brutal acts of ISIS and agreeing with them. Although very alarming, we had to very quickly think of a solution to stem this tide and push back this shift in attitude.

This proved a challenge due to having in place contractual obligations to deliver upon pre-established objectives and outcomes for that financial year. Failure to deliver on those would mean we are slipping on agreed outcomes. It was clearly evident that our approach and indeed attention needed to shift rapidly in order to address the emerging challenges posed by ISIS *et al.*

The academic and practitioner base is geographically and institutionally very diverse, but there has not been adequate interaction between the two for the necessary mutual learning to take place for better understanding. Without an accepted, standard framework for the evaluation of effect and the expression of results, reports can be very subjective, prone to unsubstantiated opinion and personal interpretation, and can be influenced by financial and commercial considerations: for example, the pressure to apply a prepared template solution inappropriate to local circumstances, or to exaggerate success and, in some cases, cover up failure.

The fact that the issue of violent extremism is, in most countries, highly politicised seriously influences the debate. Coupled with the lack of an accepted methodology, this can hinder objectivity and calm assessment and can influence the choice of measures in response, sometimes encouraging inappropriate responses, short-term success and the search for 'silver bullet' solutions.

The unease that some countries feel in acknowledging both the scale of the problem of violent extremism which they face, as well as in acknowledging the Prevent methods they resort to, creates a further gap in the knowledge. The fact that many afflicted countries suffer from bad governance, corruption, weak national and local government structures and poorly developed societal structures only compounds the problem itself. It also greatly hinders the gathering of factual data and its subsequent interpretation.

The acknowledged difficulty of coming up with a convincing measure of negative effect (*ie* measuring the value of preventing something from happening), which is common to many fields of endeavour, leads to a focus on outputs (and sometimes inputs: money, for example) instead of making the difficult decision to try to measure actual outcomes and long-term impact.

Enduring principles to take into account when planning or delivering a Prevent intervention programme

My first point here would be to accept and work with the many risks associated with preventing extremism and terrorist recruitment. We cannot – indeed, must not – allow political ambitions to take precedence over this critically important work. It is risky business and it will certainly require the practitioners or those on the front line to take certain risks. Although it is important to be mindful and considerate of life-threatening circumstances which must be avoided, it is equally important that governments and their institutions support, protect and share the risks and the challenges with the practitioners working on the front line whenever they arise.

It is difficult, and in certain cases dangerous, to rely solely or completely on evidence learned from previous experiences when trying to describe the rapid evolution of the circumstances of recruitment into violent extremism. However, there are some enduring principles which it is advisable to take into serious consideration when planning a Prevent programme. They are grouped here under the headings: *Understanding*, *Investment* and *Implementation*.

Understanding
Of these three stages in the process of developing a Prevent intervention programme, understanding is the most important. Everything depends on it. The pre-requisite for establishing any programme is to achieve a thorough and accurate understanding of the situation before you start, and to maintain the currency of that understanding for the lifetime of the intervention. This demands, firstly, a well-informed and totally dispassionate analysis based on a systematic examination and assessment of the latest evidence and taking into account the relative importance of the impact or influence of relevant factors (*eg* economic, military, political, ideological, religious, social, cultural) on the individuals involved, on their relationships and on the situation as a whole. Secondly, the analysis process must never cease, but must particularly include an ongoing assessment of the dynamics of the situation: how rapidly is it developing; how is it evolving and mutating; what is the sequence of events as they unfold?

Most difficult of all, understanding requires the exercise of judgement: where are things heading? We are mindful at this point of Mark Twain's famous dictum to the effect that it is notoriously difficult to predict the future. It is also notoriously difficult in real life even to follow, understand and make sense of what is going on in the present or recent past.

Investment
Commit to long-term engagement and build trust with all actors. Exclude no one faction, however awkward they might be to deal with and however they might complicate the situation – excluded actors tend to spoil tidy solutions downstream; actors who trust you will give you the information you need.

Measure the evolving situation appropriately so that you can see, map and understand the impact of changes as they occur.

Invest in a capacity for planning, rather than investing in a plan. Ensure your programme has adaptability and flexibility, knowing that you hold a huge degree of responsibility; be prepared to change your plans in rapid response to a new situation arising. This will require you to maintain a reserve of resources to be able to respond to the unexpected. Funding organisations often make this difficult to do by insisting on efficiency rather than enabling effectiveness; demanding a blueprint with rigid schedules, tied budgets and long lead times

Consensus is more reliable than compromise in dealing with conflicting views and interests, even though it means slower progress. Compromise can store up perceptions of injustices prolonged and create destructive resentment.

Implementation
Avoid the temptation of quick fixes and silver bullets; these offer an illusion of progress and sometimes do more harm than good. Be cautious of relying on low-hanging fruit; ask: why hasn't someone picked it already?

Avoid single, simple solutions to complex problems. It is too naïve to say, for example, 'Give someone a job and they will not engage in violent extremism'. There will rarely be one solution, as rarely as there is one cause. Interventions where practical improvements in living conditions are made without changing the mindsets of the individuals involved are as futile as trying to change minds without offering hope of improved living conditions. Programmes which are only 'bottom-up' do tend to be more often successful than programmes which are only 'top-down'. But there is far more likelihood of success if your programme does both.

Prevent is a risky, uncertain area to be operating in and a certain degree of experimentation is essential. Do not be beguiled by risk-avoidance masquerading as risk-management – although I appreciate that this is easy to say but hard to do, especially when statutory institutions and funding agencies are themselves chronically risk-averse. Do not confuse your readiness to take an institutional risk, which is in fact what is needed here, with the unwarranted acceptance of physical risk. This is something that can happen too often with those who work regularly in hostile environments.

It is our collective duty to overcome these challenges and to support, indeed participate with, those who we encourage to rise stronger and are at the cutting edge. And let us always be ever so mindful: *Extremism is sustained through a set of ideas – something that will potentially allow the most brutal terrorist groups to survive even after they are defeated on the battlefield.*

PART B
TACKLING EXTREMISM

THE REALITY OF THE THREAT – THE IDEOLOGY OF EXTREMISTS

I'm sure everyone reading this book has already grasped the severity of the problem. However, if you haven't fully appreciated the grim reality of the threat of extremism and terrorism in its current dimension, especially after witnessing hundreds of plots, many actual attacks, including those attacks in Europe, then the contents in this chapter may help you realise the actual certainty of the problem.

Over the past 14 years, since the Second Gulf War in particular, there have been hundreds of actual terrorist attacks across the globe, and an untold number of foiled plots. Every attack or plot has been an attempt to divide and destabilise communities. Although it is often hard to understand and accept, many of these terrorist attacks were launched by young men and women who have been born, raised and educated in the UK or elsewhere in the western world. What is even more worrying is that we have seen most of these plots unfold and executed by young men and women who have otherwise led ordinary lives, and have been part of the fabric of their respective communities. The threat of extremism and terrorism has become so real that we are experiencing an exodus, of sorts, of young men and (perhaps even more so) young females who are leaving their families and their homes behind to go and join a group of people they have otherwise not known or even met before. All this is based on misconceptions, internalised grievances and a serious lack of understanding, supported by a narrative they do not fully understand, but certainly feel that they can definitely relate to.

In order to fully acknowledge the reality of the threat, as well as the narrative being applied, the following few pages will give you a deep insight into one of the *fatwas* given by an ISIS 'scholar' known as Abu Muhammad al-Adnani al-Shami (now deceased), who has set out a full-on 'call of duty' and to initiate attacks wherever possible. The first read (for those who have not read it before) will probably send a shiver down your spine. However the attentive reader will be able to examine and identify the deviant nature to which it is applied, and notice how this cunning and devious man is manipulating historical and deep-rooted scriptural chords to his own evil means. It is important to pick out where, and how, he is referencing past and recent conflicts, a lot of which do actually resonate with millions of young minds across the world. He uses very limited theological references, completely out of context, where he feels the impact will be deeper. He fails completely to produce the complete verse, when and where it was revealed, and the circumstances around the revelations. This is common practice for such unscrupulous individuals.

I use this *fatwa* as an indicator for the reader to fully understand and grasp the manipulative methods and the actual potency of the problem. My approach in this chapter is for you to analyse the contents of this *fatwa*, and to demonstrate how this one example is a reality of the threat we all face. This *fatwa* was released in 2015 and has been followed by more, with an equally powerful call to arms. Events, such as those we unfortunately witnessed in Paris and in the US, are very likely to be followed by more in other parts of the world, including here in the UK, unless we identify ways and means of turning the tide against these determined and brutal groups.

AN ISIS *FATWA*

Abu Muhammad al Adnani al-Shami
O soldiers of the Islamic State, what a great thing you have achieved by Allah! Your reward is upon Him. By Allah, He has healed the chests of the believers through the killing of the nusayriyyah (alawites) and rāfidah (shiites) at your hands. He has filled the hearts of the disbelievers and hypocrites with rage through you. What a great thing you have achieved by Allah! Who are you? Who are you O soldiers of the Islamic State? From where have you come? What is your secret? Why is it that the hearts of the East and West are dislocated by their fear of you? Why is it that the chest muscles of America and its allies shiver out of fear of you? Where are your warplanes? Where are your battleships? Where are your missiles? Where are your weapons of mass destruction? Why is it that the world

has united against you? Why have the nations of disbelief entrenched together against you? What threat do you pose to the distant place of Australia for it to send its legions towards you? What does Canada have anything to do with you?

O soldiers of the Islamic State and its sons everywhere, listen and comprehend. If the people belie you, reject your state and your call, and mock your caliphate, then know that your Prophet (blessings and peace be upon him) was belied. His call was rejected. He was mocked.

If your people fight you, accuse you with the worst of accusations, and describe you with the worst of all traits, then know that the people of the Prophet (blessings and peace be upon him) fought him, expelled him, and accused him with matters worse than those you have been accused with.

If the parties have gathered against you, then know they gathered against your Prophet before (blessings and peace be upon him). This is the established way of Allah, the Blessed, the Exalted. Or did you think that the people would greet you by saying "Allah is the greatest" and "There is no god but Allah"? And that they would joyfully bid you welcome? {While such trial has not yet come to you as came to those who passed on before you} [Al-Baqarah: 214.. Quranic verse], whereby you taste what they have tasted?

No! You will be shaken. {But We have certainly tried those before them, and Allah will surely make evident those who are truthful, and He will surely make evident the liars} [Al-ʿAnkabūt: 3... Quranic verse].

Allah has given you might and honor after your humiliation. He has made you rich after your poverty. And He has aided you despite your weakness and small numbers. He showed you that victory is from Him, the Glorified. He grants it to whomever He wills and whenever He wills.

So know that – by Allah – we fear not the swarms of planes, nor ballistic missiles, nor drones, nor satellites, nor battleships, nor weapons of mass destruction. How could we fear them, while Allah the Exalted has said, {If Allah should aid you, no one can overcome you; but if He should forsake you, who is there that can aid you after Him? And upon Allah let the believers rely}

How could we fear them, while Allah the Exalted has said, {So do not weaken and do not grieve, and you will be superior if you are [true] believers}

How could we fear them, while you have proven yourselves to be the knights and men of war? When you defend, you are like the firmest mountains. And when you assault, you are like predatory warriors. You face death with bare chests, while the worldly life is beneath your worn feet. I swear by Allah that I have not known any of you except to be a forerunner towards every battle sound, eagerly searching *for the place of death in every fight. I see the Quran walking alive amongst you. What a great thing you have achieved by Allah! The weak one of you is a brave warrior, and the merciful one of you is ferocious in battle. We have not known you to be except jealous and angry. Your jealousy is not but for the religion of Allah. And your anger is not but for the violation of Allah's sanctities. You say the truth and according to it you judge. You love Allah and His Messenger (blessings and peace be upon him). And you are the most careful to follow his tradition (blessings and peace be upon him). You are harsh against the disbelievers, merciful among yourselves. For the cause of Allah, you do not fear the blame of a critic.*

Therefore Allah will give you victory. Indeed, Allah will give you victory. By Allah, Allah will give you victory. So guarantee for us two matters, and we will guarantee you by Allah's permission constant victory and consolidation. First, do not oppress anyone nor be content with oppression by being silent about it and not raising the matter [to those in authority]. Second, do not become conceited or arrogant. This is what we fear from you and fear for you. So if you gain victory, then attribute it to Allah alone. Continue on with modesty, humbleness, giving praise and thanks to Allah. If you fail, then attribute the cause to yourselves and your sins. And attack the enemy again after asking Allah for forgiveness and repenting to Him with remorse.

And we declare our innocence before Allah of injustices that could be carried out by any of you and did not reach us. And we declare our innocence before Allah of any injustice one of you conceals or turns a blind eye to.

Thereafter know that a trial, sifting, and selection, are necessary between one period and another, for some people have entered your ranks who are not of you and are only claimants. And thus some disorder has occurred. So it has become necessary for a trial to come, expel the filth, and purify the ranks. We ask Allah for forgiveness and wellness.

Also, pride and conceit has entered some of our souls, and thus some of us transgressed and oppressed others. So it is necessary for the sins to be expelled, so that you may return to your Lord. Allah has loved the mujahidin, and so there is no choice but for Him to take some martyrs. We ask Allah to make us of them, not from the disgraced nor those afflicted [in their religion].

O soldiers of the Islamic State, be ready for the final campaign of the crusaders. Yes, by Allah's will, it will be the final one. Thereafter, we will raid them by Allah's permission and they will not raid us. Be ready, for by Allah's permission you are befitting for it. The crusaders have returned with a new campaign. They have come so that the dust clears, the fog disappears, and the masks fall, and thereby the hoax of falsehood is exposed and the truth becomes clearly visible, {That those

71

who perished [through disbelief] would perish upon evidence and those who lived [in faith] would live upon evidence}

O America, O allies of America, and O crusaders, know that the matter is more dangerous than you have imagined and greater than you have envisioned. We have warned you that today we are in a new era, an era where the State, its soldiers, and its sons are leaders not slaves. They are a people who through the ages have not known defeat. The outcome of their battles is concluded before they begin. They have not prepared for a battle since the time of Noah except with absolute conviction of victory. Being killed – according to their account – is a victory. This is where the secret lies. You fight a people who can never be defeated. They either gain victory or are killed. And O crusaders, you are losers in both outcomes, because you are ignorant of the reality that none of us is killed but to resurrect the dead amongst us. None of us is killed but to leave behind him a story that awakens the Muslims from their slumber by its recount. And then you see the weak one of us – he who has no experience in fighting and thinks he cannot contribute anything practical on the ground, having no goal except to be killed, so that he can illuminate the path with his blood and thereby enliven the hearts with his story, generation after generation. He makes his body and remains a bridge for those who awaken after him to pass over. This person has realized that the life of his nation is through blood and the honor of his nation is through blood. So he went on with a bare chest and bare head towards death eagerly searching for life and honor. If he survives, he lives as a victor with freedom, might, honor, and authority. And if he is killed, he illuminates the path for those after him and goes on to his Lord as a joyful martyr. He has taught those after him that might, honor, and life are through jihad and being killed, and that humiliation, disgrace, and death are through submission and subservience.

O crusaders, you have realized the threat of the Islamic State, but you have not become aware of the cure, and you will not discover the cure because there is no cure. If you fight it, it becomes stronger and tougher. If you leave it alone, it grows and expands. If Obama has promised you with defeating the Islamic State, then Bush has also lied before him. Indeed, our Lord, the Mighty and Majestic, has promised us with victory, and here we are now victorious. He will grant us victory at every event. He is glorified and He does not fail in His promise.

And so we promise you by Allah's permission that this campaign will be your final campaign. It will be broken and defeated, just as all your previous campaigns were broken and defeated, except that this time we will raid you thereafter, and you will never raid us. We will conquer your Rome, break your crosses, and enslave your women, by the permission of Allah, the Exalted. This is His promise to us; He is glorified and He does not fail in His promise. If we do not reach that *time, then our children and grandchildren will reach it, and they will sell your sons as slaves at the slave market.*

On the authority of 'Abdullāh Ibn 'Amr Ibn al-'Ās (a companion of our beloved prophet) (may Allah the Exalted be pleased with both of them), who said, "We were with Allah's Messenger (blessings and peace be upon him) writing down what he was saying, when he was asked, 'Which of the two cities will be conquered first? Constantinople or Rome?' So Allah's Messenger (blessings and peace be upon him) said, 'The city of Heraclius will be the first to be conquered.'" Meaning the city of Constantinople. It was reported by al-Hākim in "Al-Mustadrak" according to the conditions of the two sheikhs (Bukhārī and Muslim) (Hadiths a book of references from the prophet) and declared authentic by Imam adh-Dhahabī.

So mobilize your forces, O crusaders. Mobilize your forces, roar with thunder, threaten whom you want, plot, arm your troops, prepare yourselves, strike, kill, and destroy us. This will not avail you. You will be defeated. This will not avail you, for our Lord, the Mighty, the Prevailing, has promised us with our victory and your defeat. Send arms and equipment to your agents and dogs. Prepare them with the most modern equipment. Send them very much, for it will end up as war booty in our hands by Allah's permission. You will spend it, then it will be a source of regret for you, then you will be defeated. Look at your armored vehicles, machinery, weaponry, and equipment. It is in our hands. Allah granted it to us. We fight you with it. So die in your rage. {Indeed, those who disbelieve spend their wealth to avert [people] from the way of Allah. So they will spend it; then it will be for them a [source of] regret; then they will be overcome. And those who have disbelieved – unto Hell they will be gathered}

And O Obama, O mule of the jews. You are vile. You are vile. You are vile. And you will be disappointed, Obama. Is this all you were capable of doing in this campaign of yours? Is this how far America has reached of incapacity and weakness? Are America and all its allies from amongst the crusaders and atheists unable to come down to the ground? Have you not realized – O crusaders – that proxy wars have not availed you nor will they ever avail you? Have you not realized, O mule of the jews, that the battle cannot be decided from the air at all? Or do you think that you are smarter than Bush, your obeyed fool, when he brought the armies of the cross and placed them under the fire of the mujahidin on the ground? No, you are more foolish than him.

You claimed to have withdrawn from Iraq – O Obama – four years ago. We said to you then that you were liars, that you had not withdrawn, and that if you had withdrawn that you would return, even if after some time, you would return. Here you are; you have not withdrawn. Rather you hid some of your forces behind your proxies and withdrew the rest. Your forces will return greater in number than they were before. You will return and your proxies will not avail you. And if you are not able to return, then we will come to your homeland by Allah's permission.

O mule of the jews, you claimed today that America would not be drawn to a war on the ground. No, it will be drawn and dragged. It will come down to the ground and it will be led to its death, grave, and destruction. O Obama, you claimed that the hand of America was long and could reach wherever it willed. Then know that our knife is sharp and hard. It cuts off the hands and strikes the necks. And our Lord – the Majestic and Exalted – is watching over you. {Have you not considered how your Lord dealt with 'Ād and [with] Iram who had lofty pillars, the likes of whom had never been created in the land? And [with] Thamūd, who carved out the rocks in the valley? And [with] Pharaoh, owner of the stakes? [All of] whom oppressed within the lands and increased therein the corruption. So your Lord poured upon them a scourge of punishment. Indeed, your Lord is ever watchful} [Al-Fajr: 6-14... Quranic verse]. {As for 'Ād, they were arrogant upon the earth without right and said, "Who is greater than us in strength?" Did they not consider that Allah who created them was greater than them in strength? But they were rejecting Our signs. So We sent upon them a screaming wind during days of misfortune to make them taste the punishment of disgrace in the worldly life; but the punishment of the Hereafter is more disgracing, and they will not be helped}

O Americans, and O Europeans, the Islamic State did not initiate a war against you, as your governments and media try to make you believe. It is you who started the transgression against us, and thus you deserve blame and you will pay a great price. You will pay the price when your economies collapse. You will pay the price when your sons are sent to wage war against us and they return to you as disabled amputees, or inside coffins, or mentally ill. You will pay the price as you are afraid of travelling to any land. Rather you will pay the price as you walk on your streets, turning right and left, fearing the Muslims. You will not feel secure even in your bedrooms. You will pay the price when this crusade of yours collapses, and thereafter we will strike you in your homeland, and you will never be able to harm anyone afterwards. You will pay the price, and we have prepared for you what will pain you.

O Muslims, America claimed when it first began this crusade, that it was defending its interests in Erbil and Baghdad and defending its citizens. Thereafter its blunder became clear, and the falsehood of its claims became obvious. It claimed that through its airstrikes it would save those expelled and left homeless in Iraq, and defend the civilians. Then it became clear to America that the matter was more dangerous and greater than it expected. So it started shedding crocodile tears over the Muslims in Shām (the Levant). It promised to save them and support them. It promised to save them from the terrorists. While at the same time, America and its allies remained watching the plight of the Muslims upon the hands of the nusayriyyah. They watched with happiness seeing the killing, abuse, expulsion, and destruction, neither interested in, nor concerned about, the hundreds of thousands of dead, wounded, and imprisoned Muslims, and the millions displaced – including men, women and children – all over the world at the hands of the jews, crusaders, rāfidah, nusayriyyah, hindus, atheists, and apostates, in Palestine, Yemen, Syria, Iraq, Egypt, Tunisia, Libya, Burma, Nigeria, Somalia, Afghanistan, Indonesia, India, China, the Caucasus, and elsewhere. Its sentiments were not stirred during the long years of siege and starvation in Shām, and it looked the other way when the deadly and destructive barrel bombs were being dropped. It was not outraged when it saw the horrific scenes of the women and children of the Muslims taking their last breaths with their eyes glazed over due to the chemical weapons of the nusayriyyah – scenes which continue to be repeated everyday, exposing the reality of the farce of having destroyed chemical weapons belonging to its nusayrī (alawite) dogs, the guardians of the jews. America and its allies were not emotionally moved or outraged by any of this. They closed their ears to the cries of distress from the weak, and turned a blind eye to the massacres carried out against the Muslims in every one of those lands for years and years.

But when a state emerged for the Muslims that would defend them, take revenge for them, and carry out retribution, America and the crusaders started shedding crocodile tears for the sake of a few hundred rāfidī (shiite) and nusayrī criminal soldiers that the Islamic State had taken as prisoners of war and then executed. The hearts of America and its allies were broken by the Islamic State when it cut off the rotten heads of some agents, spies, and apostates. It was terrified and its allies were terrified when the Islamic State would flog and stone the fornicator, cut off the hand of the thief, and strike the neck of the sorcerer and the apostate.

So America and its allies rose in order to save the world from the "terrorism and barbarity of the Islamic State" as they allege. They rallied the entire global media, driving it with false arguments to delude the masses and lead them to believe that the Islamic State was the root of evil and the source of corruption, and that it was the one killing and displacing the people, arresting and murdering those who are "peaceful," demolishing houses, destroying cities, and terrorizing the women and children who were previously safe. The media portrayed the crusaders as good, merciful, noble, generous, honorable and passionate people who feared for Islam and the Muslims the "corruption and cruelty of the khawārij (a deviant, extremist sect) of the Islamic State" as they allege. To the extent that Kerry, the uncircumcised old geezer, suddenly became an Islamic jurist, issuing a verdict to the people that the Islamic State was distorting Islam, and that what it was doing was against Islamic teachings, and that the Islamic State was an enemy of Islam. And to the extent that Obama, the mule of the jews, suddenly became a sheikh, mufti (Islamic scholar that issues verdicts), and an Islamic preacher, warning the people and preaching in defense of Islam, claiming that the Islamic State has nothing to do with Islam. This occurred during six different addresses he made in the span of a single month, all of them about the threat of the Islamic State. They turned into Islamic jurists, muftis, sheikhs, and preachers, standing up for Islam and the Muslims, so it appears that they no longer have confidence in the ability or sincerity of their sorcerers in the various committees of senior scholars working for the rulers – committees of the supporters of the tawāghīt (rulers ruling by manmade law).

Dear Muslims, America hasn't come with its crusade in order to save the Muslims, nor does it spend its wealth in spite of the collapse of its economy and burden itself in order to arm and train the sahwah councils in Shām and Iraq out of compassion and fear for the mujahidin from the "cruelty of the khawārij," and out of support for them as they allege. Do the crusaders rush to the support of the mujahidin fighting on the path of Allah, and rush to rescue and save them from the khawārij? "Live long enough and you'll see strange things!" Woe to my people! When will they remember? Allah the Exalted said, {Neither those who disbelieve from the People of the Scripture nor the polytheists wish that any good should be sent down to you from your Lord} [Al-Baqarah: 105]... Likewise, Allah the Exalted said about the people of the scripture (jews and christians), {And they will continue to fight you until they turn you back from your religion if they are able} [Al- Baqarah: 217].

So America has not come for any reason other than to wage war against Islam and the Muslims. It has not gathered its allies and spent its wealth for any reason other than to break the strength of the mujahidin. So you have the statement of Allah on one hand, and the claim of the crusaders on the other. Who are you going to believe, O Muslims? Then will you not reason?

The hearts of the crusaders did not denounce anything, nor were their sentiments stirred or their tears shed, except when they saw the rāfidī-safavid army and their dogs in the Iraq war collapse in the face of the strikes carried out by the mujahidin, fleeing like rats, and being crushed like insects under the feet of the muwahhidīn (monotheists). Indeed, America went mad and its allies lost their senses when the nusayrī forces, guard dogs of the jews, began collapsing in terror and fleeing in panic in the face of the mujahidin's advance. America and its allies had their hearts broken when they saw a group of nusayriyyah being herded by the soldiers of the Islamic State like animals, and slaughtered like sheep, in the *largest battle the nusayriyyah had lost in their entire black history, so that the Islamic State could begin its march towards Damascus. It was only then that the crusaders realized the extent of the threat. It was only then that their emotions and sentiments were stirred. It was only then that their hearts spoke and their tears flowed. It was only then that they suffered pain and anguish. It was only then that America and its allies rose in alarm and summoned one another, terrified. The jews! The jews! Save the jews! This is the reason they came. This is the purpose of their mobilization.*

And, I wish my people could know! I wish my people could know!

Indeed, the reality of their opposition and resistance has become very clear, and the nusayriyyah and rāfidah were not able to contain themselves. The nusayriyyah began openly calling for America's help, and welcoming their strikes against the Islamic State, completely forgetting their alleged sovereignty, their imaginary strength and capabilities, and their enmity towards America, which in fact was just a lie. Likewise Iran, as it emerged that it had allied itself with its "great Satan," when the uncircumcised old geezer, Kerry, recently declared that Iran had a role in the war against the Islamic State. So it became clear that their opposition was for the sake of protecting the jews and the crusaders, and that the resistance was a resistance against Islam and the mujahidin.

O Sunnis of Iraq, the time has come for you to learn from the lessons of the past, and to learn that nothing will work with the rāfidah other than slicing their throats and striking their necks. They make themselves out to be helpless so that they can take power, they conceal their hatred, enmity, and rage towards Sunnis, they plot and conspire against them, and they trick and deceive them. They display false affection towards them and flatter them as long as Sunnis are strong. And they keep pace with them, compete with them, and work hard to weaken them when they are on equal footing. But if one day they overcome them, they bare their fangs and reveal their claws, biting them, tearing them apart, killing them, and humiliating them. History is right there in front of you, O Sunnis, so read it. How many times have the rāfidah conspired against the Sunnis, and what do they do to them when they gain power? Read their history and look at how they are in the present. Indeed, their idiot Nouri has shown you their true face, so do not let their new snake deceive you with his soft touch and sweet tongue. You have been stung through the hole of reconciliation before with Nouri, so beware.

Our dear people of Shām, you can see the reality becoming clearer day after day. Take a lesson from our people in Iraq, for history repeats itself. Indeed, the crusaders began building the Iraqi-safavid army by training its core in Jordan, with a few thousand soldiers, as they have decided to do today with regard to

Shām. So what did the Sunnis get out of that army other than to have the rāfidah completely gain power over them? They tasted humiliation, disgrace, and many misfortunes at the hands of that army over a period of ten years. Furthermore, what did the sons of the Sunnis get out of joining that army other than apostasy from the religion of Allah, the destruction of their homes, and having their heads cut off? And those of them who lived, lived in continuous terror and a persistent state of fear, not knowing when he'd be taken by a bullet, or have his joints cut by an adhesive IED, or be deformed by an explosive or bomb, or be suffocated to death, or have a knife cutting his neck, or when he would return to find his home demolished, left in pieces after it was once whole. And for what would all this have been for? So take a lesson, O people of intelligence. So pay attention, O Sunnis. For the army that they have decided to prepare today by Āl Salūl (the Saudis) is nothing more than a new set of guard dogs for the jews, and a stick in the hands of the crusaders to be used against Islam and the mujahidin. Therefore, we advise the mujahidin in Shām to target anyone who joins that army or intends to join it. And he who has given his warning is free of blame. As for the sahwah councils and their political sponsors, they will not be able to hide their reality after today. Their reality, that they are the sahwah councils and the shoes of the crusaders, will emerge very clearly.

So rally around the mujahidin, O Sunnis of Shām, and stop your sons from joining the army and the sahwah councils, for what good is there in an army built by the crusaders which they then train on the laps of the tawāghīt. So prevent your sons, and whoever of them refuses to listen, let him not blame anyone but himself if there comes to him a day in which he digs his grave with his own hands, his head is cut off, and his house is demolished. And the blessed one is he who learns from the lessons of others. To Allah belongs honor, and to His Messenger, and to the believers. And the final outcome will be in favor of the righteous. Let us not forget before ending to praise our mujahidin brothers in the bold Sinai Peninsula, for hope has emerged in Egypt and good news has loomed with their blessed operations against the guards of the jews, the soldiers of Sisi, the new Pharaoh of Egypt. Carry on upon this path, for it is the correct path, may Allah bless you. Disperse those behind them wherever you may find them. Rig the roads with explosives for them. Attack their bases. Raid their homes. Cut off their heads. Do not let them feel secure. Hunt them wherever they may be. Turn their worldly life into fear and fire. Remove their families from their homes and thereafter blowup their homes. Do not say it is a fitnah (tribulation). Rather the fitnah is that their tribes defend them and do not disavow them. {He said, "O Noah, indeed he is not of your family; indeed, he is [one whose] work was other than righteous"} [Hūd: 46.. Quranic verse].

And to our brothers the muwahhidīn in beloved Libya, until when will you remain dispersed and divided? Why do you not gather your groups, unify, unite your word, and solidify your ranks? Why do you not identify who is with you and who is against you? Your division is from Satan.

We also call out to the muwahhidīn in the robbed land of Tunisia, follow the footsteps of your brothers in Egypt. O brother in tawhīd (monotheism), what do you wait for while the tawāghīt have prevented you from making da'wah (calling to the religion)? They prohibited you also from emigrating and opened for you their prisons of false freedom. They arrest your brothers every day and kill them. What do you wait for? Do you wait for the life of humiliation and disgrace? Or do you love the worldly life and hate death? Rise against them for the muhwahhid (monotheist) is an army by himself. Where are the descendants of 'Uqbah, Mūsā, and Tāriq?

As for Yemen, then O alas for what has come upon Yemen. Alas! Alas for Sanaa. The rafidī houthis have entered it, but the car bombs have not roasted their skin, nor have the explosive belts and IEDs cut their joints. Is there not in Yemen a person who will take revenge for us from the houthis?

O muwahhidīn (monotheist)... in Europe, America, Australia, and Canada... O muwahhidīn in Morocco and Algeria... O muwahhidīn in Khorasan, the Caucasus, and Iran... O muwahhidīn everywhere upon the face of the earth... O brothers in creed... O people of walā' (allegiance to the Muslims) and barā' (disavowal of disbelievers)... O patrons of the Islamic State... O you who have given bay'ah (pledge of allegiance) to the Caliph Ibrāhīm everywhere... O you who have loved the Islamic State... O you who support the Caliphate... O you who consider yourselves from amongst its soldiers and patrons...

Your state is facing a new campaign by the crusaders. So O muwahhid (monotheist)..., wherever you may be, what are you going to do to support your brothers? What do you wait for as the people have become two encampments and the heat of the war increases day by day? O muwahhid, we call you up to defend the Islamic State. Dozens of nations have gathered against it. They began their war against us at all levels. So rise O muwahhid. Rise and defend your state from your place wherever you may be. Rise and defend your Muslim brothers, for their homes, families, and wealth are threatened and deemed lawful by their enemies. They are facing a battle which is of the decisive, critical battles in the history of Islam. If the Muslims are defeated, they will be humiliated in such a manner that no humiliation compares to. And if the Muslims are victorious – and this will be the case by Allah's permission – they will be honored with all honor by which the Muslims will return to being the masters of the world and kings of the earth.

So O muwahhid,... do not let this battle pass you by wherever you may be. You must strike the soldiers, patrons, and troops of the tawāghīt. Strike their police, security, and intelligence members, as well as their treacherous agents. Destroy their beds. Embitter their lives for them and busy them with themselves. If you can kill a disbelieving American or European – especially the spiteful and filthy French – or an Australian, or a Canadian, or any other disbeliever from the disbelievers waging war, including the citizens of the countries that entered into a coalition against the Islamic State, then rely upon Allah, and kill him in any manner or way however it may be. Do not ask for anyone's advice and do not seek anyone's verdict. Kill the disbeliever whether he is civilian or military, for they have the same ruling. Both of them are disbelievers. Both of them are considered to be waging war [the civilian by belonging to a state waging war against the Muslims]. Both of their blood and wealth is legal for you to destroy, for blood does not become illegal or legal to spill by the clothes being worn. The civilian outfit does not make blood illegal to spill, and the military uniform does not make blood legal to spill. The only things that make blood illegal and legal to spill are Islam and a covenant (peace treaty, dhimma, etc.). Blood becomes legal to spill through disbelief. So whoever is a Muslim, his blood and wealth are sanctified. And whoever is a disbeliever, his wealth is legal for a Muslim to take and his blood is legal to spill. His blood is like the blood of a dog; there is no sin for him in spilling it nor is there any blood money to be paid for doing such. {And when the sacred months have passed, then kill the polytheists wherever you find them and capture them and besiege them and sit in wait for them at every place of ambush} – {So when you meet those who disbelieve [in battle], strike [their] necks} "The disbeliever and his killer will never gather in Hellfire.".... "Whoever kills a disbeliever, then he can have his loot [which is on his person]."

So O muwahhid... O you who believes in walā' and barā' will you leave the American, the Frenchman, or any of their allies to walk safely upon the earth while the armies of the crusaders strike the lands of the Muslims not differentiating between a civilian and fighter? They have killed nine Muslim women three days ago by striking a bus transporting them from Shām to Iraq. Will you leave the disbeliever to sleep safely at home while the Muslim women and children shiver with fear of the roars of the crusader airplanes above their heads day and night? How can you enjoy life and sleep while not aiding your brothers, not casting fear into the hearts of the cross worshippers, and not responding to their strikes with multitudes more? So O muwahhid wherever you may be, hinder those who want to harm your brothers and state as much as you can. The best thing you can do is to strive to your best and kill any disbeliever, whether he be French, American, or from any of their allies.

If you are not able to find an IED or a bullet, then single out the disbelieving American, Frenchman, or any of their allies. Smash his head with a rock, or slaughter him with a knife, or run him over with your car, or throw him down from a high place, or choke him, or poison him. Do not lack. Do not be contemptible. Let your slogan be, "May I not be saved if the cross worshipper and taghūt (ruler ruling by manmade laws) patron survives." If you are unable to do so, then burn his home, car, or business. Or destroy his crops. If you are unable to do so, then spit in his face. If your self refuses to do so, while your brothers are being bombarded and killed, and while their blood and wealth everywhere is deemed lawful by their enemies, then review your religion. You are in a dangerous condition because the religion cannot be established without walā' and barā'. (Enjoining the good & Forbidding the evil)

Finally, we do not want to forget to direct a message towards our Muslim people and brothers from the Kurds in Iraq, Shām, and elsewhere. Our war with Kurds is a religious war. It is not a nationalistic war – we seek the refuge of Allah. We do not fight Kurds because they are Kurds. Rather we fight the disbelievers amongst them, the allies of the crusaders and jews in their war against the Muslims. As for the Muslim Kurds, then they are our people and brothers wherever they may be. We spill our blood to save their blood. The Muslim Kurds in the ranks of the Islamic State are many. They are the toughest of fighters against the disbelievers amongst their people.

This fatwa should be seen as a significant demonstration of the reality of the threat. It resonates with many Muslims and non-Muslims, and especially young people. The genesis of arguments surrounding a lack of justice, and the harnessing of religious references, mean that it is emotionally relatable. But I emphasise that the writer has used theological references without actually going into detail. It is clearly used out of context. Most of his references are based on events in the early days of Islam, when it was in its infancy. Without context, clarity and understanding, a young, impressionable mind may wander loosely and consider the fatwa as legitimate and current, and in line with theological rulings. Interestingly, not only does it strike a chord with young Muslims, in fact evidence shows that far-right groups are using this fatwa to garner more support and rally communities against Muslims. It is essentially causing greater division, disenfranchisement, and hatred whilst also directly offering extremist groups from all sides a powerful recruitment tool.

This fatwa has generated a lot of attention from many diverse individuals and groups. The fact that opposing sides of the extremist spectrum are using the same fatwa demonstrates that the threat picture has changed significantly and that a much more intense and focused approach is needed across the board. We should not just read the fatwa and allow our minds to wander; rather we must read it over and over in order to seek out flaws and identify opportunities to use these against those who are using the fatwa to fuel hatred and terror. And indeed to diffuse the young mind from internalising it.

INFORMATION DUMPING STRATEGIES

I will explain how the average young person looks at some of the issues raised in the *fatwa*, and how they are further exacerbated by 'information dumping strategies' deployed with huge impact upon vulnerable and often naïve communities. These strategies are, in effect, designed with an understanding that those very communities desire an alternative narrative other than the obvious and the factual. Common conspiracy theories may help you understand which direction the susceptible mind will most likely travel in. A simple internet search using keywords such as 'arrivals' or 'Illuminati' or 'the truth behind 9/11' will reveal videos put out by conspiracy theorists regarding 9/11 and other designs to destroy Islam and Muslims. There, you will find compelling narratives that push the impressionable mind towards a completely different world view. Other videos put out by many terrorist networks are equally compelling and attractive to thousands of young men and women from all walks of life.

One important factor to consider is that young people will very often default back to a position where they feel comfortable, driven by their love and respect for their country of origin or their faith. This means it can be common for them to begin to think, 'How can any righteous Muslim carry out acts of violence and terror? There must be a good reason for it…' A typical example would be the barbaric acts carried out by Jihadi John, more commonly known to young people as 'JJ', when he brutally killed Alan Henning and others under the ISIS banner in Iraq in 2015. The narrative of 'misinformation' that was being dumped suggested that Alan Henning was actually a spy and was trying to pass on information to western secret services that would ultimately disrupt the attempts of 'God-fearing Muslims' trying to re-establish the caliphate and the application of Sharia (the law of God Almighty) in a Muslim country.

As a result, in personal conversations, I have witnessed young people ask questions such as 'What is wrong with implementing the law of God and why won't the non-Muslims allow us to establish our own state?', arguing that if Israel could have their own 'Jewish state' then why can't Muslims have an Islamic state? Another argument often brought forward by young people is that 'Not so long ago in the UK, the sentence for the act of treason was death by hanging, so if Alan Henning was a spy, then ISIS were right to execute him'.

That's when we see a complete change in attitude and, more worryingly, a greater acceptance of the actions of Jihadi John or groups like ISIS. It is because of this kind of narrative for the killing of Alan Henning that it sadly became acceptable in certain quarters. This example demonstrates how effective the narrative and propaganda information dumped by extremist and terrorist groups can actually be.

When Malala Yusufzai was shot by the Taliban it caused an uproar by millions of people within Pakistan and from across the world; even those who supported the Taliban were shocked and disgusted at this attack. I remember delivering a project in Kashmir at the time and tried to generate a mass support for Malala and to challenge the Taliban. The idea was to get as many young females from across the country to stand up in solidarity to Malala. What happened during this process was alarming and unexpected. In one session with over 50 young females one young girl received a text message claiming that Malala was Christian and worked with foreign agents, almost immediately another girl received a similar message claiming Malala was working for the Israeli spy agency. One by one over 12 similar messages were received in the one room which turned my plans to dust. In fact the girls unanimously felt that if any one of those messages are true, then Malala deserved getting shot, to a point that they all were hoping she would die.

This is how information dumping changes the attitudes of people, especially an unsuspecting community who would rather blame external sources for their problems. The environment already existed where the natural default position of such a community is that 'it cannot be Islam or Muslims, therefore it can only be the enemies of Islam'. It gets passed off, just like that.

We have witnessed first-hand, members loyal to the extremist self-proclaimed cleric Anjem Choudary as asking young people: 'Do you accept that Sharia is the law of God?' Knowing that any Muslim who disbelieves in this is considered out of the fold of Islam, when the young person accepts that Sharia is in fact the law of God, the secondary question is then: 'Would you want Sharia implemented in your country?' *ie*, Britain or anywhere else in Europe. Now if the young person says no, he faces criticism or, in some cases, hostility and abuse, but if he says yes, then he is asked 'So why aren't you doing something to get Sharia implemented?'. This line of questioning continues until a desired outcome is achieved. As you can see from this one single questioning, the young person faces a double-edged sword, no matter how he or she responds.

All the narratives applied by these groups aim to create a sentiment of affiliation, and when a young mind has a lack of context, clarity and understanding, they may easily consider these narratives to be legitimate. I suggest that the major challenge is for us to assist our young people in critical thinking skills and emotional logic training, which will develop their capacity to analyse information more critically and eventually become more resilient to the information dumping techniques applied by extremist groups.

WHO ARE THE EXTREMISTS AND HOW DO THEY RECRUIT?

Professor Peter Neumann, of the International Centre for the Study of Radicalisation (ICSR), at King's College, London, admirably describes the historical context of the extremism problem. The starting point of the present threat is linked to the Russian invasion of Afghanistan. The invasion had the capacity to mobilise the call for fighters from foreign countries to come to Afghanistan as *mujahideen* combatants to repel the invasion of a Muslim land. This move was, ironically, supported by both the USA and the UK governments, who were concerned about Russian motives. That call was answered by many Muslims, who were also reminded that it is in fact *jihad*, and who then travelled to support and fight against the Russians as a unified front. The Russian withdrawal was seen as a huge victory for Muslims but, after the war ended, this sense of unity created a void amongst those foreign fighters, who felt they had become redundant and were disillusioned as to what to do next.

The cascading effect is that the foreign fighters began to appear in other conflict zones like Bosnia, Chechnya, Kashmir, Pakistan, Iraq and Africa. Some simply returned home with an understanding that they were part of an international network of *mujahideen*. Part of the role of such returnees was to mobilise interest in their respective lands into the Muslim plight abroad. Another part of this mobilisation process was finance and action. In those days, structures were developed to move funds and assist in logistics, creating networks in domestic areas that were later to be termed as 'cells'. Those responsible for mobilising people also developed narratives to recruit people for physical participation and other means of support. In this sense they became the recruiters.

It is worth noting that since a time before the 1980s, in the UK there has been an organised recruitment process that supports the Muslim plight abroad. For example, the plight of the Kashmiris in Indian-held territory saw many individuals travel from the UK, and elsewhere, to fight as well as provide financial and logistical support. This was happening more than 30 years ago.

It would be wrong of course to infer that all returnees from conflict zones will be extremist or terrorist recruiters, or likely to contribute to any attacks on the UK. My personal experience, however, is that in the past many of the recruiters operating in the UK or Europe were returnees, or those who had travelled to the country from abroad.

Recruitment methods have evolved over the years, but although they are now much more intense and specifically targeted, the actual delivery itself has not changed greatly. However, it is inevitable that clever individuals will adapt to the speed of change and apply the most recent and effective ways of delivering their idea or message.

Terror groups are well informed and understand the dynamics of communication technology and how it has become the norm across the globe. They have effectively moved with the times and joined the masses on social media platforms, where social networking is now the conventional way of linking up. Young people, who live in the virtual world far more than other sections of society, are therefore more vulnerable than those who do not understand or are not connected to these new communication platforms.

In short, the extremist recruiters have become more 'virtual' than ever. This does not mean that physical interventions do not happen or that recruiters do not operate within communities. On the contrary, they still do so, but in a much more careful and suggestive manner, pushing individuals towards another platform where they can easily indoctrinate without many obstacles.

The *fatwa* in the previous chapter is a typical example of how the clever recruiter will remind those who may have forgotten about certain conflicts or who may not know their full extent. This *fatwa* was aimed at penetrating the hearts and minds of the vulnerable, moving them into the right space, where they can be picked off by the foot soldiers or another online recruiter.

At the start of the 21st Century, Al Qaeda recruiters were very much operating in local communities. Wherever there was a gathering, be it in a gym, street corners, college, university or a mosque, they would exploit these opportunities to engage, understand, identify, relate to, and challenge existing or conflicting opinions and views; to deconstruct, inform and apply their narrative and ideology, and then repair and reconstruct the individual's new understanding in accordance to their objectives. Once they had a receptive audience, it would be followed by support and safeguarding their investment, before finally guiding and instructing their recruits with a physical plan of action. To a recruiter, they would then have a remote-controlled device that could pinpoint its target and destroy at will. The London bombings, 9/11, the Overt plot in 2006, and many others, are real-life examples of an effective strategy being applied and executed with precision, and with disastrous effect.

We have named this strategy as ICE: Intellectual, Cultural (religious) and Emotional intelligence. George Bush Jnr understood his audience very well, and used this strategy to great effect by informing the world of a threat that would change our lives forever in the most harmful way, and that millions of people would lose their lives. He explained how it was every decent human being's responsibility to support him; he used biblical references when he stood in front of the US troops, reminding them of their duty to God and to protect life. He charged the whole world with his rhetoric and garnered the support of almost every nation to launch attacks on Iraq to neutralize the threat of 'weapons of mass destruction' (which, of course, did not materialise). Ironically, these events are used to radicalise many young people from across the world against the West. Terror groups constantly send out reminders of the shock-and-awe tactics that were used by the Coalition Forces during that war.

Past events are now dictating the future rapid pace of change we are experiencing, and it is those events that have generated a lot of resentment towards the West. Even worse, the vacuum that has been created by those events has been filled with arguably the greatest threat ever. ISIS is calling upon everyone who has a bitter taste from both Gulf Wars and the War on Terror, and they have rich pickings. The stories and images from these conflicts are deeply internalised by millions of people around the world and not just those who are Muslim. In fact there is a lot of evidence that many of the ISIS recruits are converts and, in many cases, lack the essential Islamic knowledge to be resilient enough to absorb and deflect the recruiters' ICE strategy. Even those who are Muslim by birth have been unable to see the wood for the trees and have fallen prey to the very powerful and potent narratives that are applied by groups like ISIS.

When young people are not given the importance, time or the opportunity to discuss their grievances or concerns by those who can guide them positively, then we are failing them by giving free rein to those who will listen, entertain and value them, only to exploit and abuse them. A journey then begins where circumstances are only in the control of the recruiter and no other. The personality of the young person will change, long-standing and cemented relationships begin to crumble, and a disregard for their own life slowly sets in. It reaches a point where they consistently fail to appreciate that the country where they have previously enjoyed life has now become the main focus of their 'revenge'. More significantly, their sympathy towards others in conflict zones pulls on their inner humanitarian emotions to such an extent that violence becomes the only means for expressing their feelings.

But this does not happen without an intervention of some kind, by someone who has managed to identify key vulnerabilities. This leaves us with a challenge: to re-evaluate our current practices and look at the ICE model more closely. Many may find it strange or difficult to accept, but it is evidently a largely successful model. The methods I have applied over many years have been proven and successful, and they are the very same tactics used by the recruiters. In fact, we all use the ICE strategy in many different ways and for all sorts of reasons, often without realising we are doing so. But the difficulty is in applying it with impact, in these most important and troublesome of circumstances. Those with responsibility for potentially vulnerable and at-risk people in their care need to use their knowledge of the model to identify where and when ICE may have been applied by a recruiter – and to then apply the same model to turn around the situation in a positive way.

Every individual has a certain intellect, adopts some kind of cultural or religious understanding, and of course each one of us has emotions. By engaging with someone and getting to know them a little more, and by posing certain 'targeted' questions, it is possible to establish, to some degree, the individual's personality, and certainly a greater understanding of their intellect, their cultural and religious identity, and eventually their emotional position. At this point, with the relevant information obtained, the recruiter will begin to push their idea. By applying emotional logic, in a well-established and well-practised method, people can be ignited in various ways. But still, there is likely far to go before a person can be fully manipulated. For example, simply getting someone angry will likely not establish full control. Similarly, prompting only sadness or even depression would likely not generate the desired outcome for the recruiter. For many, these are everyday emotions, imbedded within every single human being, and depending on circumstances and events might be commonly aroused. However, if the recruiter can manage to instil anger, empathy and sadness simultaneously, and massage them equally, it is an established fact that together these emotions can cause an individual to become violently driven.

Our job in preventing extremism would be made much easier if there were evidence that those at risk of recruitment came from one social background. But that is not the case. The attacks in Paris were carried out by marginalised young men and women, and there is evidence that they were socially excluded and from deprived neighbourhoods. But it must be understood that in France, there are factors at play that have led to a decades-long, festering bitterness within the Muslim communities. Historical grievances surrounding colonisation, recent laws preventing people from wearing the headscarf and the Charlie Hebdo cartoons depicting the Prophet are just some of the reasons why there are deep-rooted issues for many socially deprived French Muslims, and this has significantly contributed to the radicalisation of those individuals. But from the UK perspective, there is no real evidence that those who are recruited mostly come from a deprived or socially excluded background. Although there are certainly some cases that can be cited, most extremists recruited in the UK have not come from such backgrounds. In fact, if you look at some of the backgrounds of those who have plotted terrorist attacks in the UK and abroad, over many years, they were well-integrated, educated and financially sound individuals.

One common factor we do see is that young recruits rarely, if ever, travel by themselves. Recruiters know that the aspiration to join an extremist group develops within a small social circle: a tight group of friends or relatives. These small group dynamics influence our young people greatly and are often central to the processes of radicalisation. Intimacy with a small group of like-minded individuals is polarising, and encourages individuals to take a step they would not otherwise have taken. In many cases of extremism, individuals have a friend, or a friend-of-a-friend, who has previously joined an extremist group, who then use the many known (and some more secretive) social media platforms to encourage participation. Experience shows us that the most charismatic, vocal, influential or dominant personality within a particular group will be targeted first, in the hope that if he or she is recruited, then others will certainly follow. Opinions are then measured and subsequently shaped to conform to the recruiter's objective, and if given the space to sustain their attack on the young person, the consequences are in most cases disastrous.

VIOLENCE-JUSTIFYING IDEOLOGY

Of course, and ever more so now than before, most recruiters deploy religious arguments to legitimise their enterprise, as the *fatwa* earlier demonstrated. In almost every case I have worked with, the individual described their '*jihad*' as an obligation rooted in justice. *Jihad*, they say, is religious, although it often becomes a personal and social obligation to protect the weak and fight non-Muslim aggressors. This is becoming more common. For example, the Syrian refugees flooding into Europe are carrying stories about the horrors in their homeland, and these stories are easily manipulated by the recruiters. In so many cases we have learned that the narrative of the recruitment changes to suit the moment and the individual. Where refugees talk about ISIS as the main culprit or reason for fleeing to safety, these facts are distorted and translated to suit the recruiter's narrative, sending a different, false message to the innocent, often very emotional, sympathetic and frustrated, young mind.

An example: 'When Saddam annexed Kuwait or when he killed the Kurds, America intervened, and in Libya, the West intervened and killed Ghadafi because he was attacking his own people. So why didn't they intervene when Assad is killing the Muslims instead of fighting those who are fighting the Assad regime?'

This psychology outlines how extremism functions and the perception of grievance that drives the search for a violence-justifying ideology, not the other way around. In the case of Islamic extremism (though by no means is it unique to Islam), the language of *jihad* legitimises the grievance; it offers a religious or sectarian culprit and a method for righting the wrongs. Joining an extremist group, like ISIS or Al Qaeda, provides the young person with an opportunity to fight injustice, prevent further bloodshed of Muslims or the people of their cultural or religious background, and to restore the honour of the dishonoured. The narrative applied by the recruiter, that Islam is under attack and that Muslim brothers and sisters are being raped, brutalised and killed by the enemy, makes the individual convince themselves that they have an obligation to go. The same can be said of far-right extremists who will use the narrative that, 'our way of life, our country and our womenfolk are under attack'.

The impressionable young mind then believes he/she has a unique and special role to deliver justice and protect the sanctity of Muslims and Islam or even Christianity. This thinking goes as far back as the Marxist Sayyid Qutb and Hasan al Banna (founders of the Muslim Brotherhood), and supports the view that when Muslims are under attack by infidels, *jihad* becomes the main individual obligation (*Fard Al Ayn*) of all Muslims. It gives more emphasis and the primary focus of recruitment becomes the *Shabaab* (the youth).

The role of religion as a recruiting tool often seems to be mixed. Most of the cases I have worked with were, in my opinion, and according to themselves and others who knew them, not particularly religious before, or even after being recruited. The final decision to join extremist and terrorist groups is not always about a particular interpretation of one's religious obligations. It is often more of an emotional response to injustices perpetrated by an identified religious or sectarian enemy, which is then 'justified' by religion. This narrative seems to trigger multiple identities and perceived religious obligations to defend Islam, as well as defending Muslim women and children.

Take the Paris attackers as an example. While their stories varied (one was a student, one was a bus driver, a third was a bar owner) they mainly came from Muslim families that were neither radical nor extreme. Their radicalisation appears to have happened in a very short period, perhaps as little as a couple of months. Even MI5 have indicated this understanding, saying that most of those involved in terrorism are 'far from being religious zealots'. MI5 goes on to say that, in fact, 'there is evidence that a well-established religious identity actually protects against violent extremism'.

While religion, rather the interpretation of it, may very well be a significant contributing factor in radicalisation today, to insinuate that it is the main or only driver is dangerous. It enables attackers, like those in Paris, to remain undetected until they quite literally start shooting and throwing bombs right at us.

THE ACCIDENTAL RECRUITERS

On occasion we will experience young people themselves being the accidental or incidental recruiter, without intent and not in a harmful manner, but by simply and openly championing a cause which they are sympathetic or passionate about. For instance, when a young person has been exposed to the ongoing Palestinian or Syrian crisis and begins to look deeper into the situation, he or she may expose themselves to images or narratives that affect them in a particular way, where they can manage or process that information in the way others cannot. Some people are naturally stronger than others.

Exposure to this deeper knowledge of conflict often prompts the individual to ask themselves certain questions, some of which I have found very common amongst the cases I have worked with. 'Is this a war on Islam and Muslims? What can I do to prevent this? What is my role or purpose in life? Why is this even happening? How can I as a Muslim stand by and watch this happen without doing anything?' The individual searches for the answers to these questions and will try to find ways of how they can contribute to the solutions. And when they begin raising awareness about the issues they feel strong about, they try to convince others about the importance and the depth of the matter. This is a natural default position of many people, where raising awareness of an issue they are passionate about becomes such an important part of their life.

Unfortunately, the ones who are weaker or more vulnerable struggle to comprehend what they have been exposed to by these often 'well-meaning' individuals. The more naïve or emotionally weak can find it very challenging to deal with, and in some cases an emotional breakdown occurs. These often 'emotionally charged' individuals digest the same information very differently, and in some cases they internalise it so much that it becomes difficult to control how they can express their feelings. Anger, shock, depression and sadness become overwhelming, and they can turn to 'ungoverned spaces' as they look for solutions to these injustices and atrocities. Of course, it is on these dark platforms where recruiters often lurk. Here the radicalisation process takes a sinister turn and quickly they are completely engulfed by the recruiters and their ideology. Unintentional recruitment is particularly difficult to detect, and can be enormously powerful. Issues being raised by siblings, friends or parents are almost immediately acknowledged as credible.

HOW AND WHY EXTREMISTS DISMANTLE INSTITUTIONS

To aid and speed up the recruitment process, and to legitimise their own strategy of misinformation, extremists will often use their experience to prevent young men and women from accessing factual evidence-based information from within faith institutions. Mosques or other educational institutions will be attacked by rhetoric calling them 'grave-worshippers', misguided sects, 'the unfortunate ones who Allah hates' or government stooges and spies. We have also seen cases of infiltration where the extremists will deploy their own kind within the establishments. This is a powerful way of strengthening their network:

a. By preventing the possibility of the vulnerable individual accessing information and gaining guidance from a notable religious source;

b. By keeping the authorities in check by 'playing the game' of 'compliance with the agenda' and blending in;

c. By securing a platform for generating both support and funds for their cause;

d. By enabling the recruiters to identify and recruit further at-risk individuals; and

e. By exploiting the institution's platform where individuals who want more guidance on matters will only be subjected to the narrative of the recruiters.

Ultimately it also allows the extremists to generate an anti-Prevent, anti-government voice, by generating suspicion towards local groups or the government's programme to address extremism, which further alienates communities.

A recruitment strategy supported by the ICE model would look like this:

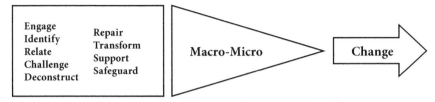

This is a basic method applied by extremist recruiters to effectively isolate and manipulate young people and to create the change they need from a macro level to the micro level. **Engagement** is the key: it allows recruiters to **Identify** the intellect, cultural, emotional, values and belief systems, the vulnerabilities and indeed skills of their potential recruits. **Relating** to their subject on matters they may or may not agree with is very important in order to continue establishing common ground, through conversations and sharing ideas. The **Challenge** aspect begins to take shape once they have built enough credibility, respect and understanding between themselves and their subject; it is designed to question and criticise the individual's established views.

'Do you know how many Muslims have been killed since the war on terror?' Or 'Don't you feel saddened by the thousands of innocent Muslims being killed?' This then allows the recruiter to subtly **Deconstruct** these existing values and belief systems. The **Repair** phase is when the recruiter rebuilds trust and suggests an alternative consideration, new values and beliefs, which are soon completely indoctrinated into the individual. This is when the **Transformation** process takes shape, and where the individual looks at their whole life differently, believes in matters other than those that he/she did previously. **Supporting** and **Safeguarding** by the recruiter or the network is a vital follow-up process in order to protect their investment. In many cases over the years, we have seen the recruiters encourage and on many occasions force the subject to disengage from their existing social networks and indeed their families. The narratives they use are often initially geared towards severing ties of relationships and kinship, claiming that 'in order to protect yourself from sin or deviating from the path, sacrifices must be made'. This can result in the individual trying to convince friends, siblings and parents to join him or her.

This is in many cases followed up by finding a husband/wife or partner for their subject, which is generally from within their network and is designed to pin down the individual where relapse becomes virtually impossible. Employment, housing and financial support is also a general process of support and safeguarding and in fact a way of fully guaranteeing that their investment will not be lost.

CHANGES IN ATTITUDES AND BEHAVIOUR OF VULNERABLE PEOPLE

Changes in attitudes and behaviour can occur unconsciously, often without any real design.

Imagine you hear, out of the blue, from a trusted friend that your next-door neighbour or a work colleague, whom you have apparently known quite well over the years, has a history of paedophilia and is still being watched closely by the police. What would your initial and immediate reaction be? How would you process this information? Do you 'actually' know your neighbour that well at all? And following this question, do you really know anyone that well at all? We have heard of cases where a wife or a husband finds out their partner for over 20 years is a serial killer or a rapist. So do we really know the other person that well?

Although some would feel that they wanted more facts and evidence before they came to a conclusion, many would immediately react negatively to the news. Often we don't realise that when multiple strands of information, often false information, are dumped upon us, it can shift our attitudes and behaviours in an instant, and without consideration of whether the information is fact-based or not. Our natural human instinct kicks in and pushes us in different directions, which then shapes our behaviours and our thinking.

As mature, educated and rational thinkers, we too find ourselves responding to certain information in accordance with the agenda of the one delivering the news, and sometimes without exploring or even considering the actual truth.

94

So consider how a young mind will respond when hearing or reading about a cause that they are already developing strong feelings towards; an attitudinal and behavioural shift is inevitable.

The media, in whatever shape or form, plays a fundamental role in changing attitudes and behaviours on a national and international scale. In recent years, it is clear that millions of people have completely changed their attitude towards Muslims and the faith of Islam. Terrorism is considered now 'a Muslim thing', more so than ever. This, of course, is understandable to a degree, because most attacks or plots have been carried out by those claiming to represent Islam. But the mainstream media's coverage of these events, and subsequently about Islam generally, has certainly done nothing to dispel this feeling. Many young Muslims take this coverage to be a clear and obvious design to undermine their faith. This often pushes them further into a space where additional or alternative sources of information are sought. It is in these spaces where extremists dump their own propaganda in order to pull the unsuspecting mind towards their own narrative, bringing about a rapid shift in the young person's attitude and subsequent behaviour.

So, ultimately, the media stance has worked at both ends of the spectrum, further polarising communities and impressionable young people. This shift on all sides has been accelerated over the last four years, primarily due to the current situation in Syria and Iraq. The manner and context in which information about these conflicts has been shared almost instantaneously across the globe has been overwhelming and poses a great challenge to young people in particular – and not only for Muslims. The rise in far-right extremism and the rapidly growing anti-Islam movements, equally recruiting thousands to their cause, is also dramatically changing the way many non-Muslims think and believe.

Readers might recall the a video that went viral on YouTube in which an English Defence League 'supporter' was interviewed as part of a Press TV documentary in 2011. Clearly under the influence of a substantial amount of alcohol (and perhaps other substances), the man claimed he was at an EDL rally because he wanted to stop 'Muslamic law from being implemented in Britain' and that there were 'Muslamic rape gangs' operating throughout the country. (The video went viral because his slurred speech made it sound as though he was concerned about 'Muslamic Ray guns'.) To me, it seemed clear that this man had been recruited to the EDL using the same techniques that a vulnerable Muslim might have been exposed to by an Islamic terror group. He had been subjected to a lot of misinformation, and he had formed an extreme attitude based on that. Perhaps more worrying is the fact that this video became so popular. The question is, did it work for or against the EDL? Many impressionable young minds would have watched it and not all will have come to the conclusion that the man was misinformed or clueless.

In a recent case I worked on, a very young man in his early teens developed a distaste and anger towards females who do not cover their hair or wear an *abaya* or *hijab*. He showed clearly that this is something he would not allow any of his family members to get away with and was vocal about how such females should be harshly beaten and forced to cover themselves appropriately. Let's look at what this could mean from two angles: either he has adopted a very strong cultural mentality where he feels the modesty and respect of the females in his family is being undermined, which is a possibility in certain strict cultures and families; or he has adopted a very extreme interpretation of his faith and feels the need to apply it because of his religious beliefs. Both circumstances are worrying, because of the potential for threat and violence, and would certainly warrant further investigation. It could certainly be an early indicator of an individual adopting an extreme ideology, demonstrating that he believes in violence as a means to meet the ends.

Indeed, there are occasions when young men begin to adopt an inconsiderate view towards young non-Muslim females, where sexual harassment, intimidation and lack of respect becomes a commonly displayed attitude. And often, frontline staff can pass this off as a sexual harassment and a safeguarding issue. Instead, it could potentially be a case of the individual now believing non-Muslim females in a non-Islamic country during a perceived 'state of war' can actually be their 'right-hand possessed' (taken from a commonly misunderstood passage from the Quran, concerning the right of a man to have sexual relations with slave girls). This has been completely taken out of context and has been wrongly applied to suit the desires and ambitions of the groups.

I have even experienced a case where a young man completely changed his style of walking. He began to walk with his back straight, head held high and with a pronounced bounce, whilst extending his chest. I did not immediately ask him why he was walking differently; rather, I decided to stroke his ego by saying, 'I like your style, you walk like a warrior'. He smiled for a split second and afforded me the understanding that he had adopted the 'Rammel' (warrior march). This was a recommended action in the early days of Islam, when during battles against the enemy the pose and the attitude was adopted to demonstrate that the *mujahideen* were ready and willing to face the enemy with energy and confidence and were not affected by any kind of fear. Similarly, another sign that a young man has begun studying Islam can be when all of a sudden he begins growing his hair, extending to or beyond the shoulders, again common within the '*mujahideen* ranks' (but not limited to them only; and in fact it is not commonly practised but merely recommended, as the practice dates back to the noble prophet).

But while a change of behaviour is often the signifier of something deeper, it doesn't necessarily follow that this is always a step towards radicalisation, or even that there is anything of any concern. Take my recent work with a 16-year-old male, who was ordinarily considered a bully in school and someone who often caused unrest within the classroom. He suddenly began to withdraw from the spotlight and became much quieter, reading the Quran during break periods and also encouraging others to follow the religion more closely. A teacher raised these concerns with me and a local Prevent officer, who decided that I was best suited to explore further the sudden change in behaviour and subsequent gravitation towards his faith. After engaging with the young man in his school, it became apparent that there had been an incident where one of his close friends was killed in a car crash, dying instantly on impact. The young man expressed how he felt life was very short and that he wanted to keep out of trouble, keep away from committing sins, and that he found more peace through practising his faith. It shows that by applying your duty of due regard carefully, it can work without causing distress even in circumstances where the individual was not being recruited or adopting an extreme view, instead merely trying to find peace, and indeed practise his faith.

Or there is the case of the usually respectful young male, who began to ignore his teacher's requests to remain silent when she asked another student a question in class; he continues to answer the question nonetheless, loudly and without consideration for his fellow students. Perhaps it could be that he feels, as a Muslim, he has more right to be heard than other non-Muslim students, who he believes do not deserve the same respect. Or could it be simply because he felt he wanted to prove he is a better student? Or is it ignorance or bad manners? These are behavioural changes that are not just associated with extremism, but more of a general indicator that something has changed in the individual's life. Regardless, the situation is worth exploring anyway, as a matter of general safeguarding.

STAYING UNDER THE RADAR

Once an attitude has been changed, whether it was consciously or otherwise, and extreme views have formed, we have found that some people will feel that they need to apply deceptive measures to deflect attention, in order to remain undetected. In many of the cases I have worked on, I have witnessed the art of deception being used to great effect. The general attitude is often that they now feel their future as 'Muslims' is limited in the West or may have something more sinister in mind (depending upon the trajectory and the current frame of mind). It is an easy position to adopt, for someone who feels that the governments of Western countries are imposing their own version or a British version of Islam – or worse, that they are completely anti-Islam. Anger can easily develop when a vulnerable young mind feels that they are being victimised because of their faith and nothing else. In many cases, people will begin to modify their behaviour in public to allow them to operate under the radar with a design to pursue their ulterior objectives at a future time. Often, this is something recommended by the influencing recruiter, who shapes his subject in multiple ways. I have met and challenged individuals working within local schools and local councils who have been quite extreme and inadvertently supported groups like Hizb-ut-Tahrir and Al Mohajiroon. Over the years these people have hampered effective programmes and interventions and indeed tried to influence many policies to suit their ambitions.

However, I'm glad to say that many of these individuals have been uncovered and have had to either leave or resign from such roles.

Clearly, if it is noticed that an individual is behaving more arrogantly than usual, or expressing his or her views without the consideration of others, there is an obvious calling for further investigation around this change. However, there are many others who will adopt the opposite approach, and when it is noticed that an individual has become withdrawn from subjects they would ordinarily be engaged in, it is also usually a prompt for further exploration.

One point to note is that young people, in general, tend to have their own social networks, and even more so in educational institutes. It is always useful to examine the group dynamic and to see whether attitudes are changing within the whole or part of the group. Often it will be the case that the whole group will show some kind of attitudinal difference, but what is also worth questioning is whether an individual has withdrawn from his/her regular social network and adopted another. And if so, why? Radicalisation often occurs and progresses in a group dynamic and it is crucially important not to lose sight of this phenomenon.

A good example is with the young men involved in the liquid bomb plot in 2006, who planned to blow up airliners across the Atlantic. These young men initially started out as humanitarian support activists, who went out of their way to generate support for the innocent victims of famine in Africa and then later for Afghanistan. They raised awareness, funds and collected clothing and food to send overseas in containers, in order to assist the humanitarian effort. Outwardly, their attitudes did not change; on the contrary, they remained polite and well-mannered citizens. What did change was their behaviour. They became very passionate about the cause and focused more intensely on the relief efforts than anything else in their lives. This obsession changed their characters to a degree, and a sense of impatience developed as they became more exposed to the realities and level of death and destruction in Afghanistan. Each of them travelled abroad to Pakistan for a 'holiday' (fact-finding) and this is when and where their minds were made up and the process of radicalisation was truly complete. Subsequently, they decided to plot their attacks. In order to deflect the attentions of police and security personnel, the group got together every weekend for football and other general sporting activities; the idea being that they would be viewed as a tight-knit group of friends and their regular meetings would not arouse suspicion.

Later, further deflective measures were applied. When they were to travel to launch their attack, they had all agreed to prominently place *Playboy* magazines or something similar in their hand luggage, in the hope that if or when their baggage was checked, security staff would see the magazines and perhaps suspicions that they were radical Muslims would be quelled.

The key point to note in this case was that it was almost impossible to see any significant change in their attitude or behaviour, except if you were truly very close to them as a group. In this case, the group had begun to actually exclude some of their friends due to a lack of trust in them keeping everything confidential.

Those best placed to identify changes in attitudes and behaviours are usually parents, siblings and close associates. Teachers come closely behind, as indeed do others in those institutions that have access to young people on a daily basis. When there are concerns about changes in attitudes and behaviour, the challenge lies in looking at ways of exploring the rationale or reason for this change. It is a good starting point to speak with the parents or those who have close contact with that particular individual, in order to ascertain what could be the cause. This approach is best made by using a different vehicle to carry the question, to avoid being direct or seen to be intrusive or even accused of spying (quite common, given the current climate).

In saying this, I do have to offer a degree of caution that parents – although naturally best placed to recognise behavioural shifts – in some cases are not always suitable to explore the reasons for the change and are equally not often best suited to provide the intervention either, even though they should be. So I would suggest a number of actions to be taken initially.

1. Explore directly, but gently, with the young person any changes in circumstances at home or with their social network.

2. Identify whether this is progressive and if so, try to establish why.

3. Take your concerns to someone with authority and who can access the parents and external service providers.

4. If you have an opportunity to speak to the parents, then do so 'as a matter of general concern'.

5. Always be mindful that the parents or guardian may even be a part of the problem.

A recent case example: a young male follows an extreme ideology and subsequently leaves for Syria. The mother is concerned and worried, without looking at options to encourage her child's return, and also shows no immediate signs of her own radical beliefs. After a few weeks of interventions I find that her nephew has also travelled to Syria. It is then revealed that she has very close links to a very extreme network of people who completely support ISIS. We then hear of the death of her nephew and a few weeks later her son is also killed. After offering my sincere condolences, I was met with a sense of joy from her. Although it was not a deliberate, obvious expression, it was an immediate reaction and one which I noticed straight away. She now believes her son has achieved the ultimate goal of martyrdom. Obviously I had to shape my approach accordingly. My point being that parents are genuinely able to change their child's mindset, but in some cases you need to ask yourself the question, are they actually willing to do that?

As long as the parent understands your concerns as a general safeguarding issue, I believe you will find a lot more support from them and will be in a better position to understand why there is an attitudinal shift, and to apply an early intervention.

Of course, the examples given here are simply case studies I have worked on, and some general analyses. It is not an exhaustive list of indicators, nor should my own actions be interpreted as instructions to be followed blindly and without question. They are reference points to note and to take into consideration. As mentioned previously, extremists and terrorist groups are evolving and adapting to emerging circumstances and environments and it is inevitable that we will see many changes in tactics. Extremism is not always represented by someone becoming devout and suddenly beginning to practise their faith more intensely, or in changes to dress code or aggressive behaviour. It would be completely wrong, indeed misleading, of me (or anybody else) to suggest that certain attitudinal or behavioural shifts can definitively pinpoint extremism. There is certainly no defined profile of an extremist or a terrorist; that is what makes our job so difficult.

Attitudes change for reasons both good and bad, and in young people especially attitudes can change drastically. Often this is simply a part of growing up and maturing as a young adult. These changes are of course worth exploring, but our approach and manner here will ultimately determine the success or failure in our attempts to identify extremism and safeguard young people.

'PUSH AND PULL FACTORS' AFFECTING VULNERABLE PEOPLE

The 'push and pull factors' involved in radicalisation and extremism have been widely talked about for years. Sadly, it is still difficult to find in-depth understanding of these often loosely used, but very significant, terms. There are some excellent examples of the 'push and pull' factors in the case studies later in this book.

Most explanations regarding the 'push and pull factors' are in the form of faith or patriotic narratives, mindsets and global conflicts, a sense of religious duty, obligations, protecting the dignity of fellow Muslims as well as striving towards gaining atonement for their sins and the reward of paradise in the hereafter. However, we need to look at the physical aspects involved and what it actually looks like on the ground internationally and at a localised level. These are factors that everyone who has engagement with young people must appreciate and give serious consideration to. In the MENA regions and places like Nigeria and Somalia, the 'push and pull' factors will vary mainly due to political grievances and economic inequality coupled with having a sense of responsibility and indeed religious duty.

At a more local and adolescent level we sometimes unconsciously contribute to creating vulnerabilities for young people, although in a general sense and not specific to radicalisation. For example, in a situation where youngsters are excluded from school, for whatever reason, we also find this often constitutes a 'push' factor. The school calls the parents, who then realise their child has been in trouble of some sort, and consequently confront their child. This can sometimes trigger the start of a breakdown between child, parent and the school. Often we find young people wandering around the streets or going somewhere else to occupy their time when their peers are at school. In other cases, the parents have argued with their child or both parents are quarrelling over whatever reason in front of their child, who then walks out to avoid further trouble or to avoid even experiencing it. In all of these circumstances we are essentially pushing the young person out of a sterile and protected environment into an unsterile and ungoverned space.

Similarly, we have found situations where an individual has a lot on their mind, something that is affecting him or her in a particular way, so they may want to speak to someone, seek clarification or just need to express their concerns. They may look to a teacher, a dinner lady, a friend, youth worker, a parent or someone who they can relate to, but if none of these listen the young person, because they are busy or unwilling, then the young person is left with little choice but to go elsewhere to express themselves, to find an answer and a solution to their problems. At the very least, they will begin to internalize whatever is affecting them, even if it is something minor. Either way, by default we have just pushed the young person away and into an environment where circumstances are beyond their control, as well as being beyond the control of the teachers or the parents. It is in this space, both physical and virtual, where abuse in all its forms often occurs, be it sexual, drug-related, gang-related or of course extremist.

I do not need to remind anyone that in the current climate there are many networks and individuals that will also pull the young person towards them for whatever reason, and that is where all the natural protective factors break down and fail miserably. Growing up is difficult. There are many factors affecting young people and they are certainly in need of support and guidance. Why should we deny them positive engagement, when we know for sure there are many out there who are standing in the shadows, ready to take advantage and to guide them elsewhere?

And going back to the emotional, psychological aspects, let's not forget that some of the most powerful pull factors playing out within our communities are ones identified in the ISIS *fatwa*. This creates the pull and supports the individual's grievances after being pushed out of a positive space.

One particular 'pull' factor that is not universally acknowledged or accepted concerns many of those females who have travelled to Syria or joined an extremist group. A lot of young females (and sometimes young men for that matter) from ethnic, culturally-driven backgrounds struggle with being able to find a companion of their particular choice for marriage. This is primarily due to strict cultural barriers masquerading as religious beliefs and restrictions, and their parents often being keener on arranged marriages. Often, it is this very issue that pushes young people away from their families, who are rather more culturally driven than driven by the actual fundamental teachings of Islam, which actually suggest that marriage must not be forced upon anyone, rather it is recommended that the individuals have choice. Sadly, and in most cases, we still find the forced marriage issue as the most troublesome within certain cultures; this then causes breakdown and disconnect. It is an ever-increasing concern, and especially in the current climate, where extremist networks prey on this phenomenon and invite young people into their groups by attracting them through the means of providing a suitable companion of choice for marriage.

One of the calls by ISIS was specifically aimed at young females, by saying their *'mujahideen'* (warriors) are waiting for them and that they are in need of 'companions who will look after them and tend to their needs, whilst they fight for Islam'. These messages were supported with images of young muscular males wielding AK47 machine guns with palm trees in the background, with the Caliph claiming to be the only one who must be followed, even if their parents disagree. They were instructing the individuals to leave their families often in secret if need be, without revealing anything, and that this was their religious duty. This method has been proven highly successful as a pull factor for many young females and indeed young males, right across the globe, who not only decide to go because they are attracted to the offer of marriage, but because they are led to believe that they will be 'fulfilling a religious duty' as well. This will continue to be effective and attract many more young people away, especially if parents fail to change their attitudes in this regard.

There are other push and pull factors that are not being addressed as seriously as they should. The number of anti-Islamic narratives and networks that are operating in both the physical and the virtual world are pushing and pulling many individuals in very different directions; at the same time, pulling disenfranchised non-Muslims towards the far right, while pushing 'victimised' Muslims towards the Al Qaeda/ISIS narrative.

Attacks on Muslim women are common even in the UK, including attempts to kill by pushing an innocent young woman off a tube station platform and pensioners being attacked with knives in the street. Meanwhile, ethnic grooming gangs target young, impressionable white girls. The terrorist attacks in Paris killing more than 100 innocent people, and the Russian and Coalition forces carrying out airstrikes across the Middle East, are all push-pull factors which are inevitably driving young people in multiple directions.

We will bring about our own demise if we fail to appreciate what goes through the mind of an innocent person who has either lost their parents, siblings, close relatives, close friends or co-religionists, either to airstrikes by Western forces or by the actions of the terrorists, or if they have experienced racially or religiously motivated attacks. When someone has been through a trauma like that, they are unlikely to think rationally, nor will they look at a peaceful solution through religion. In fact, it is safe to say that often they will want revenge, no matter what. This is a universal concern that requires much more consideration.

An example to consider here is an attack on Muslim women by a hostile and abusive Afro-Caribbean woman on a London bus; filmed, posted on YouTube and viewed almost 750,000 times within two days. Let's look at how this will change attitudes and how it has contributed to the push factors as well as extremism.

Out of the many hundreds of thousands who viewed the disgusting behaviour of the perpetrator, there will certainly be a percentage who will subsequently begin considering whether they actually belong in a Western country or whether they would feel safer in a different country. Some viewers will want to protect their dignity and avoid being abused or disrespected, and they might see the video as part of a trend that is worrying and unsettling to them. Perhaps it is not often admitted openly, but I know that it is indeed playing on the minds of a lot of people, who see their time living in a Western country as limited.

Out of the thousands who viewed the video, there will also be a number who will see the incident as another threat to their way of life, and who then begin to internalize it in a negative way. Don't forget here the ISIS narrative, 'You will never feel accepted amongst the non-believers who despise you', may be supporting their argument. For some, this fear and anger will then begin to be expressed in a violent and destructive manner. The fight-back mentality begins to take control. Indeed, who is to predict that it could be the spark that ignites a much bigger fire on a much larger scale? Minor incidents can be the trigger for worldwide problems.

Of course, there is no doubt that there will be a huge percentage of those who will have viewed the video on YouTube who can and will have remained rational, even when exposed to such grotesque racist behaviour. Some might even find positive determination to challenge it. And equally, we should examine the narratives of extremist groups who use terrorist attacks and such aggression to indoctrinate impressionable individuals to their cause, which is an increasing challenge we all face too.

My major concern is with our inability to adapt to the changing threat of terrorism and extremism. Even though it is clear that our localised methods in the past have been effective to a degree, we are shifting towards addressing the problem in a manner that will only increase it, and this only serves the aims of the enemy or those trying to divide communities. Terrorists continue to threaten and attack our communities and our way of life, and so in retaliation and anger without having foresight or indeed hindsight, we return their attacks with air and drone strikes and ground invasions. In the midst of all this conflict, it is innocent people that are being killed the most – which then causes further gravitation towards the terrorists' narratives by those susceptible individuals who become overwhelmed with the emotion of the injustices they are seeing.

Thus the wheel of fear and hatred continues to turn. So many of our actions, be it at home or abroad, actually aid the extremists by watering the seeds 'they' have sown, allowing them to harvest their next crop with relative ease.

By failing to understand these factors, we are ill-prepared to protect both our values and our communities, especially our young people.

Case example: a teenage Asian male expresses his concern around Israeli airstrikes killing innocent Palestinians after a teacher brought up the topic in class. The teenager had been looking into this conflict and felt he had much to say when the teacher raised the issue. However, when the young man asked for an answer, the teacher completely ignored the young man, who was persistent in trying to get a response, continuing to press the teacher. After no response was given, the young man tried for a few days to approach the teacher and ask why he did not respond to his question. Unfortunately, due to the teachers eventual response blaming ISIS for what is happening in Palestine, the young man was pushed away in a manner that left him exploring the conflict in more detail, and specifically into the role of ISIS. The young man then spent days on end looking at ISIS propaganda material, trying to arm himself with information to disprove the teacher's argument. This push factor caused the young man to gravitate towards a narrative and a space where very few controls are in place and where the arguments, images and beliefs would pull on anyone's emotional and religious cords, let alone those of a young impressionable man seeking answers.

This was a real case of a young man who lost all trust in authorities including teachers and for that reason anyone who would disagree with him. Simply because the teacher failed to respond to his question on a subject the teacher brought up, but a subject the young man was very passionate about. I cannot use any better example for push–pull factors than this one, given the current climate. Ironically, the very same teacher then raises the alarm to his superiors after realising that the young man was showing extremist tendencies. Rightly so, but look at the trigger point and push factors at play in this case, and how the attitude shifted.

INTERVENTIONS: HOW TO TAKE POSITIVE ACTION

Interventions are widely understood to be schemes for mentoring and support, traditionally used in cases relating to child safeguarding, education, mental health, drug and alcohol abuse, gang and street crime and domestic violence. They are intended to safeguard individuals against potential and actual risks, vulnerabilities, or susceptibilities toward a particular negative situation. The idea being that the intervention, if delivered in time, can prevent a situation from developing further, and move the individual to a more neutral, or positive, position. In some cases, they are used to stop problems before they even start. With regards to extremism, an intervention is a most important step, before the individual is radicalised to an extent where he or she considers participation in an act of terrorism.

This chapter will look at a Prevent intervention, the aim of which is to help counter violent extremism that may lead to an act of terrorism. Such interventions are generally deployed in the 'pre-crime space', where the law has not been broken. Actions to prevent people from falling into terrorism **must** take into consideration a number of factors – including legislation, policies and strategy – in developing a coherent response. In preventing people from falling into terrorism, practitioners must have strategic, tactical and operational clarity on what they are trying to achieve. In all interventions, planning is essential but an understanding of the counter-terrorism law is equally vital.

This chapter looks at the intervention process from a number of perspectives. The first perspective examines the vulnerabilities of the institutions that hold the responsibility for preventing people from falling into terrorism. The second perspective looks at the vulnerability of recruiters and how an effective response can destroy their objectives. The third perspective considers the factors surrounding an individual and the methods applied by a recruiting force. The fourth perspective is that of the mentor or the Intervention Provider (IP) who faces a number of challenges in creating the space for transition. And the fifth perspective will show what prevent interventions have worked and how.

INSTITUTIONAL VULNERABILITIES AND CAPABILITIES

Vulnerability is a susceptibility to social and environmental stresses where the individual does not possesses the capability to adapt. We will discuss the personal vulnerabilities later; for now it is worth putting in context the institutional vulnerabilities.

Here is another reminder of the ISIS *fatwa* delivered by Mohammed al Adnani, and the call for followers to attack their enemies: 'Kill them in any manner or way however it may be. Smash his head with a rock, or slaughter him with a knife, or run him over with your car, or throw him down from a high place, or choke him, or poison him.'

The potency of such a narrative needs no further commentary, and the impact upon a sympathiser of ISIS, open to the message of the *fatwa*, could clearly be catastrophic.

How could an institution deal with this threat? How would they know if someone within their organisation might be sympathetic to such *fatwas*? What are the implications? It is clear that an institution may face a significant threat without knowing anything about it. And often there is little capability to adapt or respond to an emerging threat as there is no policy, strategy or plan to deal with someone in the institution that is receptive to extreme rhetoric. This makes institutions extremely vulnerable.

If you are responsible for an institution and someone from your institution is recruited and subsequently carries out an act of terror, be it at home or abroad, it becomes your problem. However, the 'duty of due regard' (as outlined previously) sets out a framework for institutions to take measures to protect themselves which, if applied correctly and in a timely manner, should limit any possible 'failure'. In this context, we can see the huge value in the Channel programme.

There is a wealth of intelligence-monitoring information on extremist development and terror cells here in the UK and overseas. We have already discussed how extremists use Twitter, Facebook and other social media platforms to promote their cause and ideology, and to spread ideas and join forces with like-minded individuals. In the case of Bilal Abdullah, the man behind a bomb attack on Glasgow International Airport in 2007, intelligence services quickly discovered there was a close link between this plot and a planned London car bombing the previous day.

But let's just examine the possibility of him doing something different, something that could have killed many more people. He was a doctor and had access to a huge range of materials that he could have used to achieve his goal with maximum effect. Since the ISIS *fatwa* was released we have seen numerous plots and attacks on civilians across the world, all of them low-tech, carefully planned brutal acts of terror, and some of them are 'lone wolf' style, where detection is difficult. This is where the institutional vulnerability is high and in turn exploited and this is also another area where our collective efforts need to be directed.

Working with partners is a critical part of any Prevent initiative, and this is where we have experienced huge benefits in tackling the problem. The multi-agency approach will bring together a range of services, skills and information which will assist in our assessments, support and our interventions to prevent extremism. For instance, an agency such as the police will be able to inform institutions, of an emerging threat or share concerns surrounding a particular individual, which can then allow an intervention of some sort to be implemented.

So it follows that if we are seeking the bigger picture then an institution should ask other agencies for information and assistance. This is where the multi-agency approach has substantial value. In the 'pre-crime space', the police only check the concerns of the referred person to ensure that any ongoing plan does not conflict with another, or that the referred person is not of interest in a criminal investigation. If the person is not part of a wider concern, the police recommend the case for Channel intervention. This allows for the next steps, where the Channel framework aims to protect the vulnerable person against recruitment.

Many institutions may have practitioners with the skills to prevent someone from falling into terrorism. Because the vulnerable person is within the operational reach of the institution, they have an opportunity to deploy resources swiftly and efficiently to apply safeguards. Institutions, whether statutory or civil society, should always have skilled practitioners who can mentor and coach vulnerable people and if these resources are deployed at an early stage there is a good chance that an intervention will have a successful result.

The solution to reducing the 'recruitment space' of a terrorist is actually within the operational reach of institutions. The question really is one of strategy and strategic implementation. Most importantly, it is the implementation of 'due regard' that can and will protect the institution and reduce its vulnerability.

THE VULNERABILITY OF THE RECRUITER

This considers the fact that the recruiter is in a physical form, be it online or offline.

The strategic intent of a recruiter is to create what is known as a 'beneficial product' to conduct an act or support for a physical act of terrorism. That 'beneficial product' is the successful recruitment of an individual. The individual then receives his benefits when for example he conducts an act of martyrdom, which is what he values. The recruiter receives a benefit from that act as it sends fear and terror to a wider audience, further benefiting the ideological goals of the terrorist organisation.

Like any 'product', development takes time and this is where the recruiter has to face the same challenges as our institutions or any intervention. The recruiter has to decide on what is 'reasonably practical' with their own 'duty of due regard'. And this is where the recruiters and their processes have vulnerabilities. We just need to outsmart them by exploiting these vulnerabilities.

A Prevent intervention must take account of a number of key dangers. The vulnerable person may be:

- Empathetic (towards a literalistic sense of enjoining the good and forbidding the evil)
- Emotional and angry (at death of innocents and foreign policy)
- Enthusiastic (to live in an Islamic state and under Gods law (Sharia))
- Extreme (censorious to morality or beliefs)
- Excited (eager to fight and die as a martyr)

Any one of these traits creates a vulnerability that can be rapidly exploited by an astute antagonist. However, the very same characteristics can be harnessed by an astute and clever intervention practitioner (IP), who can create the 'pull' towards a better, more positive force for good. The 'push and pull' factors depend on the environment and circumstances that can be exploited for either purpose.

There are also weaknesses in the manner in which the recruiter protects him or herself. An extremist recruiter realises that there is a cost in developing a terrorist. Trust is a huge part of recruitment development and that is reinforced through two tests:

a. A task-orientated process where the vulnerable person must prove his/ her commitment and loyalty. 'Attend meetings, send messages and bring your close friends, or read up on such and such material and let me know what you think. Stop going to a particular Mosque, watch this video on YouTube or DVD, and tell me what or how you feel.'

b. A relationship-oriented process occurs after the person passes the initiation stage and the vulnerable person must show their value (note: the value here can be pretty broad). An **example might be:** to disassociate from existing social network, or to raise some funds for a particular cause *etc.* The list can go on. The recruiter gives some latitude which the individual believes is an increased level of trust.

In this sense the recruiter must maintain engagement to develop the vulnerable person's trustworthiness. This is an exposure that we should be very mindful of and that must be carefully managed – and equally exploited.

There are a number of ways of treating and exploiting the vulnerabilities of the recruiter to take advantage of and to retake the radicalised mind of a vulnerable person without actually applying de-radicalisation steps to the vulnerable person. In this sense, the strategic option is a credible intervention provider or project.

Example: when the vulnerable person displays or shows a desire to travel to Syria, for instance, the IP can relay a message on 'the severing of ties of kinship' and its Islamic ruling. Or seeking guidance on the ruling of leaving your parents without their permission. This will inform the recruiter that there is another influencing source within the same space, which will then disrupt the recruitment or move it to another stage. Either way the recruiter will become wary and will have to either up his/her game or withdraw.

INTERVENTION STEPS

Here we will look at the necessary steps within an intervention framework. It is this framework that we will use to discuss intervention activity.

- Consideration steps
- Planning steps
- Technical steps

- Risk mitigation steps
- Governance steps

Consideration steps

There are five consideration steps necessary before taking action on an intervention:

The strategy: This concerns the transparent methods that encourage the community to follow and agree with the institutional approach of preventing extremist recruitment and safeguarding vulnerable individuals. It is a mechanism of communicating the relevance and the purpose of the intention to prevent people from falling into extremism at a local level. The transparency concerns convincing people of the genuine intent of a programme that is free of any personal or financial motivations, or any kind of corruption. An example can be people asking, what the meaning of Channel is. The answer is that Channel is an acronym for **Creating Holistic Approaches in Neutralising Negative Extremist Logic.** It is an honest and genuine approach to address the attempts of those who seek to radicalise an individual.

The conditions: An appropriate assessment must consider whether the person is actually vulnerable or demonstrates extreme behaviour or has a sense of internalised injustice. A view must be taken as to where this person is within the recruitment process. That view can often be supported by objective behaviour. On the other hand, if it is deemed that the individual has vulnerabilities, expresses extreme views then we must also take into account the individual's intent or actual capacity to cause harm. It is also of importance to recognise that, in some cases, the ones who have intent or the capacity to cause harm will be harder to identify. An example here would be the Glasgow airport bombers, who had high intent, capability and would have been harder to identify due to their social status as doctors.

The environment: Here is where consideration must be made of the different environments in which recruitment takes shape.

The question is what type of intervention techniques are required to mitigate disruption of extremist tendencies in the different environments. The first step is to scope out what those tendencies are and in what context the individual is processing the information they are receiving. Some people may be in receipt of information in a sterile environment, either in a bedroom or one-to-one meetings. Others may be in a group dynamic where they follow the consensus of the group. Environments differ and change with time. So an individual may start off in a sterile environment with online activity and then progress to attending group meetings. What are the 'push and pull factors' in the vulnerable person's life that will prohibit the success of the recruiting principles or narratives and what is the mitigation strategy?

An intervention cannot itself place an extreme pressure on a person to voluntarily comply, and must take into consideration emotional and mental health. Enforcing participation can cause breakdown and non-compliance, rendering the individual more vulnerable.

The recruiter's environment considers the individual's Intellectual, Cultural and Emotional (ICE) intelligence, in addition to the social and physical environment and the journey of change. This is why the recruiter will have the upper hand and will retain participation. The social environment must take into consideration the communication networks. The physical environment must consider the networks that can offer assistance as well as those that may impede the recruiter's success.

So it is highly recommended that any intervention to safeguard an individual must consider the opponent's strategy and application. This requires the use of 'like-for-like' methods and environments, which should be supported by the 'multi-agency' framework.

The leadership: The person or project doing the intervention must possess good leadership qualities. Charisma, humaneness and knowledge and its intelligent use are key. They must also have the courage to challenge and the charisma to apply these elements in a way that sustains engagement. They must be seen as fair and just.

The discipline: This refers to organisational coherence and efficiency. It is connected to loyalty and trustworthiness and works to the principles of rewards and punishment. An intervention has no enforceable mandate and this is where the intervention provider must create trust and have charisma. A practitioner must convince the individual that he has an effective network which is greater, stronger more equitable and transparent than anything else. In a pre-crime space the person has the right to confidence and it is the practitioner's role to ensure that the partnership actually works and is beneficial. In this sense the practitioner is the critical friend to cohabiting agencies.

Proper consideration of these steps gives a benchmark to scope the intervention. This is because the statutory institution will be in a position as far as it is 'reasonably foreseeable' at that point, to assess the threat, the risk associated to the threat and the opportunities that can be exploited to create desistance.

Planning steps

There are four planning objectives that must be achieved in order to remove the recruiter's protective grip on the vulnerable individual.

Destabilise the recruiter: It is important to unsettle a recruiter or the recruiting principle(s) using the 'element of surprise' within the intervention plan. This means that the element of surprise is the entry of the intervention at a time that surprises the recruiter. The purpose of this element places the recruiter's exposure at risk, forcing a reduction in his ability to influence and sustain recruitment or forcing the recruiter to adapt. A timely intervention often achieves this.

Place psychological anchors: An intervention must be prepared to put in place a threat of sanctions that could have a significant impact on the 'recruited' and the recruiter. In the 'pre-crime space', that could be a threat that the individual's family will intervene or he will be prevented from travelling if circumstances deem it appropriate. A person telling the recruiter that he has been told he might not be able to travel will trigger risks to the recruiter. Yet again this pushes the recruiter to either adapt or respond, which also disrupts the agenda. Safeguarding action to protect the person may be appropriate. This has the effect of either disrupting the recruitment process or even foiling any plan.

Isolate the reinforcement principle: This considers a method of deconstructing the 'constructs' of the ideology. This is where theology is an overwhelming driving force behind the recruitment; the intervention may focus on separating the faith from the actions. By utilising faith in its correct application, providing irrefutable 'suggestions' to the vulnerable person has been and can be used to great effect.

Act with speed: The intervention plan must act in a most timely fashion, with a certain degree of speed, after all opportunities and risks have been considered. It is a strategic error to act hastily without consideration and thought. Hindsight is a wonderful thing, but foresight is better. And let's not forget that bad decisions often make 'good' stories in the press.

Technical steps

Develop a process to challenge: This is a technique to avoid confrontation, building a strong counter-narrative against the recruiter. Use of language needs to be carefully considered for open questions, probing questions and consequential questions. Strong leadership is essential. To overwhelm the vulnerable person, one must use the weight of the recruiter's arguments against him, or the driving force. A strong but measured counter-narrative – if properly used – can have a positive effect. If a counter-narrative is incorrectly applied this can set back or even finish an intervention. Here are a few simple examples, presented here only as a guideline.

A vulnerable person explains:

'It is clear that there is a war against Islam and it is my duty as a Muslim to participate in the *jihad* against the *'Kuffar'*, non-believers.'

Open questions: What gives you the understanding that this is a war on Islam carried out by non-Muslims? Why do you believe it is a *jihad*? And do you understand the conditions of *jihad*?

Probing Question: Who has called for this *jihad*? Are they in the authority of leader of the Muslim *ummah*/nation? Shouldn't we consider the legitimacy of the calling for *jihad* or waging war against anyone before participation? Isn't it important that it should be the leader who has the support of the majority of the Muslims, the scholars, tribes/nations and military leaders who can call for a legitimate *jihad*?

Consequential question: If you continue on this path and are killed, shouldn't you consider whether it is heaven or hell you will be ending up? What will be the overall outcome if your participation causes the death of innocent people? Even your roles as a simple cook or cleaner will cause you to share responsibility if the actions of your network are un-Islamic. Have you considered this?

Counter narrative: It is clear that at the moment there is war, death and destruction in mainly Muslim lands, and we can consider this as the West's intervention or we can consider this as turmoil and chaos caused by Muslims rebelling against their rulers. I can relate with you in regards to Afghanistan and Iraq, where Western invasions have caused the death and destruction of thousands of lives. But calling for *jihad* or participating in acts of violence as revenge for what is happening are things we must be very careful of. Islam has strict conditions when it comes to taking up arms or responding with violence and aggression. Using bombs in civilian places or using children as suicide bombers are not ideas from Islam and there is no clear evidence of this within the faith. Killing of innocent people, destroying homes, treating prisoners inhumanely and burning people alive is far from what Islam is based upon; in fact it goes against all the rulings and commands of the noble Prophet.

Create a strong engagement platform: The intervention provider must understand the social, psychological and physical environments of the individual. Interventions require voluntary participation and the objectives must serve the individual. A sustainable intervention starts from the premise that the process is in the interest of the individual, and also that the individual believes this. To achieve this, 'selling' the intervention is vital to create the 'buy-in'.

Selling the intervention: Everything rests on the manner in which the intervention is sold. It is crucial to have an understanding of what specific needs, ambitions, goals and aspirations the individual has, in order for the intervention to provide the best solutions and the service provision to succeed. More importantly, the intervention support must far outweigh those of the recruiter so it can be seen as more beneficial in every sense.

An example: a young person feels that nobody understands his plight and his empathy towards Syrian people. He feels useless and angry and wants to do something to alleviate the suffering of Syrians. A diversion needs to look at these issues and assist in providing the young person with a sense of 'doing' something positive to help alleviate the Syrian suffering. Firstly, listening and relating to the individual is primary. This must be followed through by providing a positive means to achieve his/her goals, perhaps through further education on extremist and terrorist networks, identifying career opportunities, a job, housing, counselling and/or youth leadership courses.

Often we have found the theological argument to hold significant weight especially to divert the anger and emotional element, as well as assisting in 'raising awareness' campaigns and supporting aid agencies as a means of participating in a worthy cause. I have found the theological aspect very potent and it has proven successful in most cases.

Develop leverage: At the beginning of any intervention, the influences upon the individual – either coming from the recruiter or, in the case of a lone wolf, the recruiting principles – may be beyond the control of the intervention. However, there may be aspects to those influences that the intervention can use as leverage. An example might be poverty, which manifests itself into grievance. The intervention provider could offer to use partnership network resources to train the individual, or find them a job. So the ability to get the person ready for employment or to secure a job can be used as leverage against the grievance, and the recruiting principles. But when the young person is theologically driven, it is essential to educate him on the correct Islamic standpoint, which provides a sense of 'doing the right thing in the eyes of God' which can replace or outweigh the recruiters or the recruiting principles.

Plan access to change networks: Vulnerable people do not understand and probably cannot access the various support networks and authorities, which individually cannot address inter-woven issues. In this instance, the multi-agency approach has huge benefits. It can become a substantial force of support to the individual, and harder for recruiters to attack. Change is never a linear process: there is always going to be slippage in the tussle for removing someone from the radical influencing factors of a recruiter. That objective approach will require debunking the physical elements of the grievance where the multi-agency network can assist. In this sense the leverage is in the understanding of the individual agency to access that network and the IP stating that he can assist in both creating the access but also in the management of the process. This discussion is about wellbeing.

An individual agency, or let's say the self-recruited individual, takes into consideration everything that he values and includes matters which are not specific to his own wellbeing. He may value the wellbeing of others. The measure therefore is how the partnership network assists in achieving the wellbeing of the individual as the first step. This can then be supported by the IP to identify ways and means of the individual assisting the 'others'.

Converting passion into action: Vulnerable people are generally passionate about something that they value or a goal they want to achieve. The intervention must identify something that the person is passionate about and develop the person's organisational and personal capacity to turn that passion into positive action. This is also a question of agency in the context of the freedom to achieve the goals that they value.

An example: Mr A's grievance is with the oppressive nature of the state on him and the people from the same community. It was not originally an Islam-centric grievance; that was a later development when internet searches left him frustrated and angry. An IP needs to better explain the strategy of converting passion into action and one of the ways is a discussion about how he will evaluate for himself whether his ultimate actions have been applied correctly and in accordance to Islamic principles. Achieving wellbeing for himself is one thing, but would his acts achieve wellbeing for others? And if not, would he achieve all the goals that he values? Here is where coaching and mentoring skills need to be carefully applied – but as soon as possible.

An intervention therefore has to address both objective and subjective needs and requires the active partnership network to assist.

Risk mitigation steps

An intervention can be seen as a set of variables. The recruiter is the controlling variable, the person being recruited is an independent variable (where his core values will not change), the environment and the context are the dependent variables (which allow the altering of the perspective) and the intervention is the intervening variable which mediates between the other variables to achieve the best result which the individual values. Once a practitioner understands the issues and can see that this person will be drawn into terrorism unless something is done, he must look at the risk and put in place a plan to mitigate those reasonably foreseeable risks.

There are five risk mitigation steps for consideration. These are known as the CRIME steps and the idea is that if any step is not given proper attention, the likelihood of the vulnerable person turning to crime is greater. An intervention risk log must always demonstrate that the intervention has a mechanism in place to:

- **C**ontrol the risk of someone falling into terrorism
- **R**educe the risk of someone falling into terrorism

Isolate the risk of someone falling into terrorism

- **M**ediate the risk of someone falling into terrorism
- **E**liminate the risk of someone falling into terrorism

Governance steps

There are four components to governance:

Planning evaluation – where the policy, the planning and the organisational structure is subject to scrutiny

Intervention – where the implementation of the intervention plan is subject to scrutiny

Performance – where the measurement of the milestones within the plan and intervention are monitored

Audit – an audit of all activity including the decisions surrounding the cessation of interventions, outputs and outcomes and the contribution to improvements

THE INTERVENTION: DEALING OBJECTIVELY WITH THE SUBJECTIVE

The intervention framework sets in place a process of how to tackle the recruitment steps of an antagonist and it provides the framework to enable the practitioner to counter the recruitment steps by developing a counter-strategy. It is not a rear-guard action; it is an offensive approach without being overly & obviously 'offensive'.

Practitioners may well be less confident in dealing with a subjective principle such as that of *jihad*. In the last chapter in this book there is sufficient information that compares the activity of ISIS and Al Qaeda with the rebellious groups that the Prophet (pbuh) and the righteously-guided caliphs of Islam (*Khulfah e Rashidun*) experienced almost 1400 years ago. Those examples are effective in providing both a historical comparison and a means to contextualise the negative behaviour of the present-day extremists/terrorists.

It may be that non-Muslim practitioners or practitioners from non-Sunni sects may be uncomfortable including this within an intervention plan without further consideration. Deciding when to utilise a theological 'card' requires good planning. Wrongly applied or in the wrong context, this can render the intervention futile. In this sense I will suggest that the first point of call is not to call an imam in to tell the person the Quran says his views are wrong without first gaining a sense of the immediate and underlying theological issues fuelling their behaviour. In the examples previously, in the first meeting the practitioner can ask whether they can have a discussion on how the noble Prophet of Islam dealt with such issues and what he recommended. This is a positioning strategy. In discussing the issues and explaining his position, the individual may

- Agree with the Prophet's approach
- Take an alternative line
- Disagree with that approach
- Consider this approach to be immaterial to the modern context
- Have the ability to put the approach within the modern context

Whatever the output of that discussion, in this case the IP is able to risk-assess the theological position of the individual and can then set about discussing a theological approach with relevant practitioners. In the case of the output for the non-Muslim practitioner he will also gain information on the individual's theological understanding of sharia and from there scope out relevant practitioners to address those narratives. Both approaches reach the same result from different directions.

Any individual of concern will firmly accept that *jihad* and Sharia law are both valid and important aspects within the Islamic faith and the intervention plan must also accept that. The question for the intervention is how the plan is sold to the vulnerable person, how it is received and how it is then processed. The intervention plan looks at the 'what' and the following looks at the 'how'.

The external view is that the ISIS/Al Qaeda model will fail a spiritual health check. The Western media, rightly or wrongly, give the impression that the ISIS/

Al Qaeda ideology is in some way deficient of the spiritual nutrients required for a practising Muslim. The belief is that this spiritual illness manifests itself in violence and is contagious. To reinforce this message other Muslims (myself included) rival the narratives, intentions and approaches of these groups. This view may have its validity but it is an external perspective only for consideration. Another equally valid point of view is that people internalise injustices done to others as a motivational driver as something they value. In this sense and at some point in time a question to the individual about what it is about this that he values has to look at foreign policy in the same way we have to look at the values and contradiction in the recruiter's narrative. It is unavoidable and to sidestep this would be a strategic error. Equally, saying that such a perception is right or wrong is an error. When objectively dealing with subjective issues the rule of thumb is to show, not tell. Show them how the subjective and objective teachings of their recruiter actually differ from the individual's declared aspirations and values from a theological point of view.

The points made previously about emotional logic have set out how people are receptive to any call to address psychological pain. In this sense, if people feel the pain experienced by others, an intervention provider must also consider *them* to be in pain. A practitioner then has to consider that the rationale for believing in or supporting ISIS is to assist in the removal of injustice. The underlying cause of this injustice may be the psychological pain caused by the bombing of innocent Muslims. Here, the theological health check or counter-narrative may in some cases be deficient, because it cannot immediately compete with the pain felt by the underlying cause. In this case, the intervention may only be able to have a limited effect. Such grievances and arguments are fast-paced and immediate, so quick and succinct responses will be needed. However, rapidly going into a drawn-out debate even with evidence-based arguments will prove futile because the individual will not always be receptive. However, the intervention may have a degree of leverage if common ground is sought by way of accepting that the suffering of others is unjust, which is, at times, the best option.

Leverage is the application of a narrative that has equal force to that which fuels the underlying cause. The technique to achieve the lever is in the application of an open question: 'If the killing of innocent Muslims causes you pain, is that pain the same when ISIS or Al Qaeda kill other Muslims or even when they kill innocent non-Muslims?' An answer in the affirmative gives a probing question and a negative answer invites a consequential question. Either way the engagement is sustained, and can then allow for breathing space and longer debates at different junctures, when the individual is more receptive. It is important to remain focused on the underlying cause at all times.

To an extent, modern day extremism and terrorism disproportionally focuses on the ISIS/Al Qaeda model. This slightly differs from the Afghan Al Qaeda model, so there are two strands here. The first is the general principle used by Al Qaeda of fighting injustice brought upon them. The second is the ISIS model of the establishment of an Islamic state and a caliphate in the land of Sham (Syria). This latter has the potential of recruiting man, woman and child to make a contribution in establishing Sharia and a caliphate. In determining the 'how' to achieve everything that they value within a just and fair oppression-free concept, it is important to understand the immediacy of the ISIS selling points.

ISIS literature on *jihad* sells a promise of paradise made by Allah as a reward. In this spiritual sense God is the ultimate insurer with the promise of a pay-out in death where payment is received in the afterlife. It is commonly perceived in general by Muslims that if you strictly follow the faith and do not commit sins, even without bearing arms you are almost assured the reward to heaven.

However, those who fight (in its physical sense) for Allah's cause are guaranteed an immediate transcendence and a higher level in heaven. That narrative is the ultimate wellbeing factor that comes with legacy rights to the family, where 70 members of one's family can be taken to paradise with the individual. 'Fighting' is also used in another non-physical context. Here the migration to establish the caliphate and adopt the supportive *jihad* (struggle) fighting to establish Sharia, the law of Allah, is categorised as fighting in the *way* of Allah. This 'fight' extends to the support given by females and children learning the 'true' (in the ISIS interpretation) perspective of Islam and also includes financing.

No matter what the emotional drivers or psychological hooks may be, the intervention should explore further, through probing questions, to assess the individual's motivational factors.

However, in saying this, no matter how the practitioner plays this, it is essential that any counter-argument or narrative put forward to the individual must hold water, and it must be evidenced and credible, otherwise you will lose ground very rapidly and be unable to recover.

A good example would to be look at the many stories that circulate about certain *mujahideen* fighters who have been martyred in various battles. It has been told that when other fighters have found their dead bodies after many days, even weeks, they found them still preserved, protected from the elements and decay – even smelling of sweet scent and surrounded by flowers *etc*. These stories are readily available on the internet, with titles such as 'In the hearts of green birds' and 'Operation black lion'.

These stories have played a huge role in convincing individuals that they are on a path to paradise, which can then often be the final 'pull factor' for many.

The astute practitioner should be both knowledgeable about these stories and be completely prepared to dispel these myths in a convincing yet considerate manner. Without discounting the story initially, and without coming across as patronising, because this is something that is sensitive and has been internalised very deeply, these narratives need to be extracted with a lot of care.

Ultimately it is fact that these are mere stories and myths that lack any real authenticity – whereas we know that the prophetic hadiths are credible and authentic, due to a high degree of scrutiny by credible scholars. So a comparison should be subtly drawn between both, where the individual can look at authenticity versus myths or simple 'stories'. This gives the practitioner a more convincing argument; refutations can be seriously considered and myths dispelled as a result.

Practitioners must also understand when to stop an intervention, taking an individual to a point that merely proves him wrong is not actually the aim of the intervention. It is always to achieve the things that they value without them considering violence as a means to achieving their goals.

APPLYING AN INTERVENTION

An intervention practitioner needs to appreciate the fact that the operational environment is a highly competitive one that requires a huge amount of investment and commitment. An intervention can only prove successful (as mentioned previously) if an element of trust can be established primarily, which can then lead on to further engagement, allowing for developing more understanding and to set an actual plan in motion.

However, I have experienced a number of challenges at this early stage, which is probably the defining point of the intervention, where the environment chosen for the intervention can often prove very uncomfortable and in some cases may result in disengagement. For instance: if you are going to begin an intervention by meeting in a police station, a probation office, in any kind of closed institution or 'sterile' environment where the individual will naturally feel intimidated or 'insecure', then the chances of success become very limited. Equally, if the subject is being chaperoned by a teacher, police officer or probation worker, then it defeats the purpose in all circumstances. So it is advisable, if not strongly recommended, that interventions take place in 'un-sterile' environments and where the individual can feel comfortable, which in turn affords the practitioner a better chance of success.

For example: I was called to meet a young person in a youth hostel where he was sitting in the office. I asked that we be allowed to go out into the garden area where the young person could feel easier and without the suspicion of supervision.

Another example: A young person at school was referred to me. The meeting was to be held in a side room within the school. I was not getting anywhere with conversations, so decided that we would go for a walk outside. This changed the whole picture and within an hour I knew almost everything I needed to make an informed assessment.

This intervention took much longer to establish open and frank dialogue due to the discussions taking place in the institution from which the individual was actually referred. This young man felt that it was his school that was causing him problems (due to his expressions regarding ISIS) and no one there was to be trusted, so carrying out the intervention in the same place was not exactly the right idea. However, saying this, it does not mean the intervention will completely fail because of it being carried out in the wrong place. I am merely pointing out that it could be better and quicker if the environment was neutral. My suggestions are that if we are to use schools, or probation offices *etc*, then we consider making that environment a bit better, use the garden, playing field for a walk or something of that nature. Offer a cup of tea/cold drink or something that makes the young person feel value or at least comfortable enough to lower his/her guard. And it is not always wise to sit opposite the young person; it is better move the chair to one side or sit on the same side. I'm not splitting hairs here, rather giving simple suggestions based on my own experience.

Given the nature of interventions, it is simply a matter of how much time is being spent on the individual, compared to the time the recruiter or influencing source is giving. Consideration must be made in this regard, because it is fact that current interventions are time-restricted, whereas the alternative influencer or the adversary may have unlimited access to the individual. My experience tells me that you will always end up trying to catch up, forever behind the curve in almost every circumstance, and could potentially lose the individual if the intervention is time restricted. It may be worth considering having full-time, well-experienced intervention providers to take on numerous cases, and where the intervention provider can provide a rough estimate on the time needed for each case.

At the very least I recommend serious reconsiderations to be made on the current practice of interventions both at tactical and operational levels.

An example: a young person was being heavily influenced by a violent network of similar-aged young men known to be supportive of ISIS and sending young people to Syria. The young person barely had time to breathe without him being contacted by the extremist recruiters. Our intervention was restricted to two or three hours per week, and whilst we were making good progress, I found I had to go back over the same arguments that in fact made an impact, but were then refuted by the recruiter. Each time we made progress and felt we were bringing the young man back from the brink, the following day we had to deal with another narrative. The only thing left for us to do was to invite the influencing source to a face-to-face debate, so we could find a level playing field and to destroy the recruiter's narrative in front of the young man.

This posed huge challenges and indeed risks, and whilst we thought the recruiter would refuse any challenge or confrontation in front of his subject (which is generally the case), to our surprise, he actually agreed to have the debate. A number of issues developed here: would he (the recruiter) be accompanied by others and for what purpose? Or was the recruiter over-confident and felt he could defeat us? Was I prepared to meet the challenge? Did I need to call the police in case of a potential attack upon myself, and if I did call the police would that be helpful in my work going forward or just confirm the perceptions that we are government stooges? Finally, was I confident enough and well versed on the subject to defeat the recruiter's arguments?

For your knowledge, I could not inform the police as this would have ruined my credibility and confirmed their views. I had no choice but to prepare myself mentally and physically to face the recruiter, who by the way was completely ill-prepared for me and failed to counter any of my arguments. He was theologically defunct and mentally weak. It was a very risky strategy, but isn't our work riddled with risk anyway? What choices did I have? In my view I felt I had no choice but to take on the recruiter and give it my best shot. I was prepared and I knew my subject very well and I knew the nature of the beast very well, which is why I took the risk and which is why I am proud to say that the young man is no longer a potential threat, nor is he being hounded by extremists. This is one example of many, but ultimately I can say this is not what 'could' happen, it is what 'will' happen. Only occasionally, but we need to be prepared for this scenario. Although to reassure you, there are not many recruiters these days who are willing to blow their cover, so it will not be a common occurrence in the physical environment, rather it will be more likely through virtual platforms.

My point regarding limited time on interventions can be argued just on this one case, and I'm absolutely certain that most if not all cases would be better dealt with if there were no time restrictions and better qualified intervention providers.

The success or failure of any intervention primarily rests on the quality and experience of the IP. Being able to adapt to any change in circumstances is a vital ingredient for any intervention provider. Experienced practitioners will be well aware of the rapidly changing nature of interventions and individuals who are being recruited. New narratives, developments and emotions often can cause a lot of drag and in some cases failure.

It is crucial that intervention providers are well grounded in their knowledge and actual understanding of the phenomenon of extremist recruitment and of the many challenges associated with this. Knowing your terrain and operational leeway is also equally important and having a degree of knowledge on terrorism legislation will be helpful. Sadly, however, there is no training available on preventing extremism and interventions. There are huge gaps and flaws; this is something every government and institution must address as a matter of urgency.

The wellbeing of the intervention provider

The intervention provider holds a huge level of risk and is often exposed to many challenging situations. In many cases the IP will need to hear personal stories and listen to some terrible experiences, and at the very least they will be exposed to harboured grievances and face a number of powerful emotions, including anger, from the client. This is all happening whilst the IP is equally trying to establish a degree of trust, while maintaining composure and strength. And we must never lose sight of the intervention client playing 'hide and seek', which is highly likely.

It is obvious that interventions will vary from case to case and can quite often cause exhaustion, physical and emotional breakdown, risks and in some cases can prove to be a waste of time or fraudulent.

An example: a young female (mid-teens) is being forced to marry her cousin in Bangladesh who is not a practising Muslim and who she knows is really not interested in her, rather more driven by the possibility of obtaining a visa for the UK. She has been beaten by her brothers and forced to accept the marriage. She approaches a friend who brings her into the centre for advice and potential support. But the only support she wants or will consider is to be advised on how to get to Syria or Libya where she has identified a potential husband who is devout and God-fearing, but belongs to a terrorist network; she does not accept this as problematic, rather she feels he is a *mujahideen* fighting in God's cause. She begs for help in this and explains how she is punished by her family for rejecting their idea and if they found out she was attending our centre, they would take violent action. She does not wish for any harm to come to them or even for the authorities to know her plight. After seeing the images on her phone of the guy in Syria, it becomes obvious that there are three different images of three different men,although she is oblivious to this fact. It seems she is head-over-heels in love with those images (all three) but doesn't accept the fact that the person on the other end may or will most definitely look completely different and may not even be what she thinks.

The IP is now exposed to a lot of issues, each having their own challenges. What course of action would you take? Has she broken the law? Is she in fact telling the truth and how are you going to establish that? Do you report everything to the police? Where will you start from?

I decided to start from the three different images on her phone, trying to get her to accept that the person she is attracted to or communicating with is not the person on her phone. But I had to raise her suspicions by suggestive narratives giving similar examples of 'others' first and then slowly bringing the reality back to her personally. In short, I started from afar and brought it home.

Sometimes, someone who seems like a vulnerable target is actually nothing more than a fraud. My experience with one such case was, in brief, as follows: a young European male claimed to have converted to Islam but was experiencing difficulties in attaining employment and has nowhere to live. He also claimed that he was thinking of joining Al Qaeda in Syria as he had nothing better to do; and that way at least he could have a female companion of choice, a shelter, be provided for and in some way useful and would become a martyr if all else failed. After looking at all the support he needed I began to initiate the support package through the Channel panel multi-agency approach. Support began to reach him, but each day the individual's demands increased. Meanwhile, when we dug a little deeper we found that the individual was not practising his faith at all; in fact, whenever advised or reminded to pray, he became hostile. When we moved our attention away, he immediately demonstrated hostile anti-Jewish tendencies. We re-energised the support again and again his demands increased, to a point where his daily food and phone bills were being covered, and all the while he was both claiming benefits and working part-time in the evenings. We found this individual to falsely claim he was extreme and that he had connections with extremist networks in the Middle East, just so he could receive support in finding him a job, accommodation and even finding him a female and help in getting him married. He was not interested in Islam and we found he was certainly not thinking of joining Al Qaeda. After a period of experiencing this individual's false nature, the intervention was drawn to a close.

In such circumstances it is essential to consider the intervention provider's wellbeing and personal safety. I have found all too often we get bogged down in establishing the best outcome for the vulnerable individual and forget about the intervention provider. We also find in some cases that those in authority have a lack of trust in the intervention provider, which is seriously unhealthy in every aspect and can often cause low impact and severe burnout, indeed we should appreciate: trust is a two-way street. In some cases I have found that individuals of concern who have been given a healthy support network in order to move them into a much more positive space in physical and mental terms have then become completely dependent on this provision. They then use this as a crutch without genuinely needing to do so. The intervention provider can and should pick this up and apply measures to rectify this issue, or at the very least report it back to the Channel board for further consideration. The board must appreciate this phenomenon going forward as it is and will be a trend for those who want to abuse the system, but importantly the board has to always support and protect the intervention provider in all circumstances.

The point I am making here is that it is essential that intervention providers are appreciated and valued for their roles in deterring vulnerable individuals from extremism and they also need to be selected carefully, whilst it goes without saying that they must possess a high level of credibility and expertise in the field.

In this other example of work I've been involved in, a European female in her mid-20s converted to Islam. She was attracted to a mixed-race male, also a recent convert to Islam but someone who held very extreme views and was part of a proscribed group. The female soon adopted similar views, due to her lack of knowledge of her new faith, but also because she has her own direct experience of racism due to her European origin and for not being British or fluent in English. The female, who was also ex-military and a kick boxer and fitness fanatic, decided to wear the full hijab including face veil. Over the period of a year the female developed complete hatred towards non-Muslims, as well as Muslims who she labelled as 'moderate'. She began to believe that we are in a 'state of war' (*dar-ul-harb*) where deception and fraud is permissible and that 'enjoining the good and forbidding the evil' is literal without room for consideration. Basically, this means 'hate those who disbelieve or love those who believe for the sake of God only' (Al wala Al Bara) and she expressed this through her interactions with everyone she came into contact with.

After a year of being married to her partner, he decided he wanted to get married to a second wife due to a newly-developed attraction to Afro-Caribbean women. Sadly, the female was left with two choices: to either accept this as part of a faith which allows this, or to walk away from her husband. She approached ACF for advice and asked me to intervene and speak to her partner in the hope that I could change his mind. This sadly did not work (he was almost seven feet tall and also a fitness freak, and he was not a very friendly individual and I was not prepared to argue with him), so I encouraged her to leave him which meant she needed support. It is only then I found out her views and how warped her understanding of Islam was. It was at this point I realised she even carried with her at all times a samurai sword for her own protection. If, for instance, somebody had tried removing her hijab, she believed it would be permissible to behead them.

She became a Channel case and was then provided with all the support a young female needed. We introduced her to local female police officers (in civilian clothes at first) and local council officers, and took her on outward bound trips where she was introduced to all the people she hated due to them all being non-Muslim and a part of the authorities. However, after each one lent her support and found her new ways of looking at life and helped develop her career, the hatred turned into respect and appreciation, which allowed me the opportunity to shape her thinking, both rationally and theologically.

She needed to establish a secure future without dependency on anyone else, and the service provision allowed for this to happen naturally. It had the additional effect of taking away any of her perceptions about non-Muslims and moderate Muslims, and also allowed her to develop relationships and friendships with people who she would ordinarily stay away from, but who all contributed in changing her circumstances for the better. The intervention relied heavily upon my own professional relationships, institutional links and knowledge of service provision and networks to access for support. And this is an absolute crucial element to any intervention being successful. (We took away her samurai sword eventually.)

What community-based interventions work and how?

Over the many years, I have found through experience what actually works and how, and with this in mind I ask that you look at the extremist and terrorist groups and their models. It clearly shows that they are successful in recruiting young men and women to their cause. And this is why I have used their techniques and their approach in preventing extremism. It is simple mathematics and it works.

Our first approach is Outreach & Engagement at every single level. By employing outreach officers who are reflective of the diverse communities we operate within, we essentially deploy them at a grassroots level. They go out and reach those communities who are otherwise hard to reach and would not necessarily engage with statutory sector. Schools, colleges, streets, shopping centres, parks, housing estates and youth clubs are places where the team operate. This is done every day and at all times. It allows for a greater understanding and knowledge of the dynamics of every community and what is going on. It also allows young people a source to engage with and communicate with on matters affecting them. But more importantly it affords us the opportunity to deny the space to those who would recruit our young people.

Secondly, we have a youth leadership program known as the ACF Young Leaders Programme. This was established to give young people from all walks of life, selected deliberately to create a hugely diverse group, value and position; it enables young people to look at their roles within society and to partake in establishing solutions to their problems as well as address wider community issues. We recruit them through schools and colleges and also identify key skills of those who do not attend school, in order to create the right mix of people as well as those who need support.

We take them on a journey of understanding, where they are shown how certain antagonists are exploiting the vulnerabilities of young people. We lecture them on extremism, terrorism, gangs, drugs and other similar issues and what the objectives of such groups or individuals are. We educate them on a number of key skills, like communication, critical thinking, emotional logic and public speaking; the journey over seven or eight months establishes a network of young people wholly committed to creating a better future for themselves and others. From the initial recruitment phase, we ask that each young person identifies a 'cause' which we then assist them with and help develop their capacity to deliver it within their respective communities. More often, the cause that they identify is preventing violent extremism, which is then communicated through a young people's network and creates the domino effect in a very successful way. I call it revolutionising young people in a positive way.

Thirdly, we operate a female- and family-engagement team who work at the cutting edge and go out to meet females and families or invite them along to the centre where debates, services, classes and other opportunities are provided for those who need them. This often creates the space for concerns to be aired, mostly in private one-to-one sessions but in many cases between other females. This is the way in which community credibility and community issues are addressed and established. Being a non-governmental organisation allows for issues to be shared without fear or perceptions that the authorities will act prematurely. Creating a safe space and a community-friendly environment is key in establishing successful outcomes.

Fourthly, we operate online and create campaigns with our user groups; young leaders and other young people shape and deliver campaigns like our #NotinMyName campaign, which reached in excess of 300 million people and every single nation on the planet. It was not designed as an 'apology' of some sort because of ISIS killings, rather it was an act of defiance to show that they (ISIS) do not act in the name of Islam or Muslims, and each participant and indeed those who followed the campaign did so in defiance of ISIS. It made a huge impact and actually hurt them as one former ISIS recruit and returnee from Syria informed us, and demonstrates that complex issues are not always solved by complex solutions. Low-scale, high-impact ideas, especially when you create a growing network of young people who will champion the idea, generate the desired momentum.

These are just some examples of what really works and how, and so I leave this entirely with you to consider and hopefully follow. I conclude with one message on this: these projects have worked and continue to do so with real impact and, more importantly, they are community-focused and indeed community-led. Although many such programmes are supported, and indeed funded, by governments and it is also very important that all parties concerned, such as police and local authorities, work close together, it is equally imperative that organisations or individuals delivering counter-violent extremism or any Prevent initiative at a local level remain independent from government. This is especially important when it comes to policies and strategies that are weak and have been formulated without consideration of community sensitivities. Often it becomes the case that Prevent programmes are seen as government stooges or mouthpieces that echo one voice, that of government. It is essential to remain impartial and community-friendly, whilst also a critical friend of governments, otherwise it is not going to work, because if you cannot reach the individuals then it is obvious that change will not occur. It is as simple as that.

ANSWERING SOME KEY QUESTIONS

Here are some general questions and principles to consider and keep in mind. They may not necessarily form part of an intervention, but will always be useful when interacting with young people.

Q: What is Islam? And what is a Muslim?

Answer: Islam is the religion which was revealed to all of the prophets of God. Islam is to submit to God by worshipping Him alone without partners, to obey His commandments and to keep away from all forms of polytheism. A Muslim is a person who follows the Islamic faith and believes in one God and that Muhammad is the final messenger of God.

Q: What are the sources of the Islamic religion?

A: There are two sources of Islam: 1. The Quran, which is the book that was revealed to Prophet Muhammad (*May the peace and blessings of God be upon him*). It is considered by all Muslims to be the actual spoken word of God, communicated to mankind by revelation to his chosen Prophet Muhammad through the angel Gabriel. 2. The Sunnah, which is the prophetic tradition or path. This refers to the Prophet's speech, actions, silent approvals, outward appearance and character that was observed by his companions, written down and passed on generation after generation in written form and oral tradition. This body of literature is often referred to as Hadith. Muslims **do not** worship Prophet Muhammad in any form whatsoever.

Q: Who is Allah?

A: Allah is God Almighty. It is an Arabic word that means 'the God who alone is deserving of being worshipped'.

Q: Who are the prophets of Islam?

A: The prophets of Islam are the same as the prophets of the Jews and the Christians whom we refer to as 'The People of the Book'. The Muslims also believe in a final prophet that was born in Mecca in 570CE, whose name was Muhammad. So Muslims believe in all of the prophets of God such as Noah, Abraham, Moses, Jesus and all the others and finally Muhammad (peace and blessings be upon them all). Muslims believe they were all sent to instruct the people to worship God alone, to obey Him, to do righteous deeds and to shun idolatry. So there is a shared tradition between Islam, Judaism and Christianity in that they believe in many of the same prophets and in the revealed scriptures.

Q: How should a Muslim behave around people of different faiths?

A: God and His prophet have instructed the believers to treat people with kindness and with the best of manners. God said: 'God does not forbid you to deal justly and kindly with those who did not fight against you on account of Religion and did not drive you out of your homes. Verily, God loves those who deal with equity.' (Quran 60:8) A disciple of the Prophet Muhammad called Ibn Abbas said: 'Respond to the greeting of peace from a Jew, a Christian, or a Magian because God has said: "*And when you are greeted with a salutation of peace, then greet in response with one better than it or at least the same as it.*"' Another disciple, Ibn Mas'ood would greet the non-Muslims by waving at them (Ref books: Adab al-Mufrad of Bukhari). Muslims must be truthful, compassionate, honest, caring, charitable and neighbourly towards Muslims and non-Muslims alike. A disciple of the Prophet, Abdullah Ibn Amr cooked a goat and said to his servant: 'Have you sent some to our Jewish neighbour yet? I heard God's Messenger say: "Angel Gabriel did not cease to press on me the obligations concerning the neighbour until I began to think he (the neighbour) would inherit from me!"' (Ref book: Bukhari) When the Prophet and his disciples were in Mecca, being oppressed and treated badly by the pagan tribes, he made mention of a Christian Abyssinian King about whom he said: 'If only you were to leave out and go to the land of Abyssinia, for indeed there is a king there who does not oppress anyone and is a just king.' (Ref: Biography of the Prophet by Ibn Hisham). So this type of friendly interaction between the Muslims and non-Muslims leads to people having good thoughts about God, Islam, the Prophet Muhammad and his disciples which in turn leads to a greater understanding of the Muslim faith. The great Muslim scholar Ibn Uthaymeen said: 'Look how many people there are who first entered into Islam because of the fine conduct of the Muslims, their truthfulness and honesty in their transactions.'

Q: We see Islam and terrorism often mentioned together these days. So what does Islam say about terrorism?

A: Islam forbids all forms of terrorist activity. There are however some very extreme factions of people who, in the name of Islam, terrorise both Muslims and non-Muslims alike. The most well-known of these militant groups are ISIS or Al Qaeda in Syria and Iraq, Boko Haram in Nigeria and Al Shabaab in Somalia. These terrorist groups are called *Khawarij* (extremist renegades) in Islamic terminology because the term refers to those who rebel against Islam and the Muslims. The Prophet (peace and blessings be upon him) foretold their appearance and instructed the Muslims to stay away from them, and to defend themselves if they attack them. They first rebelled against the Prophet's disciples in the time of the third and fourth Caliphs, Uthman and Ali, killing some of the finest companions of the Prophet Muhammad.

Q: So why do these militant *Khawarij* look upon the rest of humankind and see them as worthless who can be killed without mercy and compassion?

A: Because they believe they are the only ones left with any true faith in God, and everyone else besides them is an infidel, or an apostate whose life has no value. They see themselves as God's chosen people who must punish all the 'enemies of God', cleanse the earth by the mass killing of Muslims and non-Muslims alike. That is why they believe they can stroll down a street and open fire on every man, woman and child in sight without a second thought or any compassion. One of their leaders openly claimed: 'Today the whole of the world is a land of unbelievers, even Mecca and Madinah.' These *Khawarij* are merciless killers who have no compassion; they kill innocent, unarmed civilians without any regard for life. They do not judge by God's Laws; they are a law unto themselves and they have no religion except that which they have invented for themselves; they murder Muslims and non-Muslims indiscriminately. They burn Muslims alive in cages, and then claim piety for themselves! And you have heard this yourself from the actions of ISIS. The Prophet said: 'No one punishes with fire except the Lord (*ie* the creator of the fire).' (Ref book: Abu Dawud) The *Khawarij* are people who have no mercy, so they will not be shown mercy, just as the Prophet Muhammad said: 'Whoever does not show mercy to people, Allah will not show mercy to him.' (Ref book: Muslim)

Q: What are the signs of radicalisation that I can spot in others so I can avoid it and advise them?

A: There are certain clear signs and signals that you can see in someone who is trying to radicalise others, but often they use deception to disguise themselves from the authorities and even young men and women. Here is a list of a few of the clearest signs of an extremist: 1) He will constantly focus upon the political situation of the Muslim regimes in the Middle East, and the centre point of his discussion will be as if it is the most important affair in Islam. 2) He will abuse the Muslim rulers declaring them to be unbelievers and apostates, and then justify violent revolution in Muslim and indeed in non-Muslim countries under the banner of 'judgement is for Allah!' A phrase misappropriated by the extremists and misused. 3) He will praise the leaders of extremist ideologies such as Bin Laden, Omar Bakri and Sayyid Qutb. Qutb in particular is revered by extremists all around the world from Bin Laden to Anwar Al-Awlaki and even Abu Bakr Al Baghdadi. He was a prominent leader of the Egyptian group, The Muslim Brotherhood. His writings are widespread and translated into dozens of languages including English. The US-born Yemeni terrorist Anwar Al-Awlaki once boasted that he was so immersed in the writings of Sayyid Qutb that he felt the presence of Qutb with him in his prison cell! 4) He will declare all Muslims who contradict his political world-view as unbelievers. 5) He will quite often glorify the acts of violence perpetrated by terrorists whether it be suicide bombings, beheading of hostages, killing of non-Muslims, kidnappings, *etc.* You will not hear condemnation of violent extremism or its figureheads from that person. These would be the obvious signs; however, there are other smaller signs that would need to be examined further, where the person may show anger and resentment towards Western governments, the law and even towards other Muslims who abide by the law.

Q: If I see Muslim women in hijab or men with beards who pray, should I be worried? Will they try and recruit young people?

A: This is a misunderstanding; however, recruiters come in many shapes and forms so being vigilant is always a good idea. Let's not forget that Muslims are commanded to dress modestly and pray five times a day, spend in charity, fast in Ramadan, do not sever ties of kinship and do righteous deeds. So when you see Muslim women in hijab, men wearing long shirts and growing beards, do not take these as signs of extremism. You should never confuse orthodox Islam with extremism. Many learned practising Muslims are the most vocal in opposing terrorism. Eating halal meat, praying five times a day, growing a beard and wearing a hijab are not signs of extremism! We need to be aware of the methods the extremists employ to try and recruit Muslim teenagers, both boys and girls. I am sure you've heard of cases where teenagers have run away from home to join ISIS, leaving their families behind without telling them anything. They were groomed and abused by manipulation either in our community or on the internet by extremists who convinced them to hide their true intentions and their radical beliefs; to lie to their parents, relatives and teachers, and eventually run away from home. This is *haram* (forbidden) in Islam because it involves deception, severing the ties of kinship which causes heartache to loved ones, and of course joining a militant group – all of these actions oppose the Islamic faith. The Prophet would not allow people to run away and leave their parents behind in tears. You must not be deceived by the videos and speeches of ISIS/Al Qaeda or other such groups and their supporters because they are very skilful manipulators of the truth who can easily convince people by their misinterpretation of Islam. That is why many young people who fell into their web of deceit and left their homes fell into regret later on and are now stuck thousands of miles away in a war zone where people are killing each other daily.

Q: What can I do if I know someone is trying to invite me to join ISIS or other extremist groups, or even planning a terrorist attack?

A: You must tell someone you trust; tell a parent, a teacher, a youth worker or the police. It is a duty in Islam to stamp out terrorism. The Prophet (may the peace and blessings of God be upon him) said: 'There are no people amongst whom sins are committed and they are stronger than those who commit them yet they do not prevent them except that God will punish all of them'. So when you know someone is about to commit a crime, you cannot stand by and let that happen. Allah and His Prophet have instructed us to help stop criminal acts.

Q: So what does Islam say about *jihad*?

A: *Jihad* in Islam is of various types. It is to strive in God's cause, and this begins with striving against one's self in obedience to God; to learn Islam correctly from the right sources; to act upon what you have learned; and to teach that to others with patience, even if you suffer hardship in that path. It is to apply the fundamentals of Islam, namely honesty, modesty, compassion, mercy and humility. So this is *jihad* as the great scholar of the Middle Ages Ibn Al-Qayyim (died 752AH) stated. And from the types of *jihad*, a war upon the battlefield must be a conventional and strictly legitimate war. An example of a legitimate declaration of war was the first Gulf War in 1990-91 after Kuwait was invaded by the Iraqi army under the leadership of Saddam Hussein. So Saudi Arabia defended its borders by the use of its recruited army in an alliance with other countries. The following are some of the important principles and guidelines of *jihad* as agreed upon by the Muslim scholars:

a. War is declared by leaders who have legitimate governments and not by individual citizens, or terrorists, or insurgents, or preachers (or through social media!).

b. War must be for a just cause, in obedience to God, and for His worship.

c. Civilians cannot be killed or harmed in conflict and war. This includes securing the safety of all civilians: women, children, monks, emissaries, teachers, nurses, and doctors, aid workers and so on. The claim of terrorists that all non-Muslims (and even Muslims who disagree with them) are legitimate targets goes against Islamic teachings.

d. One does not fight for personal gain, or tribalism, or to steal wealth, or for political partisanship, or to rape and pillage, or for repute, fame and adventure. The terrorists obligate what they call *jihad* in any situation and have thus hijacked the term. They fight without a legitimate ruler, they kill those whom it is not permitted to kill, Muslims and non-Muslims alike; they plant bombs in civilian areas; they kill themselves in suicide bombings, which is forbidden. They murder those whom the rulers have invited into Muslim countries under the guarantee of security and safety. So what they partake in cannot be considered as *jihad* in any sense of the word.

Q: What is the ruling on travelling to Syria and is this jihad?

A: This is turmoil and chaos; a person should not partake in this. Rather, he should stay far away from it, but he should supplicate for the Muslims over there who are suffering. He should supplicate regularly for (Allah to grant) the Muslims success and relief. As for him travelling there, then this is not permissible because firstly, he has a family and parents, and secondly, he has to have the consent of the Muslim leader. These two conditions have to be met: the consent of the Muslim leader and parental consent. Travelling to Syria to fight amongst ISIS is turmoil and chaos and a person should stay far away from this.

Q: Is it forbidden to have non-Muslim friends and to love or care for them?

A: The extremists say 'do not associate with non-Muslims and hate them' however, what is fact and indeed what is from Islam explained by the scholars is completely different.

Shaykh Ali Ibn Yahya Al Haddadi, an eminent scholar of our times, mentioned that having love and care for non-Muslims, especially if it is natural love, a worldly type of love, is permissible, and the Shaykh explained that this is the most correct opinion. If one possesses this, it neither increases nor decreases one's belief; for example, one may love an individual because it is his relative, like a mother or father, or a friend, who he would possibly love or care about because he went to school with him, went to university with him. This is a natural love: you don't love him because he is a disbeliever but you love him because of the relationship or friendship; you naturally have a bond, some type of love and respect for this person.

The Shaykh provides evidence from the Quran to show that it is permissible; the proof for that is the statement of Allah addressing His Messenger (pbuh), where Allah said to him: 'Verily, you cannot guide whom you love, but Allah guides whom He wills. And He knows best those who are the guided' (Soorah a Qasas, verse 56). This verse of the Quran was revealed pertaining to the love of the Messenger for his uncle Abu Taalib who was not a Muslim. In this verse Allah is informing that the Prophet used to love him whilst Allah is informing that you cannot guide him.

We understand why the Prophet and Messenger of Allah used to love Abu Taalib because after the death of his mother and his father, and his grandfather, the one who used to support the Prophet and Messenger of Allah was Abu Taalib. He had supported him; he had assisted him from the age of 8 until the Prophet was 50. Over a period of 42 years his uncle supported, defended, spent money on the messenger of Allah. His uncle served him and the likes of that, so the Prophet had a natural love for his uncle.

The Shaykh mentions that another proof for this being permissible is that Allah has allowed the Muslim male to marry a female from the 'People of the Book' (The Jews and Christians). Allah has allowed that; what is understood is that there is naturally going to be love between a man and his wife. This is a natural love; this is not a love for their religion. Rather, to show the fact that love is going to be there, Allah says in the Quran 'And among His Signs is this, that He created for you wives from among yourselves, that you may find repose in them, and He has put between you affection and mercy. Verily, in that are indeed signs for a people who reflect.' (Soorah al Rum, verse 21) This shows you that this natural love is permissible between Muslims and non-Muslims, in spite of what the extremists say.

I would like to thank Abdul Wahid for his contributions to the above Q&As.

CASE STUDIES

Please note: All case studies have been kept brief and limited to particular information.

Here we will look at a number of case studies where intervention strategies have been put into practice. I will outline the circumstances of each case and there will be discussion of the issues relating to each in the Analysis section. You will hopefully find most of the answers to your questions there, although you may pick out other key factors that I missed or did not consider, and which may have provided better solutions or even a more rapid transformation. The process is one of learning, and looking at other ways and means of doing things when faced with such circumstances. And always remember that every case is different. Even if they share similarities, the individual will often have a number of other issues going on, and it is for you to identify these issues in order to make the right decisions and provide the best possible solution.

In each case, consider the following questions:

1. Can you identify the vulnerability factors?
2. What are the 'push' and 'pull' factors?
3. Can you identify the key risk factors?
4. What steps would you take to minimise the risks identified?

Please note – these case studies have been written with minimal detail due to matters of sensitivity and for legal reasons.

CASE STUDY 1

Profile/Name ID: Panther

Gender: Male

Age range: Mid-to-late teens

Ethnicity: Asian

Educational profile: College drop-out

Language: Fluent in Punjabi/Urdu. Conversational English

Family: Lived with relatives as both parents and siblings were abroad.

Theological understanding: Limited understanding of Islam. Has the ability to read but not understand Arabic.

Case Background

The Name/ID was chosen due to his tag/street name being similar, which indicates he identified himself as a masculine and fearless individual. It gives you an indicator of his mentality.

Panther was an ordinary young person who was friendly with others and generally very respectful and considerate. He was a good hustler and often jumped at an opportunity to make money. He traded goods and was always on the lookout for merchandise to sell for a profit. He kept his ear to the ground for any information about what was going on in the local area. He was never afraid to voice his opinion and was not afraid of other males in the area who would often bully others into handing over cash or anything of value.

He had a good social network of decent law-abiding young people who would generally hang out together and always looked out for one another. I knew these young men very well and I always interacted with most of them via our youth centre and many of the projects we ran with young people. In fact, they helped out in the early days, when I was setting up projects and outreach work.

Panther was probably the only one of the group who hardly ever came to the centre. This was primarily due to the fact that his friends would turn up after 8pm and he needed to be home at that time. He used to mention the importance of obeying his aunt who insisted that he be home at a particular time, and it was his main priority not to let her down. She raised him and cared for him while his parents lived abroad and he felt he needed to show her respect for this.

I saw him daily, although only in passing, and he always took time out to ask me how I was and how the youth centre was progressing, often asking if he could assist. You could only describe him as decent, considerate and well-meaning. He attended mosque every Friday and often took the time out to meet and greet the elders as they would exit after prayers.

The mosque he attended regularly had groups outside handing out literature and marketing material, mainly from Hizb u Tahrir (HT), an extremist political group that has been hugely instrumental in radicalising thousands of young men and women from across the world. (It was from this group that Al Muhajiroin became an offshoot and went on to cause more disruption by promoting a very extremist narrative, led by Omar Bakri who has his deputy in the UK known as Anjem Choudary.)

Panther was handed a leaflet from one of the HT guys that was in the form of a letter, purportedly from a young Muslim female held captive by American soldiers in Iraq. The letter was both a cry for help and a grievance that the woman would take up with God on the Day of Judgement, to hold to account the millions of Muslim brothers who failed to help her and protect her from daily rape and brutal beatings by her *kuffar* (non-believing) captors.

It went into great detail about her plight and was very powerful in describing what was being done to her. It asked why her 'Muslim brothers' were not doing anything to stop her suffering, how would they feel if this was their daughter, sister or mother – and posed the direct question: 'Don't you fear the day when you will be questioned by your creator?'

Panther took this letter home and locked himself in his room. He began to imagine the girl from the letter was his own sister and what he would do if this was happening to her. It made him vomit profusely.

He began to think about how and what he should do about it. He knew he could not go to Iraq but knew the British government supported the Iraq war, so he decided he wanted to take revenge here in the UK. Any soldier, police officer or government official was his prime target. His aunt called his friends to find out what was going on with him, as he was not eating and isolated himself in his room. His friends went round and managed to talk to him; they were given the whole story and were also encouraged to seek revenge. He spent a few hours trying to convince them to support him and avenge 'their sister in Islam'. They agreed in principle but on the condition that he accompanied them to come and see me and seek guidance on what to do. Their idea was to get him out of the room and allow him to breathe some fresh air, but also to bring him to me to get some help.

When they turned up with him, it was clear that Panther was not right: he looked very pale and obviously in distress. As they walked towards me a police car drove past and Panther began shouting and screaming and started beating his chest in rage. I noticed he was frothing at the mouth, dehydrating in the process.

His friend pulled me to the side and asked to speak to me in private. I invited him into my office and then asked what was troubling them. Panther's friend asked me to take a look at Panther and see whether I noticed a change in his appearance. I acknowledged that there was a clear change and that he looked very pale and strange. It was clearly evident something was troubling him.

Panther then posed a question to me: 'Do you have a sister or a daughter?' I replied in the affirmative and mentioned that one of my sisters had passed away and how I deeply missed her. He then began to read out a script which he must have memorised word for word because he did not have any paper in front of him and he was fluent with his speech. The script he read was about an Iraqi female who was being raped seven times a day and urinated upon by the American soldiers who had her locked up in a prison. She claimed that the Americans said they were 'purifying' her and she was begging for help, asking where her millions of Muslim brothers were while this was happening to her, and that she will hold each Muslim male accountable in front of God on the Day of Judgement. Panther went into more detail about the suffering of this female, his eyes full of tears. He concluded by asking, 'What am I going to do, now that I have knowledge of this brutal act carried out by non-Muslims who have invaded this female's country and are acting violently towards innocent people?' He pointed his finger at my face and demanded I respond with an answer immediately, which I found completely out of character. I responded by politely asking him to first show me the respect he had extended to me in the past and then reminded him of how he was always respectful to me before, so why this sudden change in behaviour? He quickly replied by saying, 'Would you have patience and think about respect if this female was your own sister or your own daughter?' Would I be so calm if this was the case? Before I could respond to his question he came at me with a flurry of other questions: Was I a real Muslim? Did I believe in the final day? Did I fear God? Is the war in Iraq a *jihad* for Muslims? And finally, how could I just sit there after hearing what he had said? Then he jumped up and tried to rush outside.

His friends made him sit back down, insisting he give me a chance to answer his questions, and for him to show some respect by listening. Which, I must say, he did, and this allowed me a bit of breathing space and some time to pace my arguments in a manner that could ease the tension. I began by asking whether he had witnessed me pray in the mosque or elsewhere, which he confirmed he had. So I reminded him that this should be enough evidence for him to appreciate I was a Muslim, and therefore I do believe in the final day and do, indeed, fear

God. I then explained my understanding of *jihad* and began to take him on a journey where I explained how he must be feeling, what was going through his mind, and how he felt useless sitting here while he believed innocent people were being brutalised under the guise of the War on Terror. I then asked him whether he thought it was *jihad* in Iraq and whether he knew the fundamentals of *jihad* or not, which he could not explain. He could only reply by saying he thought *jihad* was obligatory because of what the Americans were doing.

It was obvious that if I challenged him bluntly, he would get angrier and perhaps walk out, which would not have been helpful at all. I knew he was at a critical point; his body language was erratic and his mind focused on expressing himself by avenging the plight of the woman he had read about.

Panther wanted to harm someone and it was obvious he needed support in managing his anger and his emotions, but disagreeing with him was not the way forward at that particular time. So I asked him what he wanted to do about this situation and how he intended to do it, and explain what this looked like in his mind; basically to play it out so I could get a better picture. Panther did not waste time in expressing this and began to explain in great detail what he has been thinking of ever since he heard of the Iraqi female's plight. His plan was riddled with crazy ideas and was obviously internalized to such an extent – he hadn't opened up to anyone about it – that he wanted to hurt a lot of people who he felt were the enemies. It was clear he had no Islamic understanding or even consideration; this young man was completely overwhelmed with rage.

After hearing his ideas and realising how serious this young man was, I knew I had to deal with most of his anger immediately. I could not involve any other person who would not understand the situation or even relate to this young man. I began to ask Panther the same questions he put to me, 'Are you a Muslim? Do you fear God? Do you believe in the last day and do you believe in the Qadr of Allah? (The will of God)'. He smiled and replied, 'Of course I do uncle, why did you even have to ask me these questions?' I responded by reminding him of his questions to me and why he felt the need to ask me, and that he probably felt insulted by my questions, just like I was by his. He immediately apologised for his rudeness and assured me he would not do that again, which I accepted with the words 'May God bless you' and extended my hand for him to shake. He smiled again and thanked me, which afforded me the opportunity to establish a calm and controlled environment, where Panther was obliged to listen to me and was open to my mentoring.

I then took him on a historical and factual journey dating back to the time of our beloved Prophet (peace be upon him). Step by step I asked him to acknowledge whether he had heard of these stories and if not, they were available for him to read in most of the books in almost every mosque. The stories consisted of times where our Prophet (pbuh) was persecuted and seriously hurt on many occasions, but never once retaliated with violence, and whenever there was a need for war, he commanded every single companion to avoid harming the innocent and even harming trees. These stories were intended to soften Panther's heart a bit and make him more receptive to what I was saying.

I then asked him to show me the letter he had been given, which he pulled out of his pocket and handed over to me with both hands (which showed he gave the letter a lot of respect, as if it was some kind of Holy Scripture). I examined the letter and its contents thoroughly, then dropped it on the table in front of Panther, which caused him to quickly pick it up with care. I asked if he could explain why he was handling the piece of paper with such respect and whether it had any religious significance in his opinion. His response was in the negative but it did allow him to reflect a little, so then I began to suggest if he could picture the circumstances surrounding the Iraqi female and whether or not she would have had access to pen and paper or a computer and a printer, and if so, how would she have managed to either post it out or email it across the world. I reminded him to consider that she was apparently held captive and being brutalised by the Americans and whether they would allow her so much freedom while carrying out such atrocities. I accepted the fact that atrocities were indeed happening, but wanted him to analyse this particular situation first.

I then asked if the guys who handed him this letter mentioned anything and whether they looked saddened or angry when handing out these letters to the public. My intention was to take him through the process step by step, allowing him to consider things that had never occurred to him before. Panther then went over the letter again, only this time I noticed he was holding it with one hand and once he finished reading it, he left it on his lap and lent back on his chair. He looked relieved, as if a huge burden was lifted from his shoulders.

But I felt we needed to go into much more detail about his feelings and the way they were manipulated, and the manner in which he absorbed the contents and information he was exposed to. I then decided to explain in detail my own experiences from beginning to end and brought together both his and my own grievances, drawing comparisons between the two narratives each of us were exposed to. This allowed me then to push home the reality of what was going on and how these narratives were, in fact, abusing our emotions, while feeding off the suffering of innocent human beings and our fellow Muslims.

This intervention was quite tense and detailed, but I have briefly captured it for your attention and consideration.

Analysis

Establishing communication and conversations is crucial to progressing further with an individual of concern, which can only be done through engagement. Equally important is the need to relate to the young person, whether you disagree with their grievances or not. Your attitude towards the individual needs to be of an understanding and supportive nature, rather than taking an apathetic or overly critical tone. I have found it is essential to apply a personal touch to the situation in order for the individual to at least feel there is some common ground there. (Example: a young person feels sad or angry when he reads about the plight of the female, considering it could be his own sister. Your response might be something like: Yes, I understand, I have a sister or daughter and I could not imagine how I would feel…)

The main point is to generate an environment where the individual can become receptive and where a progressive discussion can take shape. The intervention provider has to build at least a degree of trust to continue further with the case.

Panther lacked the critical thinking skills needed to look beyond the false pleas about an Iraqi female held captive, projected by HT in their attempts to radicalise impressionable young people. He fell short in questioning the motives of those who handed him the letter and failed to recognise some of the telltale signs that would have been obvious if he had awareness of the strategies employed by such groups. He was targeted outside a place of worship, where people are often unaware or fail to accept that manipulative techniques may be used. God-fearing people may be highly vulnerable at this particular point: a degree of piety is often established by people after they have prayed and sought forgiveness for their sins.

One important point to consider is that Panther did not expose himself to HT or anyone else outside of his close social group after reading the letter, and was lucky enough not to have been given the follow-up indoctrination by them or any other such group. He could have very easily been pulled hard and fast towards some kind of terrorist network. His friends were much more resilient and more sceptical about the information that was 'dumped' on their unsuspecting friend.

It's important to consider the power and influence, both positive and negative, of group dynamics. The scenario could have been so different depending on the attitude and standpoint of Panther's friends.

This case demonstrates that we have to treat vulnerable people who have such grievances very carefully. We have to consider our manner and attitude. This is so important. That initial meeting can very easily define the outcome of the intervention.

CASE STUDY 2

Profile/Name ID: Abdi

Gender: Male

Age range: Early 20s

Ethnicity: Somali

Educational profile: Home schooled

Language: Fluent in English/Somali

Family: Father absent during early teens

Other: Was taken out of school at the age of 14

Theological understanding: Intermediate

Case background

Abdi was arrested in 2006 for plotting and preparing for acts of terrorism along with a number of others. He was the youngest of the group and had been involved with them over a period of three years. He had left school and had been home schooled at the age of 14, primarily due to his mother wanting him to focus more on his faith and to gain further knowledge of Islam.

He frequented religious gatherings on a regular basis and at the age of 16 had become exposed to a very charismatic individual known as OL who introduced Abdi to others and included him in a wider network. OL spent a lot of time with Abdi, to an extent where he became a father figure, and created an environment where Abdi latched onto him and in a way became part of the family.

Abdi was a young man who was genuinely seeking more knowledge about his faith. He was quite gentle and compassionate in nature and, indeed, a very respectful person. OL offered this young man the opportunity to learn and to pass on his learning to others, known as *Dawah* work. This is to promote the faith in order to benefit others and gain the great reward for doing so. Abdi jumped at this opportunity, which is normal for a compassionate young person who loves his faith and wants to help others and reap the rewards.

However, over a period of time, the meetings and general discussions revolved around the wars in Muslim countries and the killing of innocent women and children. The Afghan war was the main talking point and drew in a lot of discussion from the entire group. Every person in that group developed a deep-rooted hatred towards the Coalition Forces due to the increase in numbers of innocent civilians being killed. The war in Iraq was also an emotional topic, and the Abu Ghraib prison images depicting Iraqis being brutalised played a huge role in radicalising thousands across the world, including young men like Abdi. So the talking point was Afghanistan, yet the imagery that was firing their hearts and minds was mainly from the Iraq war. The growing issues in Somalia brought the whole war on Islam closer, especially with Abdi being African; it was hitting him hard.

Abdi explained how he found it difficult to sleep at night while bombs were being dropped over villages in Afghanistan and while US Special Forces were operating in Somalia. He began to go out for walks at night to catch some fresh air in the hope that it would ease his anxiety. He couldn't wait until the next day to meet his friends and to identify ways of doing something to help the Afghans and his fellow countrymen. Videos were being used to show the massacre of innocent men, women and children. Fiery debates by extremist scholars like Sheikh Faisal Al Jamaikee, Anwar Al Awlaki, Omar Bakri and Abu Hamza al Masri were listened to. The group's knowledge of how to manipulate holy texts and use emotionally charged arguments took away Abdi's ability to question anything they said. The rapid process of radicalisation suppressed any chance of a third-party intervention, purely because they controlled Abdi's environment and indeed shaped the way he thought.

It came to a point where phrases like 'blood for blood' were being used and emphasised; this became the focus point of their agenda moving forward. They planned activities like paintballing, camping, orienteering and outward bounds, which is where most of the plots to attack were discussed. Abdi said that he began to play out in his mind how they would attack certain targets and how he would punch the air after they had bloodied the nose of the West again, alluding to the 7/7 attacks. Abdi was clearly on a journey as a willing participant, but unaware of what all this really meant. He was completely ignorant of the fact that the very faith he loved and was extremely passionate about does not condone such acts of indiscriminate violence. He completely lost his way with regards to his original intention of seeking knowledge purely to better himself as a human being and a humble Muslim on his journey through life.

Abdi and his group were arrested and subsequently charged for preparing acts of terror. He was given a lengthy sentence and incarcerated in one of the UK's most high security prisons, where at such a young age he was exposed to many high-profile and dangerous people. His life in prison allowed him to reflect on many things and to a degree he had a lot of regret. However, his experience in prison was also pushing him into the belief that Islam and Muslims were the real target of non-Muslims. Due to the way he was being treated and the way he witnessed other Muslim inmates being treated, he was being radicalised even more so than before. His exposure to other terrorists was something that was not considered at all by the authorities, and, as a direct result of this significant flaw in our prison system, Abdi had no choice but to gravitate towards them. Not only because they would provide him with protection, but also because he related to them and it was where he felt more comfortable and more able to express himself. The prison officers unfortunately added to Abdi's hatred as their attitudes and behaviour continuously reinforced and reignited his existing views. So, the reader can imagine how much internal conflict was brewing within this impressionable young man, especially given that other Terrorist Act inmates would apply their indoctrination almost hourly. It was an overwhelming experience for Abdi, who in all honesty could not see the wood from the trees and internalised everything. It was clearly evident that he was struggling to cope, particularly with his genuine concerns about his family, especially his mother, who he was very close to. He told me it was only because of his mother that he was able to see out his term in prison. He kept his head down and cooperated as much as he could, given the circumstances.

Two days after his release, Abdi was introduced to me in a setting that could have been better planned – a police station. The reader would need to picture this scenario in your mind to fully appreciate the situation. I was called into a room where Abdi was sitting at a table, beside his probation worker, with only one space opposite him. I had to sit right opposite him, just like in an interview room when in custody. I felt that he was now looking at me as part of the same system that incarcerated him for a long time – an enemy. Even though he greeted me with respect it was obvious he was suspicious about me and my reason for being there. The probation worker had already spoken to him about me and my work, but I decided to enlighten him in greater detail so he could perhaps get a clearer picture. I explained that I was from a charity based in East London and our aims were to assist individuals like him to reintegrate into society and mentor them as and when needed.

I could see Abdi wasn't really interested in what I was saying; rather he was grasping with the idea that maybe I was from security services or something along those lines. He even told me this many years later, and it is something we now look back at and laugh about. We were left alone for an hour or so, which allowed me to get some key points across and to further arouse his curiosity in a manner that would pick at him after our meeting. After we finished exchanging views and niceties, he actually surprised me by asking for my number and address of the centre. Although it did concern me a little, I really wanted him to contact me again so I gave him my details. I was then informed by the probation worker, who was then joined by a counter-terrorist officer from SO15 (Counter Terror Command Met Police), that Abdi had strict licence conditions and if I was successful with him wanting to engage further with regards to mentoring, then I would need to support him in conforming with his conditions. One wrong step could send him back to prison immediately, so I needed to be vigilant.

Lo and behold, four days later Abdi sent me a text to say he wanted to come over to the ACF youth centre and continue further with mentoring, so I set a date and time and we agreed to meet again. Unfortunately Abdi did not turn up at that meeting and never responded to my calls for almost a week and a half, which was worrying. In a way I expected it. Some days later I got a text expressing his apologies but also explaining why he couldn't come, which was sadly due to a bereavement in the family. This allowed me to express my sincere condolences in the correct Islamic manner and extend some prayers, which I personally believe generated a bit of respect and in a way obligated him to meet me again. Abdi turned up two days later at the youth centre, where I knew he would re-evaluate his perceptions about me and my work. I took him for a tour and gave him the lowdown on how we do things, who we help, and why. I gave him examples of cases we had worked on and the outcomes thereafter, which were hard to ignore. A few young people who were the beneficiaries of our work were in the centre at the time and came across to talk about their issues and how they had been helped by ACF. I think this was something he never expected and it gave him something to think about, which was visible from his body language and expressions.

I emphasised that we tend to look at issues beyond our own front doors and that there were people in front of us who needed serious care and support, as well as in distant lands where suffering is rife. I chose words and phrases such as 'it's all about saving and changing lives for the better', and, 'stand up for fairness and justice'. I then introduced the outreach team and left him with them for a while. Although he was only supposed to be visiting for an hour, he ended up staying for three hours. Before leaving, he walked over to me and extended his arms to hug me and shake my hand. He thanked me for the introduction into my work at ACF, and asked whether it would be OK for him to come over on a regular basis and help out wherever he could. Obviously I was not going to say no to this, so I agreed that he could, as long as his probation worker gave permission. It was vital that they knew what was going on and he could see he had decided to engage further.

My intervention with Abdi started on a good footing and for the first few months it was going very smoothly. It did however hit some challenging times. Often these coincided with times when he would come back from his meetings with SO15 officers, who, in my opinion, needed to change their attitudes towards him. Instead of pushing him backwards, they should have been much more supportive and considerate than they were. They would use language like 'We know what you are up to and we are watching your every step and waiting for you to slip up'. If I had not heard these words myself, I would never have believed Abdi. So for the following day or two after these meetings it meant I had to go back to the start and pull him back into a positive space.

Luckily I had a lot of support from a remarkable person, Abdi's case worker in the Probation Service. She really gave her best and supported both Abdi and myself through some great challenges, mostly caused by SO15 officers and their continued negative attitude towards Abdi. It was as if they wanted him to trip up so they could send him back to prison. I had to look at ways of controlling my anger every time I attended such meetings, because I knew I had to work within the partnership framework in order to move Abdi forward in a positive way. It was clear that Abdi hated the police even more, and I now needed to address this issue and to reshape the landscape, so to speak. So I called an officer from the MCU in SO15 Command who I knew would jump at the chance of helping me.

The officer came over and met Abdi for the first time and we both went through the issues that were affecting him, primarily the SO15 officers mentioned previously. As you can imagine, the officer was not entirely pleased with what he heard and genuinely expressed his apologies for what was happening. He reassured Abdi and took it upon himself to look into the matter and to find a way of changing the approach of certain officers to support, rather than harass, him.

The officer came over a number of times to discuss progress and offer any assistance where and when needed, and I genuinely believe the meetings with him gave Abdi another insight into the police. It also allowed me to reinstate the fact that there are good and bad people in all walks of life and it is inevitable that we will encounter both; it's important how we then look at the two examples and apply our judgements to each individual, rather than the whole institution. I also reminded Abdi that he was a convicted terrorist, and, in all fairness, the police needed to maintain intelligence on him and to be vigilant and cautious at all times.

Over the next few months Abdi began to steam ahead and became a 'part of the furniture' as a volunteer with ACF. One evening, during Ramadhan, we needed to have a strong presence in our local area where gangs of young guys were causing some serious tensions. It was a unique situation; we had seen a female gang develop out of nowhere within a few weeks, and they were contributing to the growing tensions. Abdi came across one of the females, who had become isolated by her female friends and ended up right outside our youth centre, where another gang of males were hanging out. These young men noticed the female alone and began befriending her, and offering her a lift. Abdi noticed something was not right and quickly ran upstairs to call me and another colleague, we rushed outside to see the female was surrounded by young men all offering her a lift. It was obvious to me what was going on here, so we quickly intervened and asked the girl to come to one side so we could assess the situation and help her in some way.

With Abdi by our side throughout, we asked the girl what was wrong and where she needed to go. Shockingly, we were exposed to the foulest language one could imagine: the girl was telling us to 'f*** off', asking who the hell we were, and why we cared if she is in a difficult situation. Abdi was horrified by her response and almost walked off, but I asked him to stick around. We tried again to find out what was going on, though this time we decided to use the same 'street language' she clearly was accustomed to, of course without using foul words. She told us she was living in foster care, and that she needed to collect some more clothes from her mother's house as she only had one set, but that her mother didn't want her to come back home because her new partner did not want his step-daughter in the house.

Finding this very awkward, we decided to call the mother ourselves and tried to talk her into allowing us to accompany her daughter and to pick her clothes up. After hearing a lot of questioning and shouting by her mother on the phone, we managed to convince her to allow us to assist. This is where we had to make a very tough decision, because we did not have another female around to accompany us; it was very late, and calling the police was not going to be a good idea. We had to respond immediately, and do what we believed to be the 'right thing' to do given the circumstances. We invited the girl to come with us in our car, so we could a) get her away from the gang of boys and b) into a safer space.

Taking the young girl home gave us an insight into the bigger picture, and as we talked we realised she was in need of some urgent and serious help. In fact, she had been raped twice, once at very young age and the second time only months beforehand, by a young guy. There was so much more going on with this young 14-year-old and I cannot go into further detail, but it was very troubling.

Of course, Abdi was exposed to every detail surrounding the young female and it completely took him by surprise. I was absolutely furious and had to express myself by directing my anger inwards. I shouted out, 'We want to go and fight a war in Afghanistan and Somalia or Iraq to fight Americans, whilst here at home we have young girls being raped and abused by fellow Muslims. Shame on us all'. This changed everything. In fact I saw Abdi drop his head in his hands and cry. I think all three of us cried.

Without going into too much further detail about the girl's case, after helping her out with a wide-ranging support plan, we saw the change in front of our own eyes. This positive transformation on the girl had an enormous effect upon Abdi. He played a huge part in helping change a young person's life. From that day on, we began to chip away at Abdi's ideology and his previously held grievances. Slowly but surely we were bringing this young man back into the mainstream and getting him to open up more about his journey. In fact he took the initiative on many occasions to step forward in front of groups of young people to talk about how he was drawn to extremism and wanting to launch an attack. We had managed to redirect his energy and compassion towards a series of obvious and very real problems, and he could witness the difference his interventions made.

Abdi made some very valuable contributions to the Prevent work we were carrying out, and actually made significant inroads with another case I will be talking about further into the book. Although Abdi faced some difficult times during his transformation, especially with regards to being stopped randomly by SO15 officers and questioned about who and what he knows right in the middle of the street, he still managed to keep strong and overcome those issues. He went on to work with ACF for two years and then moved on to pastures new, but he still remains dedicated to community and youth work and pops over when he is free to offer his support and advice to change the lives of young people.

Analysis

Abdi lacked the critical thinking skills that would have enabled him to differentiate between right and wrong. His compassion and desire to help other people was overpowering his ability to rationalise the narratives and to refer back to what he 'actually' knew existed in the holy books. He had no other social network to fall back on or even belong to. His mother relied on him to be truthful, which he regrettably and eventually exploited without consideration.

There was a complete lack of awareness around the issues of extremism and home-grown terrorism at that time, and the educational welfare system, which would ordinarily look into why a young person is continually failing to attend school, either did not work for this individual or failed to investigate further enough to identify concerns. The absence of the Channel programme was another gap in the system that would have, at some point, picked up on a number of concerning factors that were clearly visible. Due to the lack of awareness or failure in the system at that time, these concerning factors were not detected.

Even after his incarceration, Abdi was drawn further into extremism by the very system that should have considered the consequences of its attitudes and behaviour towards him. How did they think this would translate, once he would be released into society? We can see how good and bad people from all walks of life, whether they are police officers, prison guards, teachers, probation workers or normal citizens, can significantly contribute to both positive and negative transformation of an impressionable young person. It also demonstrates how change can be infectious in many ways, given the right application and creating the right kind of environment.

CASE STUDY 3

Profile/Name ID: Ali

Gender: Male

Age range: Early 20s

Ethnicity: Mixed race

Language: English

Other: Diagnosed ADHD

Theological understanding: Convert, very basic understanding, seeking more knowledge

Case Background

Ali was referred to me directly by his mother who was very concerned about her son and the people around him. She called me out of the blue one day and began explaining about her son.

Her particular concern initially was about her son being radicalised and manipulated by others to follow their religion. She mentioned that he was diagnosed and suffers from ADHD and is on medication for it. She went on to describe how she tried to communicate the same message to her local authority and the Police, and after they ignored her pleas she went to the local Mosque to try and get some help from the Imam. Everyone was failing her and shrugged her off as paranoid and angry simply because her son had turned to another faith. Although she did come across as being very worried, I never got the feeling from her that she had a problem with her son crossing over from his faith into Islam. She told me that she also suffers from anxiety and depression and was getting counselling for this condition. I continued to ask her more questions around why she thought her son was being recruited by extremists.

After hearing that he was given gifts, was going out a lot more often with new friends, had begun to slowly withdraw from the family, had started arguing with his mother about her drinking alcohol and eating *haram* (forbidden) food, all the while claiming that they will burn in hellfire, it became quite obvious that Ali was adopting an extreme view. Our conversation went on for well over an hour, so I asked her to write everything in an email and provide as much detail as possible. I received the email the next morning, which she sent in the very early hours of the morning, which also indicated she was having trouble sleeping. The contents of her email were very concerning and it meant I had to act immediately. Without wasting time, I called a good friend in the MCU SO15 Command, who I knew would advise me in the best way possible. The officer, being the good man he is, shot over to see me the same day, and after going over the email, I called the mother, firstly to establish in my own mind that this was real and not a hoax, and secondly to allow the officer to hear the mother's plight with his own ears.

I explained to the mother that I was with another person who I knew and who was from the police, just to let her know I was going to put her on loudspeaker and another person was listening. She was happy to talk frankly, even knowing there would be a police officer with me. We went through the whole story again, which included how she felt her local authorities had let her down and failed to appreciate that her son was being radicalised. After hearing from Ali's mother, both the officer and I needed to make a quick decision. We agreed that meeting with both parents was now the next step to fully understand what and where the problem was and how we could assist. Meeting Ali's parents was very useful; they seemed quite stable and both of them came across as supportive and loving parents. The father had an excellent job and was clued-up, generally.

After the meeting we established a clear fact: Ali was indeed being drawn into an extreme network and that network was now applying their indoctrination and separation tactics. Buying him new trainers, leather jackets, picking him up and dropping him off and paying for his food; these are key tactics applied by such groups as they 'invest in their asset'. The next step was to meet Ali, which I did on my own two days later, and this is where everything became crystal clear. He asked many questions about who I was and why his mother had suggested he meet me, and asked some questions which I believe were suggested to him by his friends. After answering each of his questions with ease, it seemed he was satisfied that I was 'okay'. I asked how the relationship between him and his parents was getting on and if he had any concerns or issues with them or at home generally. This is where the stories began to clash and contradict with what his mother had told us. Ali asked me to step outside so we could go for a walk, and clearly this was so he could talk to me privately. He claimed that his mother had been hostile towards him since the day he told her he had converted, and he told me that he had actually converted almost 12 months prior to telling her. The father was surprised at the conversion, Ali told me, but he had sat down and discussed everything with his son and began to accept it. However, his mother had serious problems with his conversion, because she felt she had failed her son in some way. She was a devout Catholic and could not accept her own son leaving that faith. Ali went on to explain that he didn't like going home anymore and waited until very late in the evening before returning, simply because he did not wish to argue with his mother every day. He claimed that she was becoming very abusive towards him and his new faith, and it was something he could not tolerate any longer. He told me that it was something he expected, because people like his mother will never accept Islam and will always oppose it. I asked why he thought that way and reminded him that he was talking about his mother. He looked at me in a strange way and said, '*Akhi* (brother) you should know the *kuffar* (non-believers) will never accept Islam and will not be satisfied until we are all non-believers, even our own parents will try to prevent us from following the truth'. In my view, it sounded like something he had been told over and over again; it is a standard methodology used by extremist recruiters. It is a process that is used to exploit some of the push and pull factors. Supposedly, the parents – either one or both – will object to the conversion and naturally try to convince him to reconsider, which will then cause friction, disruption and eventually the breakup of a family. The end result being exclusion or self-exclusion from the home, removing any or all the natural protective factors around the individual, and he becomes isolated from any 'other influencing' source. This then allows the recruiter to apply the pull factors, by actually encouraging this process and then welcoming him into their tight-knit group and surrounding him with support in every conceivable form.

I tried to explain a few things regarding Ali's duty towards his parents in line with his newly adopted faith, which he did take on board. But sadly, due to what was happening at home, it wasn't working well. I had many follow-up meetings with him and slowly began to achieve some real progress. Each session was a challenge because I had to literally draw pictures to get him to see things more clearly. You often get carried away in conversation, forgetting the other person isn't keeping up with what is being said (ADHD was also a problem here), so I had to restart, explaining in a lot more detail and by giving examples.

Unfortunately things were getting worse at home between mother and son, inevitably pushing Ali out completely, and he ended up moving far away, closer to the grasp of the extremist support network. This situation posed a number of challenges and I now had to liaise with three different Police forces, just so I could continue with my interventions and try to change the trajectory of this young man. It took me a few days to meet and discuss my new plan of action and to consider the increasing risks now posed to both myself and others. Eventually my interventions restarted and I was driving up and down the country almost daily to engage with Ali. Now, though, the engagement was more challenging because each time we met, you could see the eyes looking out of the windows of the tiny houses in a very narrow street. The first meeting I had with Ali in his new place completely changed the whole ball-game. He had just got married to a female he hardly knew, and who had been put forward by his now very close network of 'brothers'. This is a tactic applied as an irreversible means to secure and control the investment, and a general practice used by many recruiters worldwide. Ali explained how he needed to find a partner who would understand him and stabilise him. He told me how 'the brothers' supported him and gave him a house to live in and a part-time job. Within a week the circumstances surrounding Ali had changed, and his whole attitude began to destroy any plans I had put in place to turn him around. I used every single trick in the book and more, to try to pull him back to a space where I could breach the protective layer put around him by his network – but it was looking impossible.

It took several months and many thousands of motorway miles before I could see a chink and a potential for change. I went back to the parents many times asking for more information about his childhood or other events which I could use, but received nothing much to go on. One day his mother told me about a friend she had in Europe, where she had once sent Ali to be 'de-radicalised'. This friend had recently advised Ali's mother to use pork in his pasta every day, which would create a continuous appetite for him to eat it, in turn making it harder for him to continue as a Muslim. She asked if eating pork would take him out of the fold of Islam and whether this could be an option to consider. I asked if she had done this in the past and if Ali noticed the addition of meat in his pasta; her response was yes, and that it caused a big fight in the house. It was actually one of the main reasons why he left.

My next trip to see Ali was to be much better, as I now knew the real reason for him leaving, something I could then use in my intervention. I asked him to look at what lengths his mother was going to in order to protect him from what she cannot see, only because she is a mother. I gave him chapter and verse about the son's duty towards his mother even if she was not a Muslim, and the significance of this. After a few hours I managed to get him to agree to visit his mother and promised him that I would accompany him too. Strangely he felt more comfortable with me being with him. When I asked him why, he replied by saying, 'You understand me better'. We ended up meeting at the parents' home a few days later, where both parents and two of his siblings were present. Everything was going smoothly for at least half an hour and then suddenly his mother asked why he left home, and Ali explained everything in front of his father. This caused a serious eruption, and it looked rather like I was about to see both a crusade and a *jihad* kick off within the same household.

I met Ali a few days after the incident and urged him to think of it as a mother going to extreme lengths to protect her child. I asked him not to relay what happened to anyone else, as it was a personal family matter and nobody outside of that needed to know. This softened him up a bit. I continued my engagement for another few weeks and encouraged him to join a group of young guys on a trip we had planned, where we would be hosting a number of physically and mentally challenging activities. Surprisingly, but luckily, Ali agreed to join us, and I organised the trip as soon as I could. The general idea was to take Ali out of his support network and comfort zone in order to loosen the grip of the recruiter, and more importantly to allow him to see some things a little differently. In the end, the trip gave him an overwhelming reminder that the world is not against him, nor is it at odds with Islam. We introduced him to a number of personalities: local and other young people, police, as well as some members of the British Armed forces, who he actually became friends with – although they were not in uniform and no one knew their actual identities or careers until the last day around a dinner table. This created a very positive environment but also a situation where Ali became vulnerable to our 'positive' mentoring and afforded me, and the wider team, the space to push a message across for him to internalize and seriously consider. That message consisted of raising the questions about his actual knowledge of his faith in terms of how the messenger of God lived his life, how he conducted himself and what the actual commands of God are in terms of living and contributing to society. Ali had no knowledge of any of these theological stories, raising a number of legitimate questions about the learning he has been exposed to by his network, which was in fact centred entirely on intolerance and war. I finished the evening off by handing him a book to read about the manners of a Muslim and how crucial it was for him and every single Muslim to follow and apply those manners. Finally I urged him to protect himself from agendas driven by other people, aiming at his 'brothers' and reminding him that they are ultimately human and will not always be perfect or even truthful. How could they be sincere if they have caused or supported the division between parents and their child? I reminded him of the commands from God, 'do not sever ties of kinship'- and 'be dutiful towards parents'.

After leaving him that evening I deliberately avoided calling Ali for over a week, allowing him to absorb what I had left him with. Then I got a text message one late evening asking if I could come see him urgently the next morning. After getting clearance from all the police forces, I set out to visit him, and just as I entered the town I got a call from him asking to meet at an industrial estate behind a warehouse, which I found very strange and worrying. Carefully driving up to the gates I noticed him hanging outside with the book I gave him in his hand. He ran over to me and jumped in the car and then asked me to drive away from that area. After driving him to another area we decided to go for a walk. I asked him to leave his phone in the car because he said he had something important to discuss. Ali then took apart his phone, taking the battery and sim card out and placed everything under the floor mat in the back of the car. This was, of course, an action I was very familiar with and I questioned why he had done that. He didn't know why I questioned his action, so I asked him whether that was standard procedure when he met his 'brothers', and he said that it was. I then asked whether they went into a premises and whether he would be searched after entering a room. He affirmed he was always searched and asked how I knew these things. I then told him about my experiences and asked him to try and keep up and then compare what his experiences were. He told me exactly the same as what I had described, but this time his face was looking very pale and I noticed him rock from side to side, trying to moisten his lips at the same time. It was clear he now realised he was in a difficult situation and he became very worried. He asked for me to get him out of there as a matter of urgency and told me he would pack his belongings secretly overnight and one by one he would take his bags out and leave them by the back of a warehouse so he could collect them once I arrived with a van to extract him safely.

Exercise

1. Can you identify the vulnerability factors in this case?
2. What are the 'push' and 'pull' factors in this case?
3. Can you identify the key risk factors in this case?
4. What steps would you take to minimise the risks identified?

Analysis

Ali was a genuinely kind-natured young man who grew up with both parents taking extra care with him due to his learning difficulty and ADHD problems. This care often meant that Ali would want time away from being treated like a young child or someone with a disability, because he needed to do things he found other young men of his age doing. He was quite clever and was very athletic; he really wanted to explore his potential. The mother's inability to give him a little slack put strain on their relationship and resulted in a bit of a gap between mother and son. Ali wanted some freedom, whereas his mother was reluctant to allow that due his 'vulnerabilities'. And because Ali saw his older brother enjoy the trappings of adulthood and the freedom to go out whenever he wanted, it became a point of conflict when Ali was denied that. As this was not managed effectively it caused a shift in Ali's behaviour; he opted to go to university far away from home, purely to have his own space and time to explore life in his own way. This phase allowed him to find more friends, a group who became quite close and loyal to one another in all aspects. Ali's exploration phase drew him closer to Islam, as it was mainly the religion his friends followed. This is where commonalities began to pull him further away from the mainstream, as they discussed their strong feelings about the plight of the Palestinians and the lack of support for their cause by the West. Ali was given importance and made to feel a part of something that was exploring ways to support less fortunate people.

Once Ali converted to Islam it created a huge disconnect between mother and son – in fact it caused a lot of hostility, and subsequently resulted in resentment between them. This was ultimately a major contribution to the push factor that was constantly, although inadvertently, being applied by the mother, who could not see what additional pull factors were being deployed by the recruiters who were surrounding her son. The knowledge and understanding of the attitudinal shifts of parents when their child adopts another faith, or where there is a dramatic change in behaviour, often allows the recruiters to apply their dismantling process. A severance of the ties of relationship between family and friends becomes a natural outcome, the narrative being, 'they (non-

Muslims) will never accept your faith and will not be satisfied until you believe in what they believe, and they will become hostile towards you because they are ignorant to the truth and have been overcome by Satan and his whispers'.

The mother's criticism of her son's newly adopted faith was a critical error. But the strain that was eventually caused could have been reduced if the local authority's services had provided the support that was needed to understand the serious nature of the situation. Eventually, after so much time and hard work, and after the enormous stress and fatigue of all the various interventions, the support and the determination to continue and the joined-up approach by three different police forces allowed for a successful outcome and the protection and positive transformation of Ali.

CASE STUDY 4

Profile/Name ID: MM

Gender: Male

Age range: Late teens

Ethnicity: Somali/Bravanese

Educational profile: College drop-out

Language: English/Brava/Arabic

Family: Absent father

Other: Gang affiliation

Theological understanding: Advanced

Case Background

MM was known to me through the ACF Youth Centre and was engaged by the Outreach Team due to his gang affiliation and activity within the local area. He was part of a large group of young Somali boys who were causing a lot of disruption and unrest; in fact they were known to the local authorities as being the hardest of all young men to reach and connect with. The police requested some support to try to engage with this gang in order to stem the growing gang tensions which were spiralling out of control. I remember MM being a cool, calm individual who never really expressed himself much, but clearly had a huge influence within his clique. In my opinion he was 'the thinker' and although he wasn't the obvious leader, he was the one who they all listened to. For me, he was the one within the gang that most troubled me. I know about a few occasions where he had convinced some of his gang to go out and attack three boys from a local estate, because they had threatened him when he was in college, but the reason he gave his boys was that the other boys were trying to take over their hustling ground.

The ACF Outreach Team were successful in engaging with him and over a period of a few weeks we began to see this gang trickle in through the doors of the youth centre. This caused a lot of disruption to our daily work whilst engaging with other groups of young people, but we managed to keep things under control. The problem that was brewing was not inside the centre but rather outside, because the three guys from the estate that were attacked by MM's boys were preparing a revenge attack and were building momentum by recruiting more boys. It was brought to my attention just at the right time by a young female, who had a friend who was a girlfriend of one of the boys from the estate. Because they were both African, I instructed Abdi (case study 1) to befriend MM and others in the gang, in an effort to convince them to participate in one of our projects known as Adventurous Training. The idea was to get this gang out of the local area for a few days, whilst a few members of the Outreach Team remain behind in order to squash the conflict by engaging the other crew.

As usual, organising the trip involved numerous partners including local residents, politicians and many others. A group of over 50 people descended upon the fells of the Lake District, 30 of whom were young Somali gang members who had never in their lives experienced the beauty of the Lakes. It was also unusual for the local residents in Kendal, who had equally never seen such a sight, where so many 'dodgy-looking' hooded black boys were running up and down the hills. It was winter and the snow was knee-deep in certain parts, making the mood drift from gloom to excitement and then back to despair. After arriving at the lodge and getting the protocols in place, we shaped the following day's activities by separating the group into three teams, each selecting their own leader and each team competing against each other. Chris Donnelly was always at hand to support the project and managed to garner a lot of support from many influential locals to join in the programme. All our partners knew the objectives we had set out to achieve and were distributed amongst the three teams to engage and initiate the mentoring. Abdi was tasked to stick close to MM and soften him a bit whilst identifying other options for future positive interaction. The following day we had both snow and rain, which actually pushed every single participant to their mental and physical limit, including some of the soldiers and police officers who joined the group. This caused an unplanned but very fruitful outcome, where teamwork and supporting one another through some hostile terrain was a natural outcome within each team. Police officers being helped by young gang boys, soldiers pulling young boys back up after falling and carrying them on occasion and vice versa. It was a wonderful sight to see and hearing the stories they shared after returning was amazing. After changing up and having a big get-together dinner in the evening, everyone had to share their experience in front of the whole group. Ordinarily this would never have happened, but the environment generated the outcome. Abdi stood up and talked about his personal journey in and out of prison for terrorism. The room went very silent; in fact it was a very powerful moment which shook the whole group, especially the gang boys. After a while when everything settled down and people began drifting away to their rooms, Abdi was called outside by MM. I saw them leave but never saw them return, because they were outside for a long time.

However, in the morning I had Abdi banging on my door wanting to talk with me urgently, so I let him in and he sat down to talk, though he found it hard to express himself coherently as he was in a panicked state and was struggling to catch his breath. I managed to calm him down and then listened to his concerns. MM had spoken to him, in confidence, about his thoughts on how he wanted to make homemade explosives and letter bombs so he could deliver them to a number of people who he believed to be enemies of Islam. After Abdi enquired about his understanding of who and why he considers them to be enemies of Islam, MM replied by saying they had colluded to attack Muslim women – in fact he said they mentioned they would attack his mother first and rip her hijab off and spit in her face.

When asked who these guys were, MM said that they were from his college and had only begun being hostile towards him after he had an argument with his teacher, who was Afro-Caribbean. This teacher had refused to allow him to raise some points and listen to his concerns during a discussion in class, and then subsequently excluded him from college after MM was persistent in making his point. Thereafter, three guys who were also Afro-Caribbean began harassing MM, claiming they didn't like the fact that he had an argument with their teacher. MM felt the system seemed to be against him and his faith. Though he originally merely disagreed with his teacher on a fairly trivial matter, it ended up in a heated debate when the teacher decided to exclude him. MM felt the only way to protect himself and his mother was through the violence he had become accustomed to by being involved in gangs, and the solution was to hurt his enemy in a violent way. The gang mentality kicked in; it was in his opinion the only way he could react to such a threat.

After hearing this from Abdi, we decided between ourselves to manage this situation as quickly as possible and try to direct MM's aggression in a more positive manner. The following days were tense and stressful, but we both managed to bounce off each other and convince MM that he could respond to his situation in a calmer manner, and we encouraged him to look at his need for revenge to be harnessed and re-energised in a progressive and positive way. Abdi spent a lot more time with MM throughout the trip and explained in much more detail how he had similar feelings and the need to do something drastic. Yet after following his emotions and wanting to avenge the loss of life of innocent people in Afghanistan, he ended up being incarcerated for a long time. Abdi made this point very clearly and I followed it through with MM when given the chance, by showing an alternative to violence and taking him through a visual journey where his success in life would actually form part of his revenge, which would be clearly visible for him and his adversaries to see and feel.

I also took him through the potential consequences of his actions if he failed to accept our idea. It came to a point where MM began sketching out his future and planned how, if he succeeded in life, it would hurt his perceived enemies much more than physical harm or even killing them. This allowed MM to feel as though he was the one in control and that he was making his own choices, describing how he would follow his plan step by step and take it easy to avoid mistakes. MM felt he had devised this plan himself and seemed much more relaxed afterwards.

I gave MM chapter and verse both from an ethical as well as a theological point of view, in regards to his desire to express himself through violence. We continued with this messaging for quite some time and created the time and the space for MM to join in with some of the projects and other activities put together by the organisation. The idea was to take up his time, preventing the creep or relapse back into gang activity. We call this our '**SANCTIONS**' model, an acronym for Setting Actions, Negotiating Constraint Tactics by Implementing Observation and the Neutralisation Strategy. This is a model that we implement after going a fair distance on a positive path, and we encourage (via suggestion) the individual to conform to the process. It allows us to set the ground rules, like a license condition, except it is voluntary and agreed upon by the individual. We **S**et the **A**ctions and we **N**egotiate where he/she should or shouldn't go or who they meet, which allows for the **C**onstraint **T**actics to work in favour of the mentoring and shaping of the case. Working with other institutions, like the schools, colleges or even employers and parents, helps us to **I**mplement the **O**bservation, so we know where the individual has or will be going. This then allows for the **N**eutralisation **S**trategy to work as a natural outcome.

Both Abdi and myself followed up on a daily basis and helped MM through the process, firstly by calling a different college for a meeting to discuss MM's return to studies. However, this process had its issues and whilst I appreciate the rules set out by schools and colleges, I had to use a more convincing argument than usual to gain the principal's support, which wasn't forthcoming initially. In fact, he only came around to the idea after I told him I would be left with no option and would be forced to expose his failure to support a young person who could very easily become a statistic in the event of something serious happening. After explaining the reason for his exclusion from the other college and possibilities of repercussions if support wasn't forthcoming, the principal decided to accept MM on a course and give him the chance he needed. MM went back to college and completely followed through on his plans. Today, he is working as a trainee accountant in a financial consulting company and is married with two wonderful kids of his own.

Exercise

1. Can you identify the vulnerability factors in this case?
2. What are the 'push' and 'pull' factors in this case?
3. Can you identify the key risk factors in this case?
4. What steps would you take to minimise the risks identified?

Analysis

MM was not a naïve young man who didn't know right from wrong. He was quite the opposite: he was intelligent and had the capacity to apply himself in any given situation. The breakdown came about due to a teacher's inability to recognise a number of grievances displayed by this young man, and by an unprofessional response to these grievances. This response added more fuel to an already inflamed situation, which was exacerbated by the circumstances that followed. MM was trying to express legitimate concerns and only required an explanation to some questions in order to assess what was best needed to solve his problems. The trigger point was the lack of patience and the confrontational nature in which the teacher responded to a young man, who was by no means anybody's fool; indeed, he had quite an overwhelming personality. He was calm and spoke only when he needed to and without nonsense, and he held himself very well. So for the teacher to treat him like a child in front of the rest of the class and undermine him in such a way was a recipe for disaster. MM responded calmly to the teacher's aggression, but was then met with further ridicule which ultimately generated a similar response from MM. The result of this exchange was MM's exclusion from the college, where he was then subjected to harassment and threats by the teacher's 'perceived favoured' students. The three young men who were also affiliated to a local gang were of Afro-Caribbean origin, the same as the teacher, which is why MM believed the teacher had something to do with the threats. MM internalised this to a level where he began to plot and plan his revenge, which he continuously played out in his mind. By attacking the three boys in such a way, it would send a shocking message to the teacher and in turn make him feel responsible for what happened. Reaching out to young people involved in gangs, or a street culture, who only know limited ways of responding to such situations is crucial, and it needs to happen across the board. If we continue to fail in this aspect of outreach and engagement then we can only expect the worst to come from our societies. Young people expressing themselves can often become very challenging and will inevitably cause rebellion if we fail to address their grievances. The London riots are one prime example of collective failure where an unexpected situation evolved – gangs that ordinarily harboured deep-rooted rivalry joined forces right across the city, and even in other parts of the country, unified by either perceived or legitimate injustices. MM's situation could have very easily caused devastation if his plans were realised, which may have generated greater disruption and division within communities as a direct result of his acts of terror. Consideration must be given to the young person's credibility or status as a young man, where undermining them can develop an internalisation of grievances, directly pushing them further away beyond reach and rationale.

CASE STUDY 5

Profile/Name ID: LA

Gender: Female

Age range: Mid-teens

Ethnicity: White British

Educational profile: Unknown

Language: English

Family: Single parent/mother

Other: Muslim convert

Theological understanding: Very limited

Case Background:

As I don't want to risk giving out details that might help identify this next individual, I have to be careful not to go into too much detail during this case study. But even with certain things obscured, I believe it will be enormously useful and interesting to the reader.

Lindsey is a young teenager who never really had much stability in her life, due to the breakdown between parents and her having to live in and out of foster homes. She had a small number of friends around her, who would often cause trouble and were known by the local police; so from an early age she had a disrespect for and lack of trust in the authorities. Her friends were mostly male and spoke Arabic very fluently and she was always looked after by these friends; she became familiar with their culture and it became one of her dreams to travel to an Arab country and settle down with an Arab husband. She trusted the few friends she had and was loyal to them. Lindsey has no learning disabilities and was not a naïve person at all; she was quite bright and has excellent abilities and personal qualities.

However, her friends had a lot of strong and deep-rooted feelings for their country of origin, which was at that time in turmoil and civil war. They were exposed to extreme views against 'the West', meaning Europe, UK and the USA. Lindsey was exposed to these same narratives when her friends would repeat what they heard from their relatives or elders. The situation became such that most of what the friends talked about together was the West's intentions to destroy their lands and steal the oil. Lindsey converted to Islam and soon found a boyfriend. Naturally her mother questioned why she had changed her faith and challenged her decision and rationale for doing so, though she did eventually accept it, albeit reluctantly. One of her close friends travelled abroad with some others, communicating with Lindsey regularly while he was away, and eventually Lindsey also tried to travel abroad, which led to a lot of concern from her family. She did not understand the worries and firmly believed she was doing the right thing by supporting her Muslim brethren and close friends abroad as she attempted to live 'her dream'.

Even after I'd met her on numerous occasions and explained to her what could have happened, she still believed she was not doing anything wrong. It took a few months to get her to see a fuller picture and the potential consequences of her travelling to a war zone, which might have resulted in tragic circumstances. We went through every single detail of the potentials of what might have happened, and discussed widely her arguments in wanting to look out for and support her friends. We discussed how friends, teachers or even our own parents do not know everything and they too will be wrong at times. I had to continuously remind her how to critically analyse information, even if it is from the most credible sources. Lindsey knew nothing about the actual fundamentals of Islam, yet she believed she had a purpose in life and that she should follow in the footsteps of her close friends, who were always reminding her about what they believe is the right thing to do.

Exercise

1. Can you identify the vulnerability factors in this case?
2. What are the 'push' and 'pull' factors here?
3. Can you identify the key risk factors?
4. What steps would you take to minimise the risks identified?

Analysis

Lindsey's key vulnerability in this whole situation was simply her genuine respect and love for her friends, and her imaginary future of living abroad in an Arab country with her future husband. Her trust in this friendship and her desire to live in an Arab country almost cost her everything, including her life. Incredibly, this was something she was prepared to sacrifice for her friends and her dreams. The group dynamic in this situation is an overwhelming phenomenon that needs further investigation by practitioners and educators to fully understand. It is this dynamic that has caused a number of young people to sever ties of kinship and break away from their families and loved ones.

The three schoolgirls from east London who left to travel to join ISIS in February 2015 were exposed to a similar dynamic. The strength and power of these relationships between young people need to be considered at every level of engagement by teachers, front-line staff and parents. Something else to consider is the lack of trust in authority by young people like Lindsey, who have grown up to resent the police and the government. It is a problem across the world, where young men and women are exposed to crime or anti-social behaviour, and then harbour a natural resentment towards authorities when they attempt to crack down on it. This can only change if we change our ways of dealing with the problems and our attitude towards young people when we engage with them.

CASE STUDY 6

Profile/Name ID: Tony

Gender: Male

Age range: Early teens

Ethnicity: African

Educational profile: Drop-out

Language: English

Family: Single mother

Other: Petty crime and drug abuse

Theological understanding: Convert to Islam, virtually nil

Case Background

Tony was involved in low-level petty crime and drug abuse, and, due to this, he was well known to the police. He was caught up in a few criminal acts, which eventually led him to prison. He spent some time in a young offender's institute, causing him further issues around his drug misuse, which led to him developing some significant mental health problems. He was also exposed to some 'Muslim brothers' inside prison who encouraged him to follow Islam as his religion. At the forefront of daily discussions with fellow inmates were the usual 'them against us' theories that occur in most prison wings, with the predominantly Afro-Caribbean inmates pitting themselves against the 'white man' and believing that Islam was the 'obvious' solution to all their problems. Islam is certainly the faith of choice for most Afro-Caribbean offenders within the prison system and Tony was not an exception in this regard. He told me later that he had found a good network of brothers who looked out for him. However, due to his growing mental instability, he was soon transferred into a mental hospital prison where he could be assisted more appropriately. This is where another key, and very worrying, development was identified by doctors and other staff: they discovered that Tony had been researching firearms on the internet, and was becoming obsessed with them as time progressed. At this stage, the staff told me that he was praying almost hourly and facing different directions. Although he had no knowledge of how to pray, he knew it was at least five times a day.

I was called in to meet Tony and assess the situation with a 'Prevent/Extremism' lens and to identify any concerns surrounding extremist views or ideology. When I assessed his 'ideology, intent and capability' I found no immediate 'red flag' concerns, but I was anxious about his vulnerabilities: his mental health problem primarily, but also his affiliation with certain individuals who had criminal backgrounds, and his obsession for guns. He was clearly at high risk of indoctrination by others with an ulterior motive, and who could easily manipulate this young man's vulnerability and obsession. He was ideally placed, was easily accessible by others and was searching for more knowledge about his new faith. It was an obvious case in which I needed to intervene and help manage him away from potential risk of recruitment.

He was released on probation shortly afterwards and continued to engage with me for a while, until he was given direction by people in his area who were much closer to him than I was. He met with me on a weekly basis, whilst he was being engaged by them almost daily, and they quite easily managed to 'pull' him away, offering him the solution to his needs, and indeed to theirs too. The street dynamic works in many different ways, but is fundamentally based upon mutual needs and understanding. He was told, 'You scratch our back and we'll scratch yours', which allowed him to further his obsession for guns as well as breaking away from 'his shackles'. He was being driven to believe that he had no future in this country, firstly because of his skin colour and now more so because he was Muslim. They told him his only option was to travel abroad and join 'their' network, where not only would he be welcomed as a brother and be provided for, but he could have his own guns to keep and use.

After a week or so, Tony went AWOL and almost managed to travel abroad – luckily he was stopped at the right time. Surprisingly, Tony wasn't stopped because he was being watched by security services; it was simply because he was on probation license after early release from prison and was not supposed to leave the immediate locality. He was picked up by police who had randomly stopped him and realised he was in breach of his license. Immediately, Tony was sent back to prison to serve the remaining few weeks of his sentence. After a few weeks I visited him, at his request, because 'he needed to speak to someone other than his legal team and was in need of some positive mentoring'. He received me very well and seemed happy to talk about what happened and where he was intending to travel. I asked him why he wanted to travel to somewhere where there was a war going on, especially when it wasn't even the country of his origin. His response was not surprising, but it was a very quick realisation of my original fears for this young man. He explained how he knew friends who were already in that country and they offered to find him a partner and create a new life. Mainly, though, he would be allowed the use of machine guns, which he explained was his ultimate dream. I asked whether he felt this would lead to shooting at other people, to which he replied that he hadn't thought about it too much, he just felt too excited about the chance of using a machine gun.

The security system didn't know much about his plans and reason for travel, and of course this new information meant that sadly Tony had to serve a lengthy prison sentence, where he will no doubt find himself exposed to some more very violent individuals, and also some equally narrow-minded prison officers who will likely substantiate his existing grievances. It is not my intention to undermine every prison officer; but, simply and truthfully, there are some who are on a 'power trip', believe that they 'know it all', or are inconsiderate in their approach to dealing with vulnerable young men. All this does is continue to support the narratives of those incarcerated. It needs to be addressed.

Exercise

1. Can you identify the vulnerability factors in this case?
2. What are the 'push' and 'pull' factors?
3. Can you identify the key risk factors?
4. What steps would you take to minimise the risks identified?

Before you do the exercise, let's take a look at a potential scenario in this case and identify the possible solutions.

This young man is released after serving the rest of his license in prison, which was only a matter of weeks. And then his friends or 'brothers' wanted to use him for a violent act, by knowing his obsession, what do you think could happen? Or what about if Tony was eventually released from prison after his now very lengthy sentence, locked up with other violent individuals, often with very extreme views, and without any specific mentoring, whilst he still held an obsession for using guns?

There would certainly be individuals in the community who were aware of his desires and his mental status – in particular those individuals who have links to terrorist groups overseas, and those who have access to guns. What would be the main concern for you? What do you think should be the primary objective? How could you change the potential (or even the inevitable) scenario?

Always consider the consequences of any action or reaction; the main idea is to change the trajectory of the individual in a manner and at a time where consequential damage does not occur.

Analysis

Tony clearly had many issues and vulnerabilities: his adoption of a new faith, being led by others who may follow a very extreme interpretation of that faith, and without having any idea of how to practise it or indeed what the basic fundamentals were; his obsession with firearms; his mental status, limiting his ability to consider the pros and cons; an inability to critically analyse information or think about the consequences of his actions. It all prevented him from seeing how others were abusing and exploiting his vulnerabilities. He needed a constructive, formalised support network which could have very easily directed his obsession for guns towards something much more positive. After being released on license, he was sent back in to his usual environment, his local area where he was further exposed to circumstances beyond his control and where he had been previously involved in criminal acts. Tony's parents were completely oblivious to his current situation, and his lack of an ability to protect himself from exploitation and harm. The limits of the probation system meant that Tony was not able to move or live in an alternative area, and could only be mentored once per week.

Without constant and sustained support, Tony will remain a significant threat to society due to his vulnerabilities, in particular whilst he continues to be obsessed with using guns. It is for us, collectively, to identify such concerns and, instead of applying the usual approach of incarceration for a period, we need to address the clear and present concerns and provide the right solutions.

CASE STUDY 7

This was not a case I had worked on. But there are many references to this case on the internet and important indicators for us all to take note and learn from. I have condensed this with some questions we need to look at and learn from.

Profile/Name ID: Brusthom Ziamani

Gender: Male

Age range: 19

Ethnicity: African/Congolese

Educational profile: College

Language: English

Family: Well structured

Other: Petty crime

Theological understanding: Jehovah's Witness

Case Background

Born and bred in a family of Jehovah's Witnesses, Brusthom Ziamani had a strict religious upbringing and was also a sports enthusiast, mainly involved in boxing and parkour, but was also involved in various aspects of petty crime. As a child he was taken to knock on people's doors to 'proselytise and evangelise' in an attempt to convert people to his religion. His faith meant he never celebrated his birthday or even Christmas. As a young black guy growing up in south London he slowly grew distant from his faith. After his parents discovered that their son had become a Muslim, they offered him two options: either abide by their rules and stay within the family home, or continue as a Muslim and leave immediately. He responded to the ultimatum by continuing to follow Islam, so Ziamani was thrown out of the house and onto the streets.

Homeless and alone, Ziamani ended up staying in a local mosque in South London. This is where he was targeted by extremists, who offered him a place to stay and provided him with food and clothing and fulfilled other general needs. He was quickly pulled into their ranks. Within weeks, he was openly making extreme statements and was at the forefront of protests organized by Anjem Choudary. A few more weeks down the line, riled and inspired by the killing of Lee Rigby, he himself was involved in a plot to behead a soldier and emulate the actions of Michael Adebolajo. His initial plans were to go off to Syria and fight amongst the *jihad*ists there, but he did not have the means to do so and therefore decided to plot an attack on UK soil. Amongst all of this, he was also intent upon converting his girlfriend to Islam, but when she rejected his attempts, he threatened to 'wipe her out'.

Exercise

Here are some very critical questions for you to consider and to examine for future reference:

1. What could the parents have done differently?
2. The young man changed his faith, but did that change the fact he was still their child?
3. Did you notice any 'push factors' in this case?
4. What were the 'pull factors' surrounding this young man?
5. What do you think were the obvious vulnerability factors?
6. How could it be possible for this young man to understand a completely different faith within such a short period of time? What kind of strategy did the extremists apply?

Analysis

The rapid indoctrination of this young man is a clear example of how extremist recruiters can manipulate and change a young man's identity completely, to a point where the individual becomes careless of their own personal wellbeing and that of their loved ones. It is also evident that when the natural protective factors are taken down or fail to exist, when young people are pushed out and are exposed to circumstances beyond their control, the journey of manipulation is often a swift one. We need to examine when, how, why and where the breakdown came about and indeed what could, or should , have been done to prevent it. These are pertinent questions we all need to consider and understand, because there are clearly a lot more young men and women who are, and will no doubt find themselves, facing similar situations.

WHAT WE HAVE LEARNED SO FAR

The threat of terrorist attacks on home soil and on that of our near neighbours in Europe is high. It doesn't look likely that this will change in the foreseeable future – *unless* there is a comprehensive change in our attitude and approach in dealing with the problem, by examining both the root causes as well as the best solutions. It would be incredibly dangerous to believe that this is only a Muslim problem and to ask the Muslim world to deal with it alone. It would be equally dangerous, and unfair, to call for changes to be made in regards to how Muslims practise their faith in Western countries. It is my opinion that such 'solutions' will have the ultimate impact of actually making the situation worse, because they will further divide communities and nations. In any event, these concepts hold little water in light of the evidence and examples we have at hand, that the majority of individuals joining terrorist groups have either very limited or completely no understanding of their faith.

Having engaged with hundreds of at-risk and dangerous individuals over many years, I have found that many of them simply needed someone who they can relate to, engage with and trust. The issues they are concerned or angry about vary greatly. Western foreign policy and the ongoing conflicts in the Middle East are common themes, and I have heard often that the War on Terror amounts to little more than a 'crusade', a war on Islam. Meanwhile, some individuals have experienced social exclusion, for various reasons, or racial harassment. Their various grievances generate many responses and, in their desire to make a difference, violence can be used as a means to an end.

What I have found useful is to actively question the values and beliefs of the vulnerable person; in particular how they picture themselves responding to these grievances. Often I ask if they believe their faith permits or even 'compels' them to respond with violence. I take them on a virtual and emotional journey where they can examine their intentions and potential actions by visualising the consequences of what they actually wanted to do and achieve. The role of theology becomes more important in this process than it is in the process of radicalisation. The ideology needs to be challenged and taken apart, and it can be fought with authenticated and irrefutable theological arguments, specifically in circumstances where Islam or any other faith is used as the vehicle to convey or support their message.

In every aspect of preventing extremism, there are and will continue to be difficulties and risks. But I have learned over the years that we must apply a pragmatic approach, showing patience and determination, while finding ways to create positive environments where young people can feel valued, respected, empowered, appreciated and confident in shaping their futures. And with this kind of approach you will learn that there are many opportunities and benefits, which far outweigh the actual risks.

It is essential that we establish a nationally, or even an internationally, unified approach, because the general consensus of most young people is that there has been an erosion of trust. Almost all of the youngsters I have been asked to work with have no confidence in any authority figures at all, and especially the police and the government and its institutions.

A major part of our work at the Active Change Foundation over the years has been to establish dialogue and rebuild trust between young people and the authorities, through engagement and education. By forming links and having debates, face to face, with the police and local authorities, young people have been allowed to explain and vent their frustration. It has also afforded the police officers involved the chance to put across their side of the story and occasionally to accept that there needed to be changes in attitude and approach.

These meetings also allowed the police officers to explain to youngsters the real and present dangers and threats emanating from within their communities, and gave them the chance to explain that they were duty-bound to protect and safeguard those communities by carrying out routine operations like stop-and-search. With the ball back into their court, the young people were obliged to consider their own attitudes, to accept that there are problems in communities and that the authorities needed to be able to find ways of dealing with them.

These meetings have eventually allowed us to establish common ground, where the police have extended their hand to the young people, in order to help them shape certain aspects of their attitudes and approaches to authority and the policing of communities.

The overall outcome was often that young people felt more empowered and appreciated. They were participating in finding solutions to problems, rather than being a part of the problem. This should not be considered a 'fluffy' approach; it has been very important in actually addressing a number of challenges we faced locally. Small ideas like this can make all the difference. The varied and ever-changing landscape of extremism and radicalisation means there is no one-size-fits-all solution – but simple dialogue and engagement is more often than not the key to unlocking the problem.

Another method we have used to create resilience towards an extremist narrative has been to hold workshops with a wide range of young people from diverse backgrounds. These have allowed us to explore the conspiracy theories and to explain and uncover information and facts about various conflicts and terrorist events. As the young minds digest and process the information, some will allow it to soften their own opinions and attitudes – though, of course, some will not. We dissect and discuss the presentation of various pieces of information, the language and the channels of communication used, and demonstrate how a critical analysis could help them understand things better, in order for them to make an informed decision on the position they should take.

Over the years, the cases I have worked on have changed in nature; in particular the social backgrounds of at-risk individuals are now more varied than they ever were. In the early days, after the Afghan war, a lot of cases involved individuals from broken or disrupted families. But as the terrorist groups changed strategy, narratives and demographics, we began to notice that the number of individuals from well-structured families and backgrounds was rapidly increasing.

More recently there has been an increase in numbers of Caucasian young men and indeed a large number of young females joining the ranks of extremists and terrorist groups. What is increasingly worrying is the fact that these individuals have very limited, if any, knowledge of the Islamic faith. In fact, a lot of them were previously involved in either criminal activity or alcohol and drug misuse, which is completely un-Islamic. The additional concern in this aspect is that most if not all converts to Islam have either been shunned by their families or have chosen to leave themselves. This raises a number of other issues, where the push and pull factors play a significant role.

'Calling a terrorist a terrorist'

It also brings me to an important point, one that often polarises opinion. In my view, associating Islam with an act of terror, or using it as a label to identify an individual involved in a terror act, may cause us to deviate from where the actual problem lies. The background of the terrorists in the Paris attacks in November 2015 showed that they were heavily involved in criminal activities, drug misuse and alcohol prior to the attacks. This defined their background much more so than being Islamic, and yet they were usually referred to as 'Islamists', which is a phrase that seems to have become the conventional way of describing an extremist or a terrorist belonging to the Islamic faith.

Labelling terrorists in this way simply creates the space for attitudes to shift towards a negative space of understanding, whether you are a Muslim or not. In associating an act of terrorism with the faith of Islam, we are saying the problem is one *of* Muslims and *for* Muslims and can sometimes generate hatred and resentment towards the huge majority of innocent, decent law-abiding and moderate Muslims.

This can then support Muslim perceptions that their faith is being deliberately condemned and trashed by the Western media, leaders and academics, a grievance that naturally causes Muslim resentment towards governments and institutions. The result is a whole lot of disengagement and division and young people being 'pushed' further towards the extremist narrative as a direct result of our collective failure to 'call a terrorist a terrorist'.

A terrorist has no faith, and the ones who claim to act in the name of Islam are indeed at war with Islam in the first instance. I will provide you with clear irrefutable evidence on this in the final chapter. The accomplished mind will know that throughout the ages, men have hijacked faith for all kinds of purposes, mostly for ulterior motives. Sadly, I am sure that they will continue to do so for ages to come.

Today it is Islam being hijacked, and who knows what faith tomorrow's terrorist will claim to represent. I was recently involved in a counter-narrative workshop in Crawley with a group of young people who had joined one of our young leaders' programmes. Here, a very articulate young lady, from a white British background, raised an excellent question:

'Calling a terrorist an 'Islamist' automatically associates the act to the faith. Shouldn't we separate the faith from the act?'

This is exactly what we need to do collectively, and we encourage everyone in our networks to do the same. Together we must create environments for young men and women to be able to voice their grievances and share their opinions positively. And we certainly need to look at delivering high-impact programs to shape our young people as social enablers through leadership, critical thinking, and communication skills training in order to motivate them to become more resilient.

Moving forward, it will be the efforts by politicians, supported by the traditional organs of state, which will be key determinants in the fight against terrorism. Surveillance, intelligence and technology will be crucial. However, one of the most influential factors will be the resolve or resilience of the community as a whole to desist and resist the effects of extremism. Resilience is not about achieving permanent stability, but rather about absorbing change and disruption, and adapting. That a community can come together before, during and after a major attack, and then rebuild itself for the long term, recognizing that the *status quo* is no longer valid, is a powerful idea. It is also a powerful deterrent to the terrorists, for it guarantees that they will fail. However, such resilience does not happen without design or forethought and a unified front.

Educational institutes, local community groups and businesses are an integral part of communities and have an important role to play in any prevention and de-radicalisation efforts. Communities need to be linked together, from large businesses to the corner shop and local sports club, with families, neighbours, teachers, doctors, nurses and even the dinner ladies, all prepared to play a role both proactively and reactively, before and after any such terrorist attack.

Indeed, commerce is the glue in our cities. Commuters flood into urban centres on a daily basis – doubling the local population in some areas – whilst shopping malls thrive amongst high-rise office buildings. Businesses can take the lead in developing a local community environment and building social links.

As journalist and former diplomat James Rubin suggests: 'We must develop a highly public national resiliency programme. And I can't think of a western country better able to lead a resiliency campaign in the West than Britain.'

The statutory duty of due regard in terms of preventing extremism has been applied specifically to front-line public sector staff. But no such requirement has been placed on the private sector, despite the fact that businesses are in an important position to contribute to this, both in terms of their staffs and clients. There is a huge gap in knowledge and in the participation of businesses within the UK, Europe and elsewhere in the world in this regard. Businesses lack both the understanding of the process of radicalisation and the key skills needed both to identify the early signs and to effectively prevent the process from developing. Equally, they also lack the knowledge on how the referral processes work, especially when support is needed for any individual. Without the knowledge and the skills, they could easily and unintentionally apply the 'push factor' and contribute to the problem.

In an ideal world, businesses could be a powerful 'pull factor' and reduce young people's chances of being drawn into an extremist network. Through providing opportunities for young people to work, train, and learn new skills, by sponsoring community events, and by providing spaces for young people to congregate safely, businesses can actually be part of the solution to the problem, instead of being a potential victim.

So although the statutory duty of due regard does not fall on the private sector, it has a crucial role to play in both prevention and de-radicalisation. Businesses are key players within societies because they enjoy much more engagement with at-risk young people than most public sector organisations do. Contrary to public sector institutions, the private sector can provide spaces and environments where young people feel comfortable, and where they can let their guard down, to express themselves quite differently than when they are in a school or other closed institutions.

Failure to consider the private sector and the role it has to play in our global efforts to stem the tide of extremism and terrorism could prove costly. Bridging the gap between the public and private sector in terms of preventing radicalisation would result in the development of a most effective cross-sector, multi-disciplinary approach. Such a move can also only be good for business itself.

It is evident that the threat of extremism and terrorism is no longer limited to a particular country or ethnic group. The problem is global and requires an international, collective solution, though certain states will have more responsibilities than others. I often look at this problem and liken it to a tsunami, where the actual central point of origin is in one particular area, but the ripple effects are experienced right across the world. Do we know where the central point of origin is? And if so, do we start from the central point of origin or work backwards from where its ripple effects are being felt?

This is where the leaders of the Gulf states in particular have a bigger responsibility, especially if we want to address the problem effectively. I'm not for one minute saying or even alluding to the idea that extremism is emanating from the Middle East and Gulf states, rather my experience tells me that this region is the main target for extremists. Although there is a wealth of work being done in those regions to better understand the growth of extremism and terrorism, little in effect is being done to tackle the issue on the ground.

We acknowledge that there needs to be a collective effort, and this can only be successful if each nation works in parallel. Our current responses and efforts have been applied over decades and without any real success. In fact, the problem seems to have multiplied extensively. This should be enough evidence to demonstrate that we need to change the way we do things, because our old methods are simply not working. Using military might alone creates – and will continue to create – new ideologies and new terrorists, who will seek innovative means to apply their narratives and instigate further attacks. Our collective failures to fully understand the nature and the driving force of the current terrorist groups are not just hampering our abilities to effectually eradicate the problem, but also create a greater threat to our communities. The narrative that groups like ISIS, Al Qaeda and others are pushing will not be defeated simply by killing the terrorists themselves; there will always be others waiting to take up arms behind them.

Undoubtedly, there is need for military interventions of some kind, but it needs to be a measured approach. There is clear intelligence showing a steady collapse from within ISIS and other networks causing fighters breaking away from the ranks, whilst the inhabitants are showing much more resentment towards the leadership. ISIS is potentially doomed as a state, especially due to its unpredictable autocratic regime, which will certainly suffer due to its very nature. The governance administered by its leadership is appalling and will definitely crumble over time. The key components that sustain some degree of normality in any other state – like, health and welfare, housing, education and commerce – are all failing miserably. Any military operation in this regard needs to support its economic failure; this would prove the best way to defeat ISIS and others of a similar nature. The ideology on which they call will prove futile if it is a failed concept, and in turn will reduce the lure and seriously hamper any attempts to recruit individuals to their cause.

Being defeated by its own ideology is far better than it being eradicated via western military might alone. It's the actual 'idea' that needs to be fought and destroyed; it will always remain and pop up with a vengeance if we simply rely on the notion of killing off the terrorists militarily. It is the best way to deliver the knockout blow to terrorism for the longer term. Knowing how they think and operate, and how they want to be seen, I believe their real weakness is dissent, their ideas failing and the fear of being killed by others from within their ranks, which is slowly creeping in and is indeed what they fear the most.

Finally, I wish to relay a message to the leaders of the Gulf states, European and indeed our own UK governments. Over the years we have spent billions on our individual defence and military capabilities, on beautifying our structural landscapes where high-rise buildings seem to penetrate the skies above our cities. We have even extended our efforts in seeking sustainable resources for the future, but we are all collectively and completely failing to effectively invest in our young people. Whilst doing so, we are allowing others to 'revolutionise' our youth to suit their unambiguous and ulterior objectives. We have put at risk all the material investments made, which will crumble to the ground if and when the terrorists strike; not only will it destroy our infrastructure, it will destroy our communities. Not to mention, it will destroy the futures of our young men and women.

You must extend your hands to the very communities you serve and indeed lead, especially the young people, who are and will be your future leaders, doctors, teachers, scholars, strategists, police officers, soldiers and thinkers. Invest in them sincerely and invest in them as a matter of urgency. Unscrupulous individuals and their networks are revolutionising our youth right from under our noses. Why can't we 'revolutionise' them positively, and let them help us shape the future of our nations and indeed our world.

PART C
THE ISLAMIC STANDPOINT

THE ISLAMIC VIEW OF EXTREMISTS AND TERRORIST GROUPS

It is important to acknowledge the fact that there are many sects within Islam and each sect follows a different account or interpretation of the Quran and the examples of the Prophet Muhammad and his recommendations. But it is equally important to understand that this following chapter will focus on 'actual' facts and irrefutable arguments that are indeed universal within all of the Sunni sects of Islam. Different 'opinions' will no doubt sprout out from all quarters, which is pretty much expected and I am in no way claiming that the following arguments are the only arguments. However, they are legitimate arguments, and through hard-won experience I have found them exceptionally helpful in addressing the problems with extreme individuals. In short, what has worked for me over the years with many different cases is what I present to you, the reader.

I have been very careful in not giving 'my personal opinion' on such matters and have instead referred back to the most reliable and credible sources of knowledge to cover this chapter.

It is a clear instruction and conforms to the best of manners within Islam to leave matters of 'Criticism and Praise', known in Islam as *Jarh Wa Ta'deel*, to the people of knowledge (*ie* the scholars), and it is for the scholars who are more experienced, proficient and aware of statements of deviance within Islam and of those who make them. The students of knowledge (those still learning) or the layman cannot openly criticise or refute another person or an argument without clear and concise evidence. Otherwise, we then conform to the manners and the ideology of the extremists, who excommunicate others randomly and falsely without clear evidence.

Below is a verse from the Quran, which helps in addressing the problem but also sums up a lot with regards to what is happening today.

'O you who have believed, if there comes to you a disobedient one with information, investigate, lest you harm a people out of ignorance and become, over what you have done, regretful' – Quran- 49:6

I know this chapter will be very complicated for many to fully understand and appreciate, so I have tried to keep it as simple as possible without taking away the real substance. It will examine the rise of extremists and terrorists (known as Kharijites – extremist renegades) from within Islam and actually how far apart their ideology is from the religion itself. It will be detailed and require a lot of focus, on the facts surrounding their existence and indeed their expansion. I will give references to Prophetic teachings known as *Hadiths*: every action, recommendation or command of our noble Prophet Muhammad (peace & blessings be upon him) was captured and compiled by his companions in the *Hadiths* and preserved in order for Muslims to follow the '*Sunnah*', the way in which the messenger of Allah, Muhammad (peace and blessings be upon him), lived his life. This is where the term 'Sunni' derives from, to describe those who follow in the footsteps of the noble messenger and what was revealed to him as guidance for Muslims – the Quran.

There may be duplication of verses and sentences within this chapter, due to the varying accounts of the noble companions of the Prophet and also the different circumstances.

There are a few considerations to be made whilst reading this chapter, of which the main facts would need to be:

1. Ten of the *Sahaabah* (companions) of the noble Prophet were guaranteed paradise

2. The first four Caliphs preceding the Prophet were known as the '*Khulafā Rāshidūn*' (righteously guided); all four were very close companions of the noble Prophet and were also four of the ten guaranteed paradise.

3. The Prophet gave clear guidance to Muslims: 'Hold firmly to the book (Quran) and follow my example (*sunnah*) and that of the Rightly Guided Caliphs' noted in many authenticated *Hadiths*.

4. The Kharijites (extremist renegades) earned their name (from the root kh-ra-ja meaning 'to go out') because they exited Islam and the Muslim community due to their heretical innovations. The Prophet Muhammad said: 'They will recite the Quran but it will not go beyond their throats', meaning it will not enter their hearts and they will not understand it.

The first four Caliphs (righteously guided) were known as: 1) Abu Bakr-as-Siddique, 2) Umar Ibn Al-Khattab, 3) Uthman Ibn-Affan, 4) Ali Ibn-Abi Talib. All of them were very close to the Prophet of God and devoted their lives to the faith of Islam and for the protection of Muslims and non-Muslims alike. They ruled with the highest integrity and justly and strictly observed the fundamental principles and tenets of the faith.

To begin:

To tackle extremists and terrorists like Al Qaeda, ISIS and others, we need to tackle their narrative and their ideology and their claims that they represent the greater Muslim body. And this has to be tackled with sound theological understanding and clear proofs from the noble Quran and authentic Prophetic traditions (*hadith*) and legitimate scholarly explanations.

Since the death of the Prophet Muhammad (peace and blessings of Allah be upon him), many deviant groups and factions have arisen, introducing new methods based upon their personal opinions and often based on their desire for wealth, power and land, adding innovations into the religion and thereby confusing the masses whilst violating the commands of Allah and his messenger.

Documents like the *fatwa* mentioned previously have been a common tactic deployed by extremists throughout history, one which you will find in the following chapter. Extremists have always forged certain documents to suit their own ambitions and ultimately overthrow the legitimate rulers.

I believe you must also know that most of the greatest scholars of our time are completely refuted and verbally abused by most if not all of the *Khawarij* (extremist and terrorists); in fact it is safe to say that a lot of 'ordinary' Muslims also attack those scholars too. This is simply due to the fact that they (the scholars) are the ones who establish the truth and a clear understanding within Islam. Often resented by those who would rather practise Islam or believe in it differently, some even call them 'extreme', due to their conservativeness.

Sadly the scholars are referred to as 'scholars for dollars', meaning that they only implement Islamic jurisprudence when their rulers either want them to.

(In fact, I was formely of a similar opinion and regrettably I also championed the same phrase.) But this is actually not the case: after careful studying and meeting many of the scholars, I found it quite the opposite. I can name some whom I know as having begun their journey of knowledge during childhood, have reached beyond 90 years of age and still refer to themselves as students in the pursuit of knowledge.

With this, I suggest you either accept the following or reject it; it is inevitably your choice, though I can assure you that the contents ahead are authenticated and they are brought to us by perhaps the most creditable sources from within the Islamic faith.

The Historical roots of Extremists and Terrorists

(I would like to sincerely thank Abu Ilyad for his contributions in this section)

Prophet Muhammad (pbuh) said, 'There will appear at the end of time a people who are young of age, foolish-minded. They will speak with the best (and most-alluring and appealing) of speech (that is spoken) by people and will recite verses of the Quran but it will not go beyond their throats. They will pass out of Islam as the arrow passes through its game.' The Prophet's Companion Abu Umamah al-Bahili (ra) said of the Extremist renegades, 'The Dogs of the people of Hellfire, they used to be Muslims but turned disbelievers'. When Abu Umamah was asked whether this was his own speech or something he heard from the Prophet, he said, 'Rather, I heard it from the Prophet (pbuh)'. One of the well-noted scholars of Islam has said: 'For they [the extremists] strived to kill every Muslim who did not agree with their view, declaring the blood of the Muslims, their wealth, and the slaying of their children to be lawful, while excommunicating them. And they considered this to be worship, due to their ignorance and their innovation which caused [them] to stray.'

As prophesised by the Prophet Muhammad (pbuh), the Kharijites were the first sect to break off from the main body of the Muslims and they appeared in two waves. First, as the revolutionary *Saba'ite* (followers of Abdullah bin Saba) movement against the third caliph of Islam, Uthman (ra) and thereafter, overtly as the Kharijites, against the fourth caliph Ali (ra). They expelled Muslims from Islam on account of major sins, revolted against the rulers with arms and incited the masses to fight against them. They are mostly young in age, appear as pious worshippers, have not acquired knowledge from the scholars of Islam, make use of secrecy, and come to the people under the guise of 'enjoining the good and prohibiting the evil'" and employ faulty interpretations of Islamic texts due largely to their ignorance. The Prophet (pbuh) also explicitly stated that they will never cease to appear until the *Dajjal* (the Anti-Christ) appears in the midst of their armies. This indicates that the Muslim will always be plagued by this disease throughout the passage of time and that their war is fundamentally a war against the people of Islam. The fact that most people do not recognize the Kharijites or their ideology is reflective of another wider reality, which is that most people do not understand the reality of the creed and methodology of the Righteous pious predecessors (those who follow the *Sunnah* of the Prophet) and what opposes it. Many of the contemporary Kharijite movements nowadays make an ascription to the way of the pious predecessors whilst, in fact, they are the furthest away from it in their statements, actions and methodologies of reform. This should not be surprising since the very first Kharijites considered themselves to be superior to the Prophet's Companions, seeing themselves as the actual frontrunners and the true representatives of Islam. This leads to three affairs:

Firstly, many naïve, ill-informed, emotive Muslims who see oppression, bloodshed and war in Muslim lands are emotionally manipulated into believing that the loud, rhetorical voice of the Kharijites and their use of lofty slogans of 'Shari'ah', '*jihad*', 'Judging by Allah's Law', 'Enjoining Good and Forbidding Evil' are contextually valid, evidence-based, authentic voices when in reality they are nothing but the rantings of the ignorant, unaware of the basics of the Islamic creed and ignorant of Allah's laws in His creation. This is evidenced by their gross misdiagnosis of the causes of affliction (which they always return to and blame the rulers) but whose true roots are more foundational and lie elsewhere.

The Prophet Muhammad (pbuh) explained how the extremists would put the Muslims, their leaders and their societies to trial and tribulation. These are the Kharijites. When this group appeared, the Companions of the Prophet saw that numerous verses of the Quran applied to them.

These verses from the Quran include the saying of Allah, 'Say: Shall we inform you of the greatest losers as to [their] deeds? Those whose efforts have been wasted in this life while they thought that they were acquiring good by their deeds!' (18:103-104).

Also, the saying of Allah, '*Some faces, that Day, will be humiliated. Labouring (hard in the worldly life), weary (in the Hereafter with humility and disgrace).*' (88:2-3). Also the saying of Allah, '*And when they deviated, Allah caused their hearts to deviate.*' (61:8). And also, '*Those who break Allah's Covenant after ratifying it, and sever what Allah has ordered to be joined and do mischief on earth, it is they who are the losers.*' (2:27).

It is common knowledge to the scholars of the Muslims and their students that ISIS, Boko Haram, Al Qaeda and others are simply another manifestation of the recurring appearance of this group that was explicitly mentioned by the Prophet of Islam. They have killed exponentially more Muslims in the past 1400 years than they have killed non-Muslims in the past 1400 years. In fact, if we were to say that they have killed more Muslims in the past 20 years than they have killed non-Muslims in the past 1400 years, it would not be an exaggeration at all. Their first appearance was approximately 30 years after the death of the Prophet in 36H (after migration), around the year 657CE. This faction is indeed a great trial and tribulation for Muslims in various times and ages; the Prophet (pbuh) spoke extensively about them, their traits, activities and their great danger upon Islam and the Muslims.

Their main motive lies in matters of the world and they use Religion as a cover

The primary motivations driving Kharijite extremists return back to worldly matters including wealth and how Muslim rulers dispose of it. They desire that wealth should come to them due to their belief that giving it to the rulers is unlawful because they do not distribute it justly and do not use it for its designated purposes. In other words, they cite affairs pertaining to misuse of state capital and social, political and economic injustice. For this reason, there are strong parallels between the Kharijites who departed from Islam, and the Jacobinist, Marxist, Bolshevik and Communist movements. This, under the very same banners of social and economic injustice, launched an era of war and permanent revolution.

The ideological grandfather of all extremist renegade movements in Islamic history is a man known as Dhul-Khuwaisarah al-Tamimi. The Quran judged this individual to be from the disbelieving hypocrites, a verse from the Quran saying: 'Amongst them (the Hypocrites) is one who criticizes you concerning the [distribution of] charities. If they are given from them, they approve but if they are not given from them, at once they become angry.' (9:58).

This man and his few followers challenged the integrity of the Prophet (pbuh) in a famous incident which is documented in numerous Prophetic traditions. As the Prophet was distributing wealth to a number of tribes for certain benefits he had in mind for them, this man appeared and said, 'Be just O Muhammad' and 'We are more worthy of this than them' and also, 'This is a division by which the pleasure of Allah is not sought'. The Prophet had to prevent his Companions from striking this audacious man and as the man walked away, the Prophet (pbuh) said, 'From this man will appear a people who will recite the Quran but it will not go beyond their throats'. He went to describe in other reports that they will separate from the main body of Muslims, turn against them and fight them.

This incident is evidence that the entire issue with the *Khariijtes* is a worldly one. Religion is merely used as a cloak to legitimize their activities and serve as a means of recruiting the ignorant and unsuspecting. Thereafter, it is used as a vehicle to help them attain their worldly objectives. Ibn Kathir, the Quran commentator, said, 'For the first innovation to occur in Islam was the tribulation of the Kharijites and their (ideological) starting point was due to [a matter] of the world'. The matter being referred to was the distribution of wealth, they consider the ruling authorities to be unjust and astray in their disposal of wealth. It must be noted that 'the foundation of the misguidance of these [Kharijites] is their belief regarding the leaders of guidance and the body of the Muslims that they have departed from justice and are misguided'. As we shall see in what follows, the Kharijites employed texts of the Quran which they did not understand and built their ideology upon gross misinterpretations. By revolting against the authorities, they create civil strife and bring chaos, ruin and destruction. **Not a single Companion** of the Prophet was amongst the Kharijites which demonstrates their departure from Islam, its scholarly tradition and its main body.

The Historical events preceding the Rise of the Revolutionary Terrorists in the lands of Syria and Iraq

The activities of a particular subversive movement known as the *Saba'iyyah* led to the creation of the Kharijites. The Prophet's Companion Hudhayfah bin al-Yaman used to ask the Prophet about evil out of fear that it may befall him and he would be in gatherings in which the Prophet mentioned the various tribulations to befall the Muslim nation following his death. Hudhayfah stated, 'By Allah, I am the most-knowledgeable amongst the people of every tribulation to occur between my presence and the Final Hour (day of judgement).' Ibn Kathir, the famous historian and Quranic commentator, relates the statement of Hudhayfah: 'The first of the tribulations is the killing of Uthman (the third caliph of Islam) and the last of them is the appearance of the *Dajjal* (Anti-Christ).' Thus, the first significant event having major consequences for the Muslim nation was the revolution against the third caliph, Uthman, which culminated in his assassination.

This was executed by a group of renegade hypocrites led by a man known as Abdullah bin Saba'. His followers became known as the *Saba'iyyah* and they had been recruited and mobilized against Uthman on 'alleged' grounds of social injustice, class separation and despotism in addition to a range of what were claimed to be erroneous mistakes in jurisprudence and personal conduct. Their slogan against Uthman was the same as the slogan of the hypocrite, Dhul

Khuwaysarah al-Tamimi against the Prophet – the absence of social justice in matters of wealth – the same slogan of Marxist, Communist revolutionary movements of the 19th and 20th centuries. This is a crucial point to note as it helps to explain the circumstances behind the emergence of the Kharijite terrorists during both the dawn of Islam and modern history in the 19th and 20th centuries.

Four figures are of special note here. Jamal al-Din al-Afghani, a gnostic/esoteric, a concealed revolutionary who is spuriously claimed to be the founder of modern Salafism. He was the first to revive and spread this claim in the modern era. He launched a Marxist, Communist diatribe against Uthman, accusing him of hoarding capital, nepotism, despotism and class separation. After him, Sayyid Qutb (godfather of the Muslim brotherhood) developed this poison in more detail in a number of his writings dealing with social justice and capitalism and he also praised the revolution of Abdullah bin Saba' against Uthman and maligned Muawiyah (fifth caliph of Islam), his parents and the Banu Umayyah (a clan in the Quraish tribe) in the severest of ways, even negating their Islam. At the end of his life he spread doctrines of excommunication and hatred against all contemporary Muslim societies, whom he charged with apostasy and advocated worldwide revolutions to topple rulers and governments.

Abu A'la Mawdudi (Scholar & founder of Jamaat-e-Islami – largest Islamic movement in south Asia) also made insinuations against Uthman and Muawiyah upon the same grounds alongside his spurious claim that the primary goal of the Prophets was to 'overthrow the thrones of the tyrants'. Taqi al-Din al-Nabahani – the founder of Hizb al-TaHrir – was a former Ba'thist Communist who shared in some of this poison (particularly against Muawiyah) and also advocated a revolutionary approach to establishing economic, social and political justice. So it should come as no surprise that the writings and the ideas of these thinkers (al-Afghani, Sayyid QuTb, Al-Nabahani, Al-Mawdudi) became the inspiration behind the ideologies of excommunication (*takfir*) and revolution, leading to hatred and desertion of Muslim societies, eventually culminating in terrorism.

The Activities and Techniques of the Extremist-Kharijite Terrorists

Many of the ideas and activities of this early subversive current which put Islam and the Muslims to trial can be found today amongst the Kharijite terrorists of Al Qaeda and ISIS in the land of Sham (Syria) and Iraq – the very place from which the Prophet of Islam indicated, over 1400 years ago, that these people would first emerge and then continue to emerge. The famous historian and Quran commentator, Ibn Kathir (d.774H, 14th century CE), compiled the activities of the early Kharijites in some detail and it is worthwhile to mention them here to see the striking parallels between them and the Kharijites of today in the form of ISIS, Al Qaeda, Boko Haram and others. When the statements of the leaders and spokesmen of ISIS and videos of the activities of their members are compared with those of the first Kharijites/extremists, it becomes clear with absolute certainty that they are the Kharijite Dogs of Hellfire referred to in the Prophetic traditions.

Forging documents against the Companions

The Kharijite terrorists distributed a document in the name of Uthman (ra) in which there was a command authorizing the killing of the conspirators behind the planned uprising against Uthman during 35H (656CE). They had forged this document and the seal of Uthman with which they stamped the document to give it the appearance of authenticity. However, Uthman would have had no knowledge about these conspirators and their intentions at the time and he expressly denied he wrote this document or indeed had anything to do with it. They also fabricated documents against the Companions such as Ali, TalHah and Zubayr in which they allegedly called the people to fight against Uthman in order to aid the religion, and they wrote in these fabricated documents that fighting against Uthman was the greatest form of *jihad* and support of the religion. They also fabricated a document against A'ishah (the wife of the Prophet) in which she allegedly called the people to revolt against Uthman. Ibn Kathir comments, 'And in this and its likes is plain evidence that those Kharijites, may Allah disfigure them, would fabricate documents upon the tongues of the Companions and spread them in the horizons, inciting the people to fight against Uthman the Righteously guided caliph of Islam'.

Addressing the rulers with derogatory names

The Kharijite terrorists would address Uthman with names of Jewish and Christian leaders to imply he was not the right person to lead the Muslims as he was working for them or aligned with them, so to cause chaos, mistrust and even dissent. And they would refer to Ali with derogatory names such as *jaHid* (denier, rejecter). During their revolt against Uthman in Madinah, one of them stood up whilst Uthman was delivering a sermon and said to him, 'Stand O Na'thal and come down from this pulpit'. Na'thal was the name of one of the Jewish leaders in Madinah. And when the murderers eventually broke into his house they said to him, 'Which religion are you upon O Na'thal?' Uthman replied, 'Upon the religion of Islam and I am not Na'thal, but I am the Chief of the Believers *(Amir al-mu'minin)*'.

Stealing property and wealth

The first Extremist-Kharijite terrorists would steal the property and possessions of the rulers whom they declared apostates as they did with Uthman after killing him. They left nothing in his house and took all of his possessions. Uthman was one who was of the highest ranks in the sight of the Prophet, hence why he was to become the third Caliph of Islam after the death of the Prophet. This also demonstrates how vile the Extremists have been and continue to do so now.

Spilling blood and cutting off routes of travel

The Kharijite terrorists who opposed Ali would shed blood, cut off the routes of travel and would violate the inviolable such as the murder of Abdullah bin al-Khabbab and killing his wife and their unborn child. (Elaborated further in section on the traits & characteristics of extremists)

Motivated by personal reasons

The Kharijite terrorists of old made it clear that they were motivated primarily for personal, worldly reasons. One of the assassins of Uthman known as Amr bin al-Hamiq sat on his chest after he had already been stabbed by another and proceeded to stab him nine times in the chest, after which he said, 'Three stabs of them were for Allah and six of them were for what I held in my chest'. In reality, none of them were for Allah or for Islam at all, simply because these individuals were disbelieving hypocrites by judgement of the Prophet.

Divided in their pursuit of overall leadership

Ibn Kathir writes, 'So when they revolted in the era of Uthman, the people rallied behind them [the Kharijites], and every group had their own figurehead [leading them in the revolution]'. Many factions came to Madinah from the various cities and each one of them had their own leader. Their anticipation would be that, following the removal of Uthman, their leader would be the one to take power. This undercurrent of rivalry and pursuit of ultimate authority expresses itself today in the rivalry between the factions of ISIS, al-Nusrah, Ahrar Al Sham and many others.

Recruitment by stealth and encouraging emigration from Muslim lands

After splitting from the main body of Muslims under the leadership of Ali, Abdullah bin Wahb al-Rasibi – who was the first leader of the Kharijites – began to meet with his associates and started recruiting people by encouraging them to abandon their families and to travel to them by stealth. He said, 'Come out with us O our brothers from this city whose inhabitants are oppressive, show your rejection of these oppressive rulings'. Similarly, Zayd bin Husayn al-Ta'i – the one who threatened to kill Ali just as his group had previously killed Uthman – advised those who were upon this Kharijite ideology in various cities. He informed them that when they desire to leave Kufah (A city in Iraq) to come to their meeting place, they should not leave in groups, but in isolation so as not to create suspicion. They would write letters to their followers in Basrah and other locations giving them advice on how and where to meet. Young people in particular began to leave, abandoning their mothers, fathers, aunties and uncles and all other relatives. Ibn Kathir commented, 'Due to their ignorance and lack of knowledge and intellect, they thought this matter pleases the Lord of the Heavens and Earth and that they were now duty bound by Islam. They did not know that it is from the greatest of major sins, vices, destructive affairs, mighty transgressions and errors and that it is from what Shaytaan (Satan) has beautified for them and for their souls which command them with evil.'

This will enable you to draw clear comparisons as to what they do till this day, by recruiting young people and encouraging them to leave their families under the guise of Islam.

Waging *jihad* against Muslims and encouraging their slaughter

They have always used religious texts to demonstrate to their followers that they are correct and they are doing their duty as God-fearing Muslims. However, the following will expose how in fact they manipulate the verses of the most holy book of Islam and how they completely abuse the emotions of ignorant yet innocent people.

These Kharijites considered the Muslims to have strayed and abandoned Islam, despairing of bringing them back and thus they enjoined *jihad* against them. When the heads of this movement gathered in a house, each one of them was presented with leadership and they all refused except Abdullah bin Wahb al-Rasibi who said, 'By Allah, I do not accept [leadership] desiring the world and nor do I abandon it out of aversion of death'. When he had been made leader, they gathered together in the house of Zayd bin Husayn al-Ta'i who gave them a sermon. He encouraged them to enjoin the good and forbid the evil and he recited verses from the Quran to them such as, 'O David, we have made you the vicegerent upon the Earth, so judge between the people with truth and do not follow desire lest it misguide you from Allah's path' (38:26) and also 'And whoever does not judge by what Allah revealed, they are the disbelievers' (5:44) and '...they are the oppressors' (5:45) and '... they are the sinners' (5:47). These verses are the foundation of all Kharijite movements without exception and the central affair that unites them all. Thereafter, the Kharijites have differences. Some of them do not excommunicate Muslims on account of sins at all. Others excommunicate Muslims on account of some sins exclusive to others. And yet others excommunicate Muslims on account of every sin, large or small. This is a refutation of the terrorist sympathizers who say that the likes of ISIS, Al Qaeda and other Kharijites do not excommunicate Muslims on account of drinking, fornication, gambling and other major sins. The reality is that neither did the very first Kharijites/Extremists.

Then he said, 'So bear witness against the people subjected to our call from the people of our *qiblah* (direction of prayer) that they followed desire, shunned the judgement of the Book, have transgressed in speech and deed and that waging *jihad* against them is a duty upon the believers'. Then he encouraged them to attack the people and in his speech he said, 'Strike their faces and foreheads with swords until Allah the Most-Gracious, Most Merciful (al-RaHman, al-RaHim) is obeyed'. Ibn Kathir commented upon this: 'These types of people are from the strangest of species amongst the offspring of Adam, and sublime is Allah who created variations in His creation as He desired... The intent here is that they are misguided ignoramuses, wretched (despicable) in both statements and deeds.' One should note that though the Kharijites split and became into many sects, acquiring other deviant beliefs; what is common between them and unites them all is the issue of *takfir* (excommunication) in relation to rulership and judgement by Allah's law. This is the foundational basis of all revolutionary political movements taking form in the innovated 'Islamic political groups': judging Muslims with disbelief on account of matters that do not constitute it.

The ignorant Kharijites excommunicated Ali and accused him of being a polytheist because he deferred judgement to men, a reference to the arbitration between Ali and MuAwiyah during the battle at Siffin. They said, 'O Ali, you have ascribed partners to Allah in His religion, judgement belongs only to Allah'. This is despite the fact that arbitration – such as in marital disputes and in reconciliation between two contending or warring parties – is permitted, indeed recommended in the Quran, and this is how Ibn Abbas, the Quranic scholar, refuted those Kharijites. Thus, they accuse Muslims with disbelief through matters that are not even considered sins in the Islamic Shari'ah, let alone disbelief itself, but rather commended.

Their opponents condemned to Hellfire if killed by them

The Kharijites of old also believed that whosoever was killed by them was automatically condemned to the Hellfire. The companion of the Prophet Abu

Ayyub al-Ansari said, 'I pushed a spear into a man from the Kharijites and pushed it through till it came out from his back and I said to him, "Glad tidings O enemy of Allah for you will be of the Fire". So he replied, "You will soon come to know which of us is more worthy of being burned therein".' This is keeping in mind that some of the Companions of the Prophet are guaranteed Paradise by the testimony of the Quran and the Kharijite dogs are condemned to the Hellfire by testimony of the Quran and the Prophetic traditions.

Claiming Paradise for their dead

When Ali came to them at Al-Nahrawan, admonished them and warned them severely that they intended battle, they began chanting, 'Judgement is for Allah, departure, departure to Paradise!' Thus, they claimed automatic entry to Paradise for their dead, whereas the Prophet had judged them Kharijite dogs of Hellfire who exit from Islam as an arrow passes through its game.

Violating the rights of the people under protection

The Kharijites violated the rights of the Christians, Jews and other non-Muslims, who were under guarantee of protection from the Muslims. Ali had sent Ibn Abbas, the most knowledgeable companion of the Prophet of the Quran, to debate the Kharijites and as a result one-third of them changed their ideology and entered back into the main body of Muslims. To the remaining two-thirds Ali announced that there is 'an agreement between us and you, that you will not spill inviolable blood, you will not cut off the pathways and you will not oppress [the non-Muslims] under protection'. Later, when they broke the covenant and murdered those under protection Ali had fought them, A'ishah (wife of the Prophet) said to Ibn Shaddad (a companion of the Prophet), 'He (Ali) killed them' and Ibn Shaddad replied, 'By Allah, he (Ali) did not dispatch his army to them until they cut off the pathways, spilled blood and made lawful [the killing] of the [non-Muslims] under guarantee of protection'. This portrays a clear example and indeed evidence that the Muslims fought those [Extremists] for what they were doing and to protect innocent people Muslim and non-Muslim alike.

They comprised of the ruffians, hooligans, the dregs of society and the young and foolish of age

The Prophet described them, 'young of age and foolish-minded'. Historians Ibn Sa'd, al-Dhahabi, Ibn Kathir and others recount from earlier authorities that those, the revolutionaries mobilized against Uthman, were the dregs of society, ruffians, foolish-minded, naïve and brainless savages and that the Kharijites comprised of ignorant masses. The Paris attackers and those in Tunisia and elsewhere are examples of this very statement.

Find fault with scholars in irrelevant matters

When Ali sent Ibn Abbas to debate with the Kharijites after they abandoned his army and camped at Harura', he was wearing a fine garment. They began to debate with him about it and why he was dressed so nicely, so he replied with the verse of the Quran, 'Say: Who has forbidden the adornment [of clothing] given by Allah which He has produced for His servants and the good lawful things of provision?' This indicates their resentment against both the rulers and the scholars for the good things Allah has bestowed upon them and that these underlying currents of jealousy are what drive the instigators amongst them.

Fault-picking against the rulers and twisting everything that they do

During the two-year period between 36H and 38H before Ali eventually fought the Kharijites, after they continually tried to find faults with Ali in every issue possible, criticize him and twist his words to present them in the worst possible light. Ibn Kathir relates through al-Tabari that the Kharijites 'began to confront Ali regarding his statements, make him hear their slurs (revilements) and making all sorts of interpretations of his statements'. Similarly, it was the case with Uthman, who made some personal judgements in matters of jurisprudence and these issues were raised against him too as part of a wider agenda to stir up revolution. Likewise, when they fabricated a letter upon Uthman in which he allegedly gave orders to have them killed and Uthman stated his complete innocence, they responded by saying, 'If you did write it, you are treacherous; and if you did not write it, it shows you are powerless and incompetent and the likes of you therefore are not fit for leadership due to either treachery or incapacity'. The ISIS *fatwa* and other material are examples of how they manipulate documents and texts, including the very words of God Almighty, to suit their vile agendas.

Doctrines of prominent early Extremist sects

The heresiographers specializing in documenting the ideas and practices of the deviant sects note the following about the very early extremist Kharijite splinter groups: The Azariqites declared the killing of the wives and children of Muslims they considered apostates to be lawful. Some of them also made it lawful to violate contracts. They also held that whoever resides in the lands of disbelief is a disbeliever, keeping in mind that a land of disbelief is any land other than theirs. The Najadites made it lawful to kill non-Muslims under covenant with the Muslims and to take their wealth. Some of them also believe that dissimulation (*taqiyah*) in speech and deed is permissible even in killing people.

The Bahaisites asserted that when the ruler becomes a disbeliever (according to them), all of his subjects also become disbelievers. Another group, the Ajaridites make secret assassinations lawful and they also make it permissible to enslave women and kill the children of the disbelievers (that includes Muslims). From the above, which is but a glimpse of their activities, one can clearly determine that these people are at war with Islam primarily, its lands and its inhabitants, rulers and the ruled. And therefore anyone who equates the ideology of the modern Kharijites – from the Qutbists, Al Qaeda/al-Nusrah, ISIS and others – with the Islam brought by Muhammad or with the noble scholars of Islam, who have always been at the forefront of fighting against the Kharijites, deserves a rank of ignoramus.

The Prophet's Description of the Extremist-Kharajite Terrorists

From the well-known, authentically related statements of the Prophet about this group include his saying, 'They depart from the religion (Islam) like an arrow passes through its game and they do not return back to it until the arrow returns back to its bow-string' and 'Their faith does not pass beyond their throats' and 'They recite the Quran but it does not go beyond their collar-bones', indicating ignorance and false scholarship. He also said, 'They speak with the best speech of the creation', meaning, beautified, alluring speech, and '(They are) young of age, foolish of mind' and 'Their actions are evil' and 'They are the most evil of the creation' and 'They call to the Book of Allah, yet they have nothing to do with it'. The Prophet went further and also said 'They are the most evil of those killed beneath the canopy of the sky' and 'They are the Dogs of Hellfire'. These very severe and harsh descriptions of the Kharijite extremists came alongside a mention of their devotion which would surpass and excel that of the Prophet's Companions themselves. Despite this, the Prophet signalled his intent to kill them should he have reached them.

The Traits and Characteristics of the Extremist-Kharajites

On the basis of the Prophetic traditions and the activities of the Extremists, the noble and highly credible scholars of Islam have detailed their traits and characteristics, which are summarized below:

Complaining and supplicating for change despite living in relative affluence and safety

From their ungratefulness is that despite living in sufficiency, affluence and safety, they would always demand for change. In the reign of Uthman, people would come to the state treasury (Bayt al-Mal), take their portion, and then complain and supplicate for a change in their circumstances for the better.

Many of those who are upon and promote the ideology of the Kharijites in the UK or other Western countries and who enjoy state benefits, even in the Muslim countries, particularly those of the Gulf states, live in relative affluence, have jobs and live in security. They forget that this comfortable situation came about for them through the efforts of the rulers, ironically whom they resent and even judge with disbelief.

This indicates the nature of the heart residing in the body of an extremist-Kharijite, vile and putrid, ungrateful and filled with scorn. One look at the extremists–terrorists of today and you will see clear parallels with those mentioned above.

Their first act of terrorism against the Prophet's companions and their display of fake piety

After they broke off from the army of Ali, their first act of terrorism was against the Companion of the Prophet called Abdullah bin Khabbab, near Basrah in Iraq in the year 37H (around 658CE) after they had split from Ali's army and set up their own state in al-Nahrawan. An illustration of their fake piety is that when a group of them took Abdullah bin Khabbab captive and led him to his eventual slaughter, they passed by some date-palm trees owned by a Christian where one of them took a date and ate it. So the others said to him, 'You have (unlawfully) taken a date which belongs to the people of the covenant'. Another killed a pig that belonged to a Christian and they ordered him to pay compensation. Whilst observing these actions, Abdullah said to them, 'Shall I not tell you who has a greater right upon you than this?' (Meaning that he should be shown clemency by them because he is a practising Muslim and a human being, and that they have a duty to respect this and free him) They said, 'Who?' and he replied, 'Me, because I have not abandoned a single prayer nor have I abandoned neither this nor that (meaning various forms of worship)'. However, they killed him without thought and without mercy.

So they showed overt piety and fear of Allah in taking a date unlawfully and killing a pig which was the property of a Christian; however, it was clearly a fake type of piety, because they paid no regard to human life, especially that of the Prophet's companion. Despite giving Abdullah an assurance of safety at the first encounter, they acted treacherously towards him. Because he did not agree with them that Ali, the fourth caliph, was an apostate, they excommunicated him thereafter, they laid him on the ground and slaughtered him whilst his blood flowed into the nearby water stream. Then they murdered his wife who was at the peak of pregnancy. She pleaded for her life and that of her unborn child, but they sliced her open and spared not even her child. Then they killed numerous others who were present in his caravan. It was here that the cousin and son-in-law of the Prophet, Ali, followed the Prophetic traditions, ordering this group to be fought and killed.

They consider themselves to be more righteous and superior to the people of knowledge

The first of those who went astray in this regard are the renegade Kharijites when they judged that they alone are holding fast to the Book of Allah and the Prophet's *Sunnah*.

Considering that the Kharijites have not one single noteworthy or genuine scholar amongst them, it is clear that they consider themselves more learned and superior to the scholars.

Treating what is not a sin to be a sin

They have two well-known traits by which they departed from the main body of the Muslims and their rulers. The first of them is their departure from the *Sunnah* (example of and the way of the Prophet) and making what is not a sin to be a sin or what is not a good deed to be a good deed.

They declare Muslims as disbelievers on account of sins and subsequently legalize their murder

The second of their two well-known traits is that they declare Muslims to be disbelievers on account of sins and evils and built upon the excommunication (*takfir*), they make lawful the shedding of the blood of the Muslims and taking their wealth and claim that the land of Islam is a land of disbelief and war and that the land inhabited by them alone is a land of faith *ie* Islam.

Take a look at Syria (Raqqa) where they have currently established the 'Islamic state', calling every other place the land of disbelief; they have even included Makkah & Madinah, the two holiest places in Islam.

Their gross ignorance of the religion and absence of scholars amongst them

This is manifest when Ibn Abbas was sent to debate with them and to repel their doubts. It became clear that, amongst the 12,000 or so of them, there was not a single Companion of the Prophet. In their debate they demonstrate their ignorance of the Quran and its interpretation. They do not have the ability to make *istidlal* (inferences and deductions from the texts) and they rely upon generalizations and absolutions. Imam al-ShaTibi (an Andalusian Sunni

Islamic legal scholar) said, 'From following ambiguities is to take unqualified absolutions before looking at their qualifications and taking generalizations without reflecting as to whether they have specifications or not. Likewise, the opposite, to take a text which has been restricted and to generalize it.' There are no scholars to be found within the Kharijite terrorist networks of Al Qaeda/al-Nusrah, ISIS and others. Certainly those who feign knowledge amongst them did not take knowledge from the well-known, credible and notable scholars of this era. Rather, they were nurtured upon the books of Sayyid Qutb and Mawdudi and the books of ideology (*fikr*) and Harakah (political activism) that are circulated amongst the Qutbiyyah, Sururiyyah, Haddadiyyah – all factions of Takfiris (Accusers) who came from the direction of the Muslim Brotherhood (al-Ikhwan Al Muslimoon).

They subject the Quran and *Sunnah* to faulty analogies and interpretations

Ibn al-Qayyim said, 'Whoever subjected the Quran and the *Sunnah* with a form of interpretation such as the use of analogy (*qiyas*) or one's taste (*dhawq*) or intellect (*Aql*) or emotional state (*Hal*) then he has a resemblance to the Kharijites, the followers of Dhul Khuwaysarah'. Ibn Taymiyyah said, 'The very first innovations such as the innovation of the Kharijites arose due to their evil intentions whilst misunderstanding of the Quran. They did not deliberately intend to oppose it, but they understood from it what it did not indicate.'

They are the worst of those killed beneath the canopy of the sky

This is textually stated in the Prophetic tradition related by Ibn Majah: 'They are the most evil of those killed beneath the canopy of the sky.' Anas ibn Malik reported: 'They are the worst of the creation. Blessed are those who fight them and are killed by them. They call to the Book of Allah but they have nothing to do with it. Whoever fights them is better to Allah than them.'

They murdered the Prophet's cousin and son-in-law

The Kharijite extremists accused Ali bin Abi Talib of becoming an apostate because he agreed to an arbitration by which reconciliation was intended between himself and MuAwiyah. Due to their severe ignorance and the absence of a single scholar amongst them, the Kharijites held this arbitration to be an act of disbelief because in their misguided view it entailed judging by other than Allah's law. Hence, they excommunicated the Companions and split away from the main body of Muslims. It was only after their murder of Abdullah bin Khabbab that Ali bin Abi Talib recognized these were the very people spoken of by the Prophet decades earlier and mobilized himself to fight them. A number of years after battling them, one of the extremist Kharijites called Abd al-RaHman bin Muljam plotted to assassinate Ali and attained his evil objective in the year 40H (661CE). This was one of three assassination plots but the only one that was successful. The Kharijites had desired to kill the main leaders of the Muslim nation following their defeat at al-Nahrawan. Abd al-RaHman bin Muljam agreed to assassinate Ali in Kufah (Iraq), al-Barrak bin Abdullah al-Tamimi agreed to assassinate MuAwiyah in Syria and Amr bin Bakr agreed to assassinate Amr bin al-As in Egypt. The latter two failed in their mission. One can see that the Kharijites were intending to destroy the Muslim nation by assassinating its rulers in the three major capital regions of the then legitimate Islamic caliphate after having split away from the main body of Muslims and then established their own mini-state in al-Nahrawan close to Bagdhad (Iraq).

This is the way of these people throughout the ages until this day of ours: to pursue wealth and power by undermining the Islamic authorities and bringing chaos, destruction and bloodshed through murder, assassination, terror and chaos. In the Prophetic traditions, the Muslim rulers are commanded to fight these Kharijites whenever they appear because their evil ideology and terrorist mindset are the primary enemies of the religion of Islam and run contrary to it from every angle. The Mufti of Saudi Arabia, Shaykh Abd al-Aziz Al al-Shaykh, remarked, 'The terrorism of ISIS/Daesh/A.Q *etc* is the very first enemy of Islam'. The leaders amongst them are motivated by wealth, land, power and politics and simply use Islam as a hijacked vehicle or a donned, beautified garment through which they pursue their interests.

Through beautified speech, they recruit the young, ignorant and foolish. Whilst the noble Prophet of Islam, Muhammad, commanded that these evil and most harmful of people to Islam and its adherents be fought, killed and cut off, we see on the other hand that they are most beneficial in serving the purposes of those who oppressively ascribe their destructive activities to the Prophet of Islam and satirize him upon falsehood. This is despite the historical record showing that the Prophet of Islam was challenged by their ideological grandfather, Dhul Khuwaysarah, that his Companions were slaughtered and murdered by them and that the Islamic tradition throughout history is squarely against them. Despite being defeated by Ali at al-Nahrawan, many of them escaped to various Islamic lands and continued to sow the seeds for the Kharijite (extremist) ideology which has continued to this day.

The Azariqah Sect: Forerunners of ISIS

Many early Islamic scholars from the third, fourth and fifth centuries of Islam who specialized in the study of deviant sects (heresiography) documented the beliefs and actions of one of the most extreme sects of the Kharijite terrorists known as the Azariqah. ISIS are reminiscent of this group. Their founder was Abu Rashid Nafiʻ bin Azraq (d. 65H around 685CE). The Azariqah split off from the Kharijites and made their way to Basrah, taking control over it and other areas in Persia. Their evil doctrines included the belief that the excommunication of Ali was valid and correct and that Ali's assassin, Ibn Muljam, was correct and praiseworthy in his action. In their view, all sinful Muslims are apostates who will reside in Hellfire for eternity should they die without having repented from their sins. Whoever opposed their opinion was considered a polytheist and they threw the children of such people alongside them – all of them were considered disbelievers whom it was permissible to fight and kill.

The land inhabited by those outside their group was considered to be a land of war (*dar al-Harb*) and whatever was permitted with respect to a land of war was permitted to them against the Muslims inhabiting such a land. Anyone who did not join them by emigrating to them, even if he shared their evil view, was also considered a polytheist. They also held the necessity of eliminating every 'disbeliever' from the Earth, and by 'disbeliever' they mean everyone, including any Muslim who does not agree with them. They would interrogate Muslims on their views towards the rulers and whoever did not agree with their excommunication of the Muslim rulers of the time would be killed. They would lay in wait for Muslims, slaughter them and also slaughter their children mercilessly, on the flimsiest of grounds until they instilled terror in the hearts of civilians who would be scared to leave their homes or embark on journeys.

Their main focus is the issue of judging by Allah's law and excommunication (*takfir*) of the rulers

From what has preceded, it is clear that the central focus of the Kharijites is around the issue of rulership and judgement by Allah's law. Their ignorance in this regard became manifest when they treated something permissible in the Shari'ah – namely, arbitration between two warring parties as a means of conciliation – to be major disbelief. This same compound ignorance remains a trait with them to this day and indeed the Messenger of Allah characterized them as 'youthful' and 'foolish-minded' and stated that 'the Quran does not go beyond their throats', meaning, that whilst they recite it, they do not grasp and understand it. Today, the Kharijite movements, parties, groups and sects show their ignorance in this matter in their interpretation of the verses related to judgement and rulership in order to elicit generalized *takfir* of the rulers without any detail or elaboration. This in turn allows them to justify their revolutionary methodology clothed with the lofty slogan of 'enjoining the good and forbidding the evil' thereby mimicking the speech and action of the heads of the Kharijites. This is after our knowledge that due to their compound ignorance they have grossly misdiagnosed the actual causes of decline and deterioration in Muslim societies and nations which are not restricted just to the rulers alone. As for the centrality of their focus around this issue, Abu al-Muzaffar al-SamAni (d. 489H) said, 'Know that the Kharijites seek evidence through this verse and say that whoever does not judge by what Allah has revealed is a disbeliever; but true Muslims, who follow the *Sunnah* of the noble Prophet, do not make *takfir* on account of abandonment of judging alone'. And Ibn Abd al-Barr said, 'And a faction of the people of innovation from the Kharijites have strayed in this field and used as proof verses which are not to be taken apparently, such as His saying, the Mighty and Majestic, "And whosoever does not judge by what Allah has revealed, they are the disbelievers". (5:44).'

Ibn Taymiyyah said, 'They (the Kharijites) said that Uthman and Ali and whoever allied with them had judged by other than what Allah revealed, "And whosoever does not judge by what Allah has revealed, they are the disbelievers". (5:44). Thus, they declared Muslims to be disbelievers on account of this and other than it.' The misguided and ignorant Kharijites treat matters pertaining to trade relations with non-Muslim governments and bodies, matters of loyalty and disloyalty, tyranny and oppression, absence of fulfilment of the subjects' rights, commission of major or minor sins to comprise major disbelief without any qualification and detail (*tafsil*), but rather upon generalization and absolution. Upon that basis, they stir up societies against rulers and governments, thereby causing instability. In all these subject matters there are details and elaborations in the statements of the people of knowledge from the Companions and those after them from the scholars, right until this day of ours – all of which the Kharijites either feign ignorance of or are ignorant of because, and as mentioned previously, they have no genuine scholars amongst them.

Regarding the rise of the Black banners/standards/flags

The prophetic traditions which mention the appearance of black banners/flags (*rayatun sudun*) are all weak and inauthentic. As such, we cannot accept them as evidence in matters of Islamic creed in which we must believe. Muslims should not be fooled by groups carrying black banners intending to attribute themselves to the righteous ruler Al-Mahdi, but rather such groups must be judged on the basis of their actions, not the colour of the flags they wave.

First, there is the *hadith* attributed to Abu Huraira (a companion of the Prophet) in which the Prophet (peace and blessings be upon him) supposedly said:

'Black standards will come from Khorasan, nothing shall turn them back until they are planted in Jerusalem.' Source: A book of Hadith: Sunan At-Tirmidhi 2269

This narration was declared weak by At-Tirmidhi himself in his commentary on it; by Ibn Hajar in his compilations – Al-Qawl Al-Musaddid 1/53; by Ahmad Shakir in his verification of compilations – Musnad Ahmad 16/316; and by sheikh Al-Albani in his book Silsilat Ad-Da'eefah 4825.

Another narration:

'When you see those [Black flags], then pledge your allegiance to them even if you have to crawl over the snow, for that is the caliph of Allah, Al-Mahdi.' – Source: book of Hadith: Sunan Ibn Majah 4084

The scholar Adh-Dhahabi declares the narration to be rejected (*munkar*) in the book – Mizan Al-I'tidal 3/128; as well as the noble scholar Sheikh Al-Albani in his book – Silsilat Ad-Da'eefah 85. Ibn Al-Qayyim says in his writings – Al-Manar Al-Munif 115 – that the sub-narrator Ali ibn Zaid is weak and his traditions have been rejected.

Throughout history, groups of groups have used faith, and indeed Islam and such narrations and symbols like the black banners or the flag, to attribute themselves to Al-Mahdi, a righteous ruler who will appear near the end of time. There have been many groups who carried black banners and referred to their Caliphs as Al-Mahdi in an attempt to legitimize their rule.

Likewise in modern times was the insurgency of Juhayman Al-Otaybi in 1979 wherein his followers violated the sanctities of Islam by attacking and killing the Muslims of the most sacred mosque in Islam, Masjid Al-Haram in Makkah. They declared that a man among them was the promised Al-Mahdi and therefore Muslims were obligated to support their violent rebellion.

In the same way, we expect impostors and pretenders to continue using weak narrations and erroneous arguments to deceive ignorant Muslims into supporting their brutal and evil ambitions. Rather, any group that calls to Islam must be judged by the actions of its members and the character of its leaders.

Those who declare ordinary Muslims to be unbelievers, justify the spilling of innocent blood and the seizing of their property have nothing to do with Islam even if they recite the Quran and carry Islamic symbols. Indeed, as I have mentioned extensively, the Khariijte recites the Quran eloquently, yet they are the worst of the creation and the dogs of Hellfire. Such is the abomination of those who have taken the blessed seal of the Prophet, peace and blessings be upon him, and turned it into a symbol of terrorism in the eyes of the world.

A few other authenticated narrations to consider:

Ibn Kathir writes:

'If the Khawarij [extremist renegades] ever gained power, they would corrupt the entire earth, Iraq, and Syria. They would not leave a boy or a girl or a man or a woman, for in their view the people have become so corrupt that they cannot be reformed except by mass killing.' Source: Al-Bidayah wa Nihayah 10/584

Wherever they appear, the Kharijites cause division among the Muslims at large and even among their own groups. Whenever they form a group, it is not long before splinter groups and off-shoots appear with each one claiming to have the right to seize the Caliphate.

Abu Huraira (a companion of the Prophet) reported: 'The Messenger of Allah, peace and blessings be upon him, said: "Whoever rejects obedience to the leader of a nation and divides the community and dies will have died upon ignorance. Whoever fights under the banner of one who is blind, raging for the sake of tribalism, or calling to tribalism, or supporting tribalism, and is killed will have died upon ignorance. Whoever rebels against my nation, striking the righteous and wicked alike and sparing not even the believers and does not fulfil the pledge of security, then he has nothing to do with me and I have nothing to do with him."' Source: Sahih Muslim 1848

Ibn Umar narrated: 'I heard the Prophet saying, "Do not revert to disbelief after me by striking (cutting) the necks of one another."' Source: Bukhari. Book 89, volume 9 – 198

This is the obligation, as Allah the Glorified and Exalted said:

'And co-operate upon righteousness and piety and do not co-operate upon sin and transgression. And fear Allah, since Allah is severe in punishment.' [Quran – Sooratul Maa'idah 5:2]

And Allah the Majestic and Exalted said:

'By the time! Verily man is at a loss, except for those who believe and do righteous deeds, and those who advise each other to the truth and to patience.' [Quran – Sooratul-'Asr 103:1-3]

In conclusion to this chapter:

The extremist terrorist groups operating today are primarily at war against Islam and Muslims. Research published by the Kings College Centre for Study of Radicalisation in January 2015, entitled 'The New jihadism', shows that the equivalent of three 7/7 terrorist attacks are taking place every day and killing, on average, 180 Muslims daily in places of conflict such as Syria, Iraq, Libya, Somalia, Nigeria, Afghanistan, Pakistan and others, where this ideology is to be found, whether in the form of Al Qaeda, Boko Haram, ISIS or other insurgent groups.

The terrorist acts we see in the West – no less reprehensible – are given extensive coverage in the media leading to the faulty perception that these people are primarily at war with non-Muslims in the West. The facts are very different from what is being perceived.

As Adel Al Jubeir admirably mentioned in a speech in February 2016, ISIS or Al Qaeda are as much Islamic as the Ku Klux Klan is Christian, using the cross and believing that they are compelled by Christ to lynch and kill people of African descent. Do we ever say that the KKK are representatives of Christianity? There are many other examples that can be drawn from groups who claim to act in the name of their respective faiths: we see Jewish, Hindu and Buddhist extremists, all claiming to be acting in the name of their religion. But can we really say that their faith actually compels them? Of course not! So for anyone to align ISIS or Al Qaeda with Islam is preposterous.

Many Western academics recognise that the rejection of ISIS/Al Qaeda and other such groups is unanimous (except for those ignorant minds poisoned by them), from all sects and denominations of Islam. It is important to note that even those sects within Islam who are more conservative than others have in fact been consistent and loud in their speech against the ideology of ISIS and Al Qaeda, as can be evidenced from a survey of their writings and statements. For example, the Mufti of Saudi Arabia said that ISIS is the enemy of Islam and many other very credible scholars from across the Muslim world have stated that fighting against ISIS and Al Qaeda is a strongly recommended legitimate form of *jihad* and is actually required by Islam. This large scale rejection shows how far these extremist terrorists have removed themselves from the actual teachings of Islam and disengaged from the overwhelming majority of Muslims, even conservative brands of Islam.

There are distinct parallels to be drawn from the actions we see from today's terrorists, to the actions of those terrorists highlighted in this final chapter. They use exactly the same arguments, the same ideology as the Khawarijites, the exact same language, attitude, brutality, methodology and even the same environments. There is no argument whatsoever that ISIS and Al Qaeda *et al* are in fact branches of those mentioned by the Prophet Muhammad as explained in this chapter.

They thrive on our collective ignorance and indeed the chaos they generate or when mistakes are made.

It would appear, therefore, that in many cases where individuals are at risk of recruitment to violent extremism, a strong religious education can in fact provide a good defence against radicalisation to violent extremism. Furthermore, when an individual has been radicalised, the most reliably effective path to de-radicalisation is to move that individual into a very traditional form of religious practice, which gives them discipline and purpose.

Unfortunately, the failure – sometimes perhaps the unwillingness – to grasp the complexity of the religious element in the radicalisation equation and to engage with it, leads to interventions which prove inadequate or opportunities being lost. Automatically equating traditional or conservative forms of Islam with support for violence is plain wrong, just as to conclude that the answer lies in somehow persuading people to embrace 'moderate Islam' dooms any Prevent or counter-extremism intervention to failure.

Islam has placed great emphasis on compassion and mercy towards others. This is a fundamental religious duty of every single Muslim across the world.

I am not a scholar on religious affairs, nor do I claim to be the most knowledgeable person in this field; I have simply tried to provide as much credible information as possible in this final chapter, through research and the help of some excellent students of knowledge. It is my hope that you will be better equipped and prepared to a) dispel the myths associating terrorism with Islam, and b) alter your own perceptions around and of Islam. But more importantly, c) to fully understand the ideology of extremists and what they call for, d) to also enable you to counter the narratives espoused by extremist and terrorist networks and their sympathisers and finally e) to prevent young men and women from being drawn into terrorism.

CONCLUDING REMARKS

This book's objective of investigation was defined as Islamic-based radicalisation leading to violent extremism. Whilst defining this issue, I have given an insight into the dichotomy in the nature of the term 'radicalism' and have separated it from universal, often populist, definitions considering it to be a religious fervour automatically resulting in violent extremism.

Based on a detailed understanding of the phenomenon, this book has then exposed underlying issues leading to radicalisation that are, in large parts, ignored in the current state of research. While most approaches regarding the prevention of radicalisation fail to take into consideration issues such as foreign policy, specific government actions, and the need for a thorough understanding of local communities, I have justified the actual importance of these topics when examining the determinants of radicalisation. I have done so methodically through empirical, qualitative data provided by cases I have worked with, the analysis of original documents, and my personal experience. Deduced from these underlying issues, this book has then exposed the techniques used by extremist recruiters and their instrumentation of religion and grievance.

Finally, I have delivered a critical review of existing intervention programmes such as the British government's current Prevent strategy, and given detailed recommendations for principles to take into account for future interventions. These recommendations are based on the fact that what distinguishes the current global situation from past ones is the strikingly fast pace of change on the international stage and within societies, which emphasizes the need for adaptability. At the same time, interventions need to be oriented at long-term solutions rather than quick fixes. Hence, the most effective way of dealing with radicalisation and terrorist recruitment will ultimately be to create long-term strategies which simultaneously remain flexible to current and future challenges.

In order to take a look at forthcoming developments, in particular on an international scale, I would now like to emphasise a topic that I believe to be of great importance in the future. No matter which way of preventing radicalisation and terrorist recruitment is chosen, it is the aspect of governance that will be indispensable. Although many earlier studies of the causes of radicalisation to violent extremism and of Prevent interventions pay scant attention to governance, studies in the last two to three years have come to acknowledge the *fundamental* importance of governance as one of the causes of the problem. Studies on globalisation and its impact, rather than studies on preventing or countering violent extremism alone, can be a good supplementary source of understanding for this factor.

As hypothesised and elaborated on in this book, in recent years, societies across the world have been experiencing drastic change at a faster rate, more profoundly, and on a more sustained basis, than at any previous period of history other than during major war. This change is stimulated by many factors, chief among which are generally taken to be:

- A population increase, with its resultant diluting of societies' ability to transmit cultural values and to maintain economic opportunities for subsequent generations (the countries most affected by this include many where radicalisation to violent extremism has become a particular problem)
- The universal availability of information and means of transmitting it
- A near-universal access to advanced technology, including weaponry
- Ease of travel
- Uneven access to resources and wealth

States and societies can no longer isolate themselves from the competition of ideas and economics. There have always been gaps between rich and poor, privileged and underprivileged. But unlike in times past, where problems usually remained localised, now the poor and dispossessed are not only much more aware of the inequalities and injustices which create grievances, they are capable of taking effective, violent action to do something about it, and can communicate and travel to make their impact anywhere and everywhere.

This change is now so rapid, profound and sustained that it is overtaking the ability of governments to react, adapt and remain effective, including the more stable, wealthy Western societies and governments. Much greater is the truly revolutionary impact of this change on societies and governments which are inflexible and cannot or even fail to adapt. Such countries, which may have traditional tribal-based governments, dictatorships, corrupt or otherwise incompetent governments, could potentially fail under the impact of drastic change, just as countries fail and collapse under the impact of war. The 'Arab Spring' or the 'Coloured Revolutions' in Eastern Europe can be convincingly interpreted in just this way. The world is actually facing a crisis of governance.

Violent extremism, in all its forms, can increasingly be understood as a product of such failure of governance. It is shown to flourish where the state is weak or has collapsed, where extremist groups can move to fill a power vacuum, and where resentment and dissatisfaction can be fuelled by the consequent social, political and economic grievances.

Failure of governance can also be found in states where the government creates resentment by its efforts to enforce conformity, limit expression and repress dissent, including by the excessive or inept use of force. Corruption, abuse of power and impunity to justice are the main causes of outrage, anger and a sense of impotence on which extremism feeds.

In such circumstances, improving governance – reinforcing a state's willingness and ability to acknowledge and tackle the causes of grievance appropriately and effectively – is probably one of the most important, indeed essential, actions that can be undertaken to prevent and counter violent extremism. It must be considered an absolute priority. Security sector and justice reform is an important element of such improvement in governance. However, improving governance, of course, is difficult to do and may in practice, for political and other reasons, be impossible. But if that is the case, it should be acknowledged that Prevent or CVE interventions which are not accompanied by parallel programmes at a national level are likely to be pointless in the long term.

As a state begins to fail or collapse under the impact of change, the resulting instability and turmoil favours those individuals or groups which can adapt and react quickly, take advantage of opportunities, take daring risks, not be hidebound by previous restrictive rules or social constraints. Whereas the failing authorities by definition lose their ability to be effective, and are seen to do so, the rising new forces – the extremists – do so precisely because they can flourish in the turmoil and can be seen to deliver what the old authority cannot. One look at how ISIS have established some kind of order for the Sunni majority in Mosul (Iraq) – who were being persecuted by the 'legitimate', albeit minority, Shia government – is evidence enough to appreciate how this works.

Those seeking to recruit individuals and inspire them to violent extremism, these are our actual opponents whom we seek to defeat with a Prevent or CVE intervention, direct or indirect. That intervention must therefore take account of the adaptability and agility of the opponent, of their speed and freedom of reaction, as well as their determination. If, as is frequently the case, an intervention is slow to get off the ground, bound by budgetary or health and safety regulations or due to risk averseness, and is applied insensitively or inflexibly, then it will be very difficult to outmatch the radicalisers and counter the recruitment process and achieve the desired impact. It is exactly this ability to react fast and to remain flexible that I have recommended in this book.

Unfortunately, although a prerequisite for success in many cases, programmes to improve governance are not only difficult to contemplate because they require state-level intervention, they are also unlikely to be sufficient on their own once the process of radicalisation has taken hold within a sector of the population. They will need to be supplemented by interventions to address the mechanisms and process of radicalisation as discussed further.

Inadequate governance is a factor that heavily influences the aspect of opportunity. Although this is not much studied in Prevent or CVE literature, it is an issue now being seriously addressed in the literature of criminology, which would appear to be highly relevant here. It is that, in practice, a major cause of bad behaviour is simply that people have the *opportunity* to indulge in it, especially when there are no effective sanctions. When opportunities for crime are reduced, crime rates fall.

The opportunity for recruitment to violent extremism today is provided by several developments of recent years which spring from problems of governance and which before were simply not available. As noted previously, these include, *inter alia*: the spread of technology; the ubiquitous availability of information and communications; and the ease of travel. Together, these ensure that people know what is going on, can do something about it, and can go anywhere to do it. Any ungoverned space will rapidly be filled by trouble, which can easily be exported.

It is obviously going to be difficult for Prevent interventions alone to curtail such opportunity, although some intergovernmental collaboration will be effective to an extent. But as it stands at present, without an effective network of community-led programmes, supported by statutory sector actors, the opportunity for radicalisation to violent extremism is only likely to increase, perhaps even drastically.

Although the circumstances are particular today, the problem of how to soak up the desire for action, the propensity for risk-taking and the capacity for violence that is the hallmark of any young person's developing brain, has been a problem societies have long faced. In addition, of course, to military conscription, the totalitarian societies of the 20th Century created large-scale youth movements, such as the Nazi Hitler Youth or the Soviet Pioneers, Communist Youth organisation and military sports association. Democratic societies created, for the same reason but with a different end in mind, the Scout movement, youth clubs, leadership programmes, the UK's Duke of Edinburgh award programme, Cadet Corps, Al Wattani in the UAE, and so on. It is noteworthy that, other than the Scouts in some countries, such voluntary youth movements are largely missing in many at-risk countries and might profitably be developed as alternatives to the recruitment programmes and team-building activities offered by terrorist groups.

Certainly, experience of effective youth engagement through adventurous training activities, leadership programmes and youth clubs in countries as far apart as the UK and Pakistan has shown that this is an area well worth exploring further.

I will end my final remarks with a brief view on possibly the most acknowledged topic in the contemporary discourse on radicalisation, which is the role of religion. Although, as mentioned in previous chapters, it is evident that religion initially is more often not the contributing factor in recruitment to violent extremism, it is important to note that religion is in fact a crucial factor in also solving the problem we are addressing. Despite this, religion is actually given remarkably little serious attention in much of the general literature on Preventing or Countering Violent Extremism, as if people were not comfortable with discussing the topic.

The fact is that, in the conceptual framework of modern Western liberal intellectual thought, which insists on separating religion from politics, religion is often treated with, at best, tolerance. The EU seems to pride itself on being a post-religious organisation. The role and importance of faith in many people's lives is simply not appreciated, or it is considered as something of an aberration.

This is a real hindrance when addressing recruitment to violent extremism. The relationship between religion, society, politics and the state in the Muslim world, is everywhere complex. It differs significantly from country to country in both form and extent, and between the different branches of Islam. But everywhere religion will have a huge bearing on whether the Prevent or CVE intervention will be successful or not.

Addressing this aspect of the problem requires more sensitivity, knowledge, understanding and trust than any other area of CVE. It is something that people with no faith find extremely difficult to do because they have no internal reservoir of sympathy on which to draw and on which to base a relationship of trust with those whom they seek to influence. It is perhaps for this reason that many people shy away from addressing the issue at all.

The key case to be answered is whether violent extremism springs solely from religion or not. It used to be assumed that this was purely the case and that the more traditional or conservative the branch of Islam, the more likely it was to produce terrorists and suicide bombers. Although my experience, and that of the many cases I have worked on, proves otherwise. In fact it shows that the research in this area is flawed, and that the evidence now seems to point to a completely different reality.

I agree that religion – rather, the interpretation of religion, or the widely held belief by many young people that their religion compels them to act – has a certain role to play in some cases. But to simply pass it off as religion being the sole culprit would be totally misleading.

Ultimately, it is important to remain open to the acquisition of knowledge and understanding to be able to address all the different aspects of the problem of radicalisation, including those that might be difficult to address. Only in this way, effective interventions will be found.

ACKNOWLEDGEMENTS

In the world of Preventing Extremism and Terrorist recruitment it is undeniable that change can only happen when people, institutions and services come together and work hand in hand. I have been very lucky over the years to be supported by some very special people from a hugely diverse background and from some important institutions in the UK and abroad who wrapped their unwavering support around me, the Active Change Foundation and many of the cases I have worked on. It is therefore only right to acknowledge them in this book and pay respect and sincere thanks for their continuing support in helping me.

Every single one of these remarkable people has been profoundly instrumental in assisting in the prevention of extremism and terrorist recruitment. More often than not, in very difficult circumstances and out of normal working hours. Without their assistance it would not have been possible to achieve the many successes I can celebrate and it is safe to say that this book would simply be empty pages without their generous support. These remarkable people have essentially helped save and change lives for the better and often go unnoticed, so it is only right that I give due recognition to them. They are:

Chris Barry – Counter Terrorist Command MCU (Retired)

Governor John H Sununu – Chief of Staff White House (Retired)

Mark Whyte – Sky News Reporter

Noel Warr – CT Command MCU (Retired)

Gordon Corerra – Security Correspondent BBC/PBS News

Paul Birch – CT Command MCU

Abid Raja – CT Command MCU

Simon Cornwall – Central Extremism Division NOMS/London Probation

Liz Dickson – Restorative Justice Coordinator London Probation

Mel Waudby – Police Staff (Retired)

Linda Niamantis – London Probation

Priscilla Samuels – London Probation

Supt Ian Larnder – Met Police /NCTT ACPO (Previous)

Angus Walker – ITN News (previous)

Mariam Rashid – London Probation

Ginny Sandringham – Channel 4 News – Home affairs

Christianne Amanpour – CNN

Geoff Storey & Team – Vertical Air

Baroness Pauline Neville Jones – Minister for Security (Previous)

Jamie Martin – US Embassy London

Chris Nel & Team – Quest Leadership

Yusuf Desai – Forward Thinking

Oliver McTernan – Forward Thinking

William Sieghart – Forward Thinking

Tony Heal – Senior Civil Servant OSCT Home Office UK (Retired)

Charles Farr – Director General OSCT Home Office UK (Previous)

Dave Grant – Chief Supt Met Police (Retired)

Stewart Rivers – Chief Supt Met Police (Retired)

Peter Wickstead – Chief Supt Met Police CT Command, head of MCU (Retired)

Jim Boyling – CT Command MCU (Retired)

Asim Hafeez – Director Prevent OSCT Home Office UK (Previous)

Debbie Gupta – Director Prevent OSCT Home Office UK (Previous)

Siobhan Peters – Director Prevent OSCT Home Office UK (Previous)

Nick Jones – OSCT Home Office & FCO (Previous)

Mark Galliers – Inspector SO15 Met Police Channel (Previous)

Paul Barrie – Inspector SO15 Met Police Channel (Previous)

Jena Musa – Prevent Lead local Authority

Waqar Ahmed – Prevent Lead Local Authority

Stella Creasy – MP Labour

Kenny Bowie – Home Office

James Golshetti – Foreign & Commonwealth Office

Quinton Wiktorowicz – US Embassy London/Former White House official

Bob Lambert – CT Command MCU (Retired)

General Nick Parker – Chief of Armed Forces MOD Land UK

General Nick Carter – Chief Armed Forces MOD UK

Commander Steve Tatham – Royal Navy UK

Brigadier Mike Griffiths – MOD UK (Retired)

Brigadier David Alfrey – MOD UK (Retired)

James Montague – MOD UK

Naheem Bashir – Local Authority Prevent Lead/Former Police Thames Valley

Victoria Houghton – MOD UK

Jonathan Mullchrone – Met Police

Cllr Farooq Qureshi – Retired

Dianne Andrews – Local Authority Hate crime & Domestic Violence Coordinator

Mathew Barzun – US Ambassador UK

Nick Pickles – Public Policy Twitter UK

Farah Pandith – US State Dept EuroAsian Affairs (Previous)

Andrew Cummings – OSCT Home Office/FCO (Previous)

Paul Mott – Director RICU – Home Office (Previous)

Alex Michael – RICU Home Office UK

Alex Simm

Lesley Simm – Defence Academy UK (Retired)

Pierre Lafayeedney

Anthony & Anne Fitzherbert

Sue, Shelley, Jade & Mike Williams – My beautiful family away from home.

Claire Hensman – High sheriff Cumbria (Retired)

Paul Bevan & Team – SSC

Eleanor Gillespie & Colleagues – SECTU

Poonam Tuneja – BBC News Reporter

A special thanks to Chris Donnelly, David Gilbertson and Dan Lafayeedney who have trusted and supported me and the organisation through many a storm and have significantly contributed in my day to day work with some very extreme and high risk cases.

And all the rest of the great people I have worked with over the years and may have forgotten to add.

I would also like to thank Mike Jervis (my brother from another mother) for all his dedication and help in shaping parts of this book, and for his resolve and sincerity in assisting me on most of the cases. We have travelled across the world and driven many thousands of motorway miles, often sleeping in the car to get to the individuals needing our help.

All of the ACF team past & current, friends and family members who have worked tirelessly in our efforts to protect our communities and indeed our young people. Without them all we could not have achieved so much. Especially Balgees Barendilla for keeping me in check and managing all the case loads.

May God bless you all.